THE
MILLENNIUM
COOKBOOK

*This book is dedicated to our excellent staff
and loyal customers.*

THE

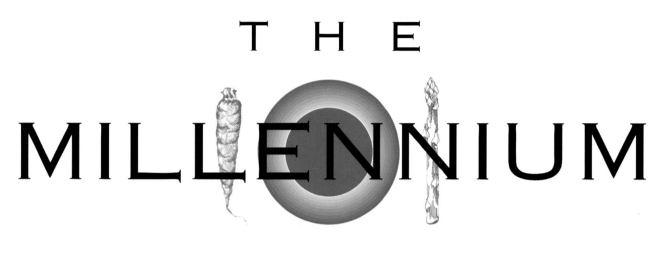

MILLENNIUM

COOKBOOK

Extraordinary Vegetarian Cuisine

Eric Tucker & John Westerdahl, M.P.H., R.D., C.N.S.

Dessert recipes by Sascha Weiss

Photography by Renée Comet

Ten Speed Press
Berkeley, California

1&

TEN SPEED PRESS
P.O. Box 7123
Berkeley, CA 94707
www.tenspeed.com

A Kirsty Melville book

Distributed in Australia by Simon & Schuster Australia; in Canada by
Ten Speed Press Canada; in New Zealand by Tandem Press; in South Africa by
Real Books; in the United Kingdom and Europe by Airlift Books;
and in Malaysia and Singapore by Berkeley Books.

Text and cover design by Nancy Austin
Photography by Renée Comet

Printed in Malaysia

Library of Congress Cataloging-in-Publication Data on file with the publisher.

1 2 3 4 5 — 02 01 00 99 98

ACKNOWLEDGMENTS

I wish to thank all of those who have helped support me and this project, especially Marilyn Nauss, Sean Chatham, Sascha Weiss, and Randall Reeves for their work at Millennium; recipe testers Kristen, Allyah, and Jason; Dennis Malone, Steve Mclaine, Gary and Colleen Tucker, Rachelle Blackman and my parents, Joan and Gerald Tucker.

—Eric

I would like to thank my wife Doris for her encouragement and support, as well as her assistance in helping me with the computer work on portions of the manuscript. Thanks also to my colleagues at Veggie Life *magazine for their support, especially Wayne Lin for allowing me to use the magazine's computer for the nutritional analyses, and Laura Nilsen for her assistance.*

—John

We both wish to thank Sascha Weiss for his unique culinary contributions, and the exquisite skill he brought to the dessert section of this book, as well as Mariah Bear and Clancy Drake at Ten Speed.

A special thanks go to Dennis and Brian Malone, the original inspiration behind Milly's, and to Margaret, whose dream it was to open a gourmet vegan restaurant in San Francisco. The authors are also greatly indebted to Chip Conley, Larry and Ann Wheat, Randall Reeves, and the entire staff of the Millennium Restaurant for their contributions, support, and dedication, all of which have helped to make Millennium so successful.

CONTENTS

ABOUT THE RESTAURANT

We are deeply gratified by the success of the Millennium, our trailblazing San Francisco–based gourmet vegetarian restaurant. The Millennium has its roots in Milly's, a Marin county restaurant created by Dennis and Margaret Malone. Millennium has attracted nationwide attention since its 1994 opening in San Francisco's Civic Center, both for its food and for its mission. That mission—to provide healthy gourmet dining that is good for the heart, the planet, *and* the palette—has certainly struck a chord, helping to accelerate America's trend toward more conscious eating habits.

Our recipes, as you will see in this book, prove that vegan dining can be delicious, satisfying, and plentiful. Historically, healthy eating has gotten an undeserved reputation for being rather spartan and unappealing. Not true! Our goal is to lighten up cooking *and* attitudes.

Too often, vegetarians are perceived as the "food police"—dogmatic, humorless, and out of touch with the mainstream. One of the joys of running this restaurant has been to see the eclectic mix of loyal customers. From the hard-charging type A executives to triathletes training for their next competition to all-American couples who discovered natural food through the market in their neighborhood, Millennium attracts a wide variety of diners you wouldn't normally see in a vegetarian restaurant. They all have one thing in common: They're here for a wonderful dining experience.

And wonderful it is. Our recipes will surprise you… this isn't your mother's old bean-sprout-filled vegetarian cookbook. Chef Eric Tucker wanted to reinvent vegetarian cuisine so that people perceived it as a path to a better and happier life, not just a political statement or monastic solution to our collective culinary guilt. By serving food that supports optimal health and restores the natural vitality to our bodies, Millennium's cuisine not only nourishes the body but is also a feast for the senses.

We've had fun along the way too, including starting a Full Moon Aphrodisiac Night once per month. This package allows couples to enjoy a collection of herbal aphrodisiacs developed into the recipes of the special menu, and then, at the end of the dinner, a complimentary hotel room upstairs in the charming Abigail Hotel. Nobody calls this vegetarian cuisine boring or lacking in sensuality! Does it work? Well, these special nights are always booked up a month or so in advance.

It shouldn't be a surprise to see that the audience for this style of cooking has grown. *Cooking Light* is America's fastest-growing gourmet magazine. Nonfat and cholesterol-free items are the fastest growing section in supermarkets. Well-known authors like Dr. Dean Ornish and Dr. John McDougall have built enormous followings by espousing a low-fat vegetarian diet, and, of course, as our population ages, Americans are increasingly concerned about health. Indeed, the general interest in health, as well as corporate America's focus on building a healthier workplace, have helped the Millennium reach out to an ever-larger audience.

In sum, the recipes in this book reflect our changing eating habits. They are not punishment, but a gateway to a healthier and happier life. Check your dogma at the door. We're not only interested in making your conscience feel good, we want your body (and especially your taste buds) to feel good as well. Try these recipes out on your Uncle Herbert who swore he'd be a life-long carnivore. He'll be surprised by how tasty and filling a low-fat vegetarian diet can be.

—Larry Wheat & Chip Conley
Owners of the Millennium Restaurant

FOREWORD:
THE MILLENNIUM EXPERIENCE

Eat more vegetables and less meat, nutritionists tell us, in order to stay trim and healthy. We believe them, and we want the benefits. Indeed, vegetarianism is actually quite stylish these days. Most restaurants are now offering a vegetarian selection on the menu, and a few dedicate their entire menu to vegetarian dishes—but none has done this so well as the Millennium. There you'll find gourmet dining, with white tablecloths, fine china, a romantic ambiance, first-class service, and food fit for a health-conscious king or queen. Image starting dinner with Bitter Greens, Figs, and Beets with Curried Almond Dressing, moving on to Roasted Corn and Hedgehog Mushroom Tamales with Mushroom-Chile Cream Sauce, and finishing with Lemon Caramel and Hazelnut Napoleons with Kiwifruit Mango Sauce. Now you don't have to only imagine this exhilarating gustatory experience, because you have in your hands a copy of the *Millennium Cookbook*.

The foods from Millennium are extraordinary because the people behind the book and the restaurant are motivated by a sincere interest in bettering your personal health and the health of this planet. We know a vegetarian diet avoids the bad things (cholesterol, saturated fat, sodium) and is chock-full of the good things (vitamins, minerals, carbohydrate, and fiber). With a plant-based diet, you'll find it much easier to lose weight and prevent or treat conditions from heart disease to cancer, diabetes to arthritis. Food truly is our best medicine.

The more vegetarian meals people consume, the better the chance of saving our planet from the many burdens of producing animal-based foods. Much less fuel, water, and land are required to grow the plant-based ingredients you will be using to make the foods from the *Millennium Cookbook*. From all viewpoints—health, appearance, personal expenses, kindness to animals, religious teachings, concern for fellow human beings and our earth—a vegetarian diet is right. The more you can incorporate delicious Millennium recipes into your diet, the better all aspects of your life will become. Whether you're new to healthy foods or a lifelong vegetarian, the *Millennium Cookbook* will enrich your life.

—John A. McDougall, M.D., Founder and
Director of the McDougall Program
St. Helena Hospital, Napa Valley, California

INTRODUCTION

My mother tells me I've been cooking on my own since the age of five, when I pulled a step stool up to the stove so that I could make my specialty, scrambled eggs. Much to my parents' delight, I was that rare kid who will eat almost everything and—thanks to them—I did! They were real food lovers, and they would drag me to restaurants all over Manhattan. So, by the age of five, I'd probably been exposed to more types of cuisine than many people experience in a lifetime.

Some of my most vivid food memories are of our regular visits to New York's Chinatown. I was (and still am!) fascinated by the sights,

smells, and flavors, and as soon as I discovered our local Chinese market, I was cooking Chinese meals for my family and, by the age of fifteen, catering a few dinner parties as well. So, my lifelong interest in cuisines of the world began early.

My interest in healthy eating, by contrast, came in high school, when I was a fledgling distance runner and, simultaneously, was diagnosed with hypoglycemia (low blood sugar). On the one hand, nutritionists were telling me to eat mainly protein (meat, to be precise); on the other, everything I read about distance running said to stick to a diet high in carbohydrates. Not knowing which way to turn, I read everything I could on dietary theory, tried out a few things—including some fads, from popping supplements to being a staunch macrobiotic—and eventually found a balance that seems to work well for me and my lifestyle.

After working for a few years in the restaurant industry, I was able to find a culinary balance that fit my lifestyle as well. That's where the Natural Gourmet Cookery School comes in. They offered the perfect program for me, focusing as it did on working as a professional chef, with a foundation of healthy, natural foods. Attending this Manhattan-based school also gave me the opportunity to work with quality organic produce, thanks to the Union Square Farmers' Market, and to sample great dishes from New York's most creative restaurants.

My schooling ended with an externship at Milly's Restaurant in San Rafael, California. The restaurant sounded great to me—creative, up-scale vegetarian cuisine twenty minutes north of San Francisco. It was everything I'd hoped, so when a month after graduation the owners called to offer me a permanent position, I was ecstatic.

When I arrived at Milly's in 1990, the restaurant was in the process of eliminating all eggs and dairy from the menu, as well as revamping its image to that of a truly fine dining establishment. Dennis Malone, founding chef and owner, had recently hired Steve Mclaine, a professional chef who came on board about the same time I did. Within three months he was promoted to head chef, while I was made sous chef. The experience of working under Mclaine in such a creative environment really accelerated my learning. We were given a great deal of leeway in terms of menu planning, and we made the most of it. We'd decide to make a manchamantal sauce and, even if we'd never made one before, it would be on the menu that night…over tempeh

baked in banana leaves. And if I'd never even seen a banana leaf before, let alone cooked with one? Well, I learned. If a dish worked, it worked. If it didn't, we made it work by the time the doors opened for dinner.

After a year and a half, I moved up to the head chef spot. The whole kitchen crew (myself, sous chef Gabe Barkin, and pastry/sous chef Catherine Burke) was really learning and refining this cuisine as we went along. One thing I learned very early on was that *everyone* in the kitchen has something useful to add—how to make an authentic tomatilla sauce, shortcuts for working with rice paper, how to make a perfect vegan pastry crust—whatever tricks they brought from their families, other cultures, or previous cooking experiences.

In the fall of 1994, I was able to bring all this experience to San Francisco, when the Millennium was opened as a sister restaurant to Milly's. As of this writing, it's been close to four years, and we're still learning and loving it. Chef Marilyn Nauss, chef Sean Chatham, and pastry chef

Sascha Weiss have brought their own ideas and influences into the kitchen. Millennium is a rare thing among restaurants, in that the entire staff—kitchen, waitstaff, and management—are really devoted to this type of cuisine and lifestyle. It's not just a job here. Not that all of us are strict vegans, or even necessarily vegetarians, but we are all dedicated to promoting this model of a healthy, innovative cuisine.

Our food is a celebration. To the uninitiated, cooking vegan may sound like it means following a lot of restrictions, but within those boundaries there is an infinite world of flavors and influences. Our food is exciting because we pay as much attention to flavor, texture, and visual appeal as we do the food's healthful qualities. Down here in the kitchen, we do what we do out of love of food and love for the creative process. Those factors come together in interesting ways, which is why at the Millennium you can find a Hispanic-inspired plantain torte next to our interpretation of a Thai curry served in a baby pumpkin, next to an African lentil stew with corn-millet crepes.

Interpretation is a key word here. We try to capture the essence of a particular cuisine and make it our own. We may not be using the meats and cheese found in traditional or avant garde dishes (and we're inspired by both), but nonetheless, we can bring you the galangal and kaffir lime leaf from a traditional Thai curry, or the haute cuisine combination of beet coulis, saffron cream, and a leaning tower of morel-stuffed filo dough, as seen in the glossy pages of *Art Culinaire.*

While we're doing all this, we don't go out of our way to make "health food," but it naturally seems to end up that way. Most of the staff have developed an innate sense of balance when it comes to composing a dish—so, I might add a legume or grain to a dish to enhance flavor or texture, and end up with a balanced protein/starch combination. Basically, when you're eating a diet based wholly on a variety of plant foods, it's pretty hard not to be healthy.

A major factor in the quality of our dishes is the quality of the raw ingredients available to us. Depending on the season, a substantial amount of

our produce comes to use straight from the farmers. In fact, the restaurant has built some wonderful relationships with farmers, to the point that some grow a special planting of a vegetable just for us, or maybe pick the baby Tokyo turnips at just the size we like them.

We've become especially close to growers like Shirley Ward, from Stoney Farms up on the Sonoma county wine country, who coddles and nurtures her broccoli plants, and then picks only the sweetest side shoots for us. Or Wayne and Lee James at Healdsburg's Tierra Farms, farmers who I call "chile archeologists," because of their passion for heirloom chiles. These relationships are important, because in a best-case scenario, chefs will introduce our customers to new and exciting kinds of produce that the customers will then want to cook for themselves—thereby guaranteeing the growers a decent market for their crops, and advancing the cause of adventurous, healthy eating a bit in the process.

One thing we've done to promote foods we care about is a series of special dinners devoted to specific types of produce. Whether the evening's star was chiles, mushroom, or wines, the dinners have been both fun and successful, and you'll find the best-loved recipes in this book. So far, the largest turnout for one of these dinners was a wine-pairing dinner hosted with our friends from the Bonny Doon Vineyard in Santa Cruz. Their wines are a bit esoteric, as is our food, so it made for an interesting and harmonious mix.

But what does all this mean for you, the cookbook reader? I hope that you'll get more out of this book than just the recipes—that you'll come to share our ideas, philosophy, and knowledge of food. I want this book to help improve your cooking skills and expand your culinary repertoire. Whether you follow the recipes verbatim or use them as inspiration, in time they should all come to be a set of guidelines, a framework for your own creativity. So, don't feel compelled to make the Pumpkin Stuffed with Thai Pumpkin Curry perfectly from top to bottom, especially when your guests will be arriving in an hour. You could, however, whip up the curry paste, and keep any extra on hand for a quick weeknight dinner. You could make the chutney and freeze it, pulling it out on some rainy evening when you want to add a little zip to your meal.

Look at how we bring ingredients, flavors, and textures together, and you'll be inspired to play around with them a bit. Make Sascha's Chocolate Midnight by the book once, then get a little creative the next time—maybe adding a shot of espresso and some orange zest to the recipe and serving it with a Grand Marnier sauce of your own devising. We've given you our best shot in these recipes—now take them, make them, play with them, and make them your own!

See you in the kitchen!

—Eric Tucker

APPETIZERS

Many of our appetizers are very brightly flavored and full of contrasting elements like the sweet of fruit with the sting of chile. They awaken the palate, and they are downright fun to prepare as well as to eat.

At Millennium, we serve a variety of grilled seasonal vegetables as an antipasto platter. This chapter contains a number of the marinades we use; you can make these versatile marinades into staples in your kitchen. Use them to grill or roast vegetables, or with protein foods like seitan, tempeh, or tofu.

Make a tapas dinner party out of an array of our appetizers, antipasto salads, and grilled vegetables—and don't forget to try one of our decadent pâtés.

SMOKED PIMIENTO PÂTÉ

MAKES 8 SERVINGS

This pâté is a mainstay at Millennium. The recipe lends itself to a number of easy variations. We smoke quality canned pimiento or, in the later summer, fresh pimientos. This pâté works equally well without smoking the peppers. Try marbling the pâté with swirls of Spinach-Cilantro Pâté (follows) or layering both pâtés. Serve with crackers or crostini and one of our salsas.

$1/2$ cup cashews

12 ounces canned pimientos with liquid, smoked (or add 1 teaspoon liquid smoke)

2 tablespoons nutritional yeast

1 clove garlic

3 tablespoons fresh lemon juice

$1^1/2$ teaspoons sea salt

$1/4$ teaspoon ground nutmeg

$1/2$ teaspoon ground black pepper

$1/2$ teaspoon dried oregano

2 cups water

1 tablespoon powdered agar agar, or 3 tablespoons agar agar flakes

In a blender, combine the cashews, pimientos, yeast, garlic, lemon juice, sea salt, nutmeg, black pepper, oregano and $1/2$ cup of the water and blend until smooth.

In a small saucepan, bring the remaining $1^1/2$ cups water to a boil and whisk in the agar agar until thoroughly dissolved. Add to the mixture in the blender and blend until smooth.

Agar agar is very reactive to acids like vinegar and lemon, so there can be some variance depending on whether the pimientos were packed with some type of acid. Test the pâté by placing a tablespoonful in the refrigerator or freezer for 3 to 5 minutes; it should set up and be firm in that time. If not, you will have to add more agar agar. Start with 1 teaspoon agar agar powder or 2 teaspoons of agar agar flakes dissolved in $1/2$ cup water.

Transfer the pâté to an 8 x 5-inch loaf pan or an 8-cup mold. Refrigerate the pâté for at least 2 hours or up to 5 days. Unmold and cut into slices to serve.

NUTRITIONAL ANALYSIS PER 3-OUNCE SERVING PÂTÉ:

76 Calories (47% from fat), 3 g Protein, 7 g Carbohydrate, 4 g Fat, 0 mg Cholesterol, 532 mg Sodium, 2 g Fiber

SPINACH-CILANTRO PÂTÉ

MAKES 4 SERVINGS

This pâté is a good complement to the Smoked Pimiento Pâté on page (above). Serve them marbled or layered together (see directions in the Variation, below), or separately, with crackers or crostini.

$1/4$ cup cashews

2 cups packed spinach leaves, blanched in boiling water for 1 minute

3 tablespoons fresh cilantro leaves

2 tablespoons fresh mint leaves (optional)

$1/2$ serrano chile, seeded and minced

$1/2$ teaspoon sea salt

1 cup water

$1^1/2$ teaspoons powdered agar agar, or 1 tablespoon agar agar flakes

In a blender, combine the cashews, spinach, cilantro, mint, chile, salt, and $1/2$ cup of the water and blend until smooth. In a small saucepan, bring the remaining $1/2$ cup water to a boil and whisk in the agar agar. Continue whisking until thoroughly dissolved. Add to the blender and blend. Test the pâté as above before using, adding more dissolved agar agar if necessary.

VARIATION:

To marble the two pâtés, pour the pimiento pâté into a loaf pan. Pour the spinach pâté on top and randomly fold into the pimiento layer. To layer the two pâtés, pour half of the pimiento pâté into the pan and refrigerate for 10 minutes. Pour half of the spinach pâté on top and refrigerate for 10 minutes. Repeat to make 2 more layers.

NUTRITIONAL INFORMATION PER 3-OUNCE SERVING PÂTÉ:

68 Calories (53% from fat), 3 g Protein, 5 g Carbohydrate, 4 g Fat, 0 mg Cholesterol, 345 mg Sodium, 2 g Fiber

MUSHROOM, WALNUT, AND ROSEMARY PÂTÉ

MAKES 8 3-OUNCE SERVINGS

Try adding minced black truffle or black chanterelles to this pâté for an even richer taste. Serve with a few capers and some Dijon mustard.

1 red onion, cut lengthwise into thin crescents

2 teaspoons minced garlic

$1/2$ quart cremini and shiitake mushrooms

1 cup regular or nonalcoholic red wine

1 teaspoon sea salt

2 teaspoons coarsely chopped fresh sage

1 teaspoon coarsely chopped fresh thyme

2 teaspoons coarsely chopped fresh rosemary

1 teaspoon ground nutmeg

$1/2$ teaspoon ground pepper

1 tablespoon nutritional yeast

1 cup walnuts, toasted (see page 234)

1 tablespoon tamari soy sauce

2 teaspoons balsamic vinegar

$2^1/2$ cups water

2 teaspoons powdered agar agar, or 2 tablespoons agar agar flakes

In a large nonstick skillet or sauté pan, cook the red onion, garlic, and mushrooms in the red wine and sea salt over medium heat, stirring often, until all the moisture has evaporated. Remove from the heat. Add the sage, thyme, rosemary, nutmeg, pepper, and yeast and stir well to incorporate.

Transfer to a blender. Add the walnuts, tamari, vinegar, and $1^1/2$ cups of the water. Blend until smooth.

In a small saucepan, bring the remaining 1 cup water to a boil. Whisk in the agar agar and turn the heat to low. Continue whisking until the agar agar is thoroughly dissolved, about 5 to 7 minutes. Add to the mushroom mixture and blend until incorporated.

Test the pâté to ensure that it sets up by refrigerating 1 tablespoonful for 10 minutes. If the test pâté isn't firm by then, dissolve another 2 teaspoons agar agar powder or 1 tablespoon agar agar flakes in boiling water and add to the pâté. Spread in an 8 x 5-inch loaf pan or 8-cup mold. Refrigerate for at least 2 hours. Unmold and cut into slices to serve.

NUTRITIONAL INFORMATION PER 3-OUNCE SERVING PÂTÉ:

120 Calories (60% from fat), 4 g Protein, 8 g Carbohydrate, 8 g Fat, 0 mg Cholesterol, 422 mg Sodium, 1 g Fiber

SMOKED BABA GANOUSH

MAKES 8 ¼-CUP SERVINGS

Our twist on this Greek classic is that we smoke the eggplant before we bake it. It gives the baba a complex smoky quality that is sublime. For this one we don't skimp on the tahini or olive oil. During the summer we use the sweet and mild fleshed Rosa Bianca eggplant. Serve this with our Chickpea Flat Bread (page 7) or toasted pita bread and a bowl of pungent olives.

2 globe eggplants or 4 Japanese eggplants, halved lengthwise, salted and smoked (see page 235)

1 teaspoon extra virgin olive oil

2 cloves garlic, minced

¼ cup fresh lemon juice

¼ cup sesame tahini

3 tablespoons extra virgin olive oil

1 teaspoon coriander seeds, toasted and ground (see page 234)

½ teaspoon ground pepper

1½ teaspoons sea salt

1 tablespoon chopped fresh parsley or cilantro, plus more for garnish

Paprika for garnish

Preheat the oven to 400°. Rub the smoked eggplant halves with the 1 teaspoon olive oil and place on a baking sheet. Bake for 30 to 40 minutes, or until the flesh is very soft. Let cool to room temperature.

Scrape the eggplant flesh from the skin into a blender or food processor, retaining some of the skin for its charred flavor. Add the garlic, lemon juice, tahini, 3 tablespoons olive oil, coriander seed, pepper, salt, and the 1 tablespoon parsley or cilantro. Blend until smooth. Serve in a bowl sprinkled with more parsley or cilantro and paprika.

NUTRITIONAL INFORMATION PER ¼ CUP SERVING BABA GANOUSH:

142 Calories (63% from fat), 2 g Protein, 11 g Carbohydrate, 10 g Fat, 0 mg Cholesterol, 475 mg Sodium, 4 g Fiber

MIDDLE EAST EGGPLANT PÂTÉ

MAKES 8 3-OUNCE SERVINGS

This is another of our agar-bound pâtés. Though similar to baba ganoush, there is much less fat in this version. For even less fat, substitute silken tofu for the tahini if you don't mind losing the tahini flavor. Serve this with our oil-free harissa sauce (page 176) and crostini.

1 large globe eggplant, cut into ½-inch dice

1 teaspoon sea salt

1 yellow onion, cut into ½-inch dice

4 to 6 cloves garlic, minced

1 cup vegetable stock or water

1 jalapeno chile, seeded and diced

2 teaspoons cumin seeds, toasted and ground (see page 234)

1 teaspoon coriander seeds, toasted and ground (see page234)

1 teaspoon dried oregano

¼ cup fresh lemon juice

3 tablespoons tahini, or 3 ounces silken tofu

2 teaspoons sea salt

2½ cups water

1 tablespoon powdered agar agar, or 3 tablespoons agar agar flakes

Combine eggplant cubes with the 1 teaspoon salt, place in a colander, and let stand for 20 minutes, rinse off salt and pat dry.

In a large skillet, cook the eggplant, onion, and garlic in stock over medium heat until the eggplant is hot and most of the liquid evaporated, about 20 minutes. Add the chile, cumin, coriander, and oregano and cook for 10 more minutes, stirring to prevent scorching. Remove from heat and set aside.

Add the lemon juice, tahini, 2 teaspoons salt, and 1 cup of the water to the eggplant mixture and purée in a blender. In a small saucepan, bring the remaining 1 1/2 cups water to a boil and whisk in the agar agar, continuing to whisk until thoroughly dissolved. Add the dissolved agar to the blender and blend until thoroughly incorporated.

Test the pâté to ensure that it sets up by refrigerating a tablespoonful of the pâté for 10 minutes. If the test pâté isn't firm by then, dissolve 1 teaspoon agar agar powder or 1 tablespoon agar agar flakes in 1/2 cup boiling water and add to the pâté. Spread the pâté in an 8 x 5-inch loaf pan or an 8-cup mold. Refrigerate for 2 hours before serving.

VARIATIONS:

Try smoking the eggplant (see page 235) or adding finely chopped black olives before the pâté sets up.

NUTRITIONAL INFORMATION PER 3-OUNCE SERVING PÂTÉ:

79 Calories (34% from fat), 2 g Protein, 11 g Carbohydrate, 3 g Fat, 0 mg Cholesterol, 571 mg Sodium, 3 g Fiber

CHICKPEA FLAT BREAD

MAKES 8 SERVINGS

This is a variation of socca, a traditional Roman bread dating back many centuries. Made from chickpea flour, it has a soft, dense, and slightly grainy texture that goes perfectly with our pâtés or spreads like our Baba Ganoush. Also try different seasonings. We have had great success with curry powder and cilantro.

2 cups chickpea flour (garbanzo flour)

1 teaspoon minced garlic

1 teaspoon cumin seed, toasted and coarsely ground (see page 234)

1 teaspoon minced fresh rosemary

1/3 teaspoon red pepper flakes

1 teaspoon sea salt

4 cups water, or more as needed

In a large bowl, combine the chickpea flour, garlic, cumin, rosemary, pepper flakes, and salt. Gradually whisk in 4 cups water. Add more water as needed to bring the batter to the consistency of heavy cream.

Preheat oven to 400°. Grease an 8 x 10-inch sided baking sheet and line the bottom with parchment paper. Pour the batter into the prepared pan and bake for 15 minutes, or until the bread is brown on the edges and firm in the center (check every 5 minutes). Let cool before slicing into wedges. Store in an airtight container for up to 4 days. To serve after the flat bread has been refrigerated, warm in a 250° oven until warm to the touch.

NUTRITIONAL INFORMATION PER WEDGE:

82 Calories (16% from fat), 4 g Protein, 13 g Carbohydrate, 1.5 g Fat, 0 mg Cholesterol, 325 mg Sodium, 3 g Fiber

MUSHROOM AND HAZELNUT-STUFFED ARTICHOKES WITH SAFFRON-GARLIC SAUCE

MAKES 6 SERVINGS

Some people claim that artichokes, saffron, and mushrooms have aphrodisiac effects. This will be up to you to decide. This dish is both earthy and elegant. The artichokes are braised in a flavorful tomato and herb mixture that can double as a sauce or be used as a garnish. If this method is too time-consuming, simply boil the artichokes in water or stock with lemon juice to prevent discoloration.

3 large artichokes

Juice of 1 lemon

16 ounces quality canned tomatoes, diced
    (reserve juice)

1 lemon, halved

1 cup dry white wine or nonalcoholic white wine
    or water

1 tablespoon minced garlic

1 teaspoon dried thyme

2 bay leaves

2 tablespoons extra virgin olive oil (optional)

1 teaspoon sea salt

FILLING

1 small yellow onion, finely diced

1 teaspoon minced garlic

2 teaspoons olive oil , vegetable stock, or dry sherry

8 ounces cremini or button mushrooms,
    cut into 1/2-inch slices

2 red bell peppers, roasted, peeled, and
    cut into 1/3-inch cubes (see page 235)

1 teaspoon dried thyme

1 teaspoon ground cumin

1/2 teaspoon ground cinnamon

1 teaspoon sea salt

1/4 teaspoon cayenne pepper

1/4 cup hazelnuts, toasted, skinned, and ground
    (see page 234), optional

1/2 cup fresh bread crumbs, toasted (see page 234)

Saffron-Garlic Sauce (recipe follows)

Minced fresh parsley or finely shredded basil
    for garnish

Remove the tough outer leaves of the artichokes and cut off the stems. Cut the artichokes in half lengthwise, and remove the chokes with a teaspoon. Put in a bowl, cover with water, add the lemon juice, and set aside.

Combine the tomatoes, lemon halves, wine, garlic, thyme, bay leaves, oil, and salt in an 8-inch square baking dish. Put the artichokes in the dish, cut-side down. Cover with aluminum foil and bake for 40 minutes, or until the artichokes are soft in the center. Drain, reserving the braising liquid. Set the artichokes aside to cool.

To make the filling: In a large sauté pan or skillet over medium heat, sauté the onion and garlic in the oil until lightly browned. Add the mushrooms, red peppers, thyme, cumin, cinnamon, sea salt, and cayenne. Sauté until most of the mushroom liquid evaporates, about 20 minutes. Remove from the heat and add the ground hazelnuts and bread crumbs. Fill each artichoke half with the filling. Bake in a 400° oven for 15 minutes, or until the artichoke and filling are heated through.

Coat the bottom of each serving plate with 1/4 cup of the saffron-garlic sauce. Place a tablespoonful of the reserved braising liquid in the center of the saffron sauce. Place an artichoke half on top of the tomato mixture. Garnish with the parsley or basil.

VARIATION:

For an even more elaborate presentation, dot the saffron sauce with a couple drops of Red Beet Reduction (page 174) and drag a knife through it to create a pattern.

NUTRITIONAL INFORMATION PER SERVING ARTICHOKE:

(With oil and hazelnuts) 266 Calories (34% from fat), 9 g Protein, 35 g Carbohydrate, 10 g Fat, 0 mg Cholesterol, 916 mg Sodium, 8 g Fiber

(Without oil and hazelnuts) 204 Calories (18% from fat), 8 g Protein, 34 g Carbohydrate, 4 g Fat, 0 mg Cholesterol, 916 mg Sodium, 8 g Fiber

Saffron-Garlic Sauce

MAKES 2 CUPS

1/2 cup Millennium Braised Garlic (page 230)
1 1/2 teaspoons minced garlic
1/4 cup cashews, or 3 ounces silken tofu
1 cup water
1/3 teaspoon saffron threads, soaked in 1/4 cup warm water
1/2 cup fresh lemon juice
1 tablespoon capers, drained
1/3 teaspoon ground pepper
2 teaspoons nutritional yeast (optional)
Sea salt to taste

In a blender, combine all the ingredients and blend thoroughly until smooth, adding more water to thin if needed. Taste and adjust the seasonings, heat until just hot enough to serve.

NUTRITIONAL INFORMATION PER 1/4 CUP SERVING:

42 Calories (43% from fat), 1 g Protein, 5 g Carbohydrate, 2 g Fat, 0 mg Cholesterol, 42 mg Sodium, 0.4 g Fiber

GRILLED MARINATED VEGETABLES

Grilled vegetables (fruits, too) are usually the centerpiece of our antipasto display at the restaurant. We display a bountiful section of seasonal vegetables grilled with any one of our marinades and served alongside a few of our grain, bean, or vegetables salads. A platter of grilled vegetables is ideal for entertaining. The vegetables can be cooked ahead of time and set on a platter drizzled with more of the marinade they were grilled with, awaiting your guests' arrival.

If you don't have a grill (or you don't somehow feel like firing up a grill during a snowstorm or in cold weather), fire up the oven or oven broiler and roast in a 450° oven on a lightly greased sheet pan. Or grab a large skillet or sauté pan, heat it over high heat with or without a little oil, and sear the vegetables. Then pour some of the marinade into the pan and let it glaze the vegetables.

What vegetables should you use and how do you prepare them? Don't fight the seasons—don't bother with some mealy dried-out corn shipped in December from some country you never knew existed when you can grill or roast slices of fresh winter squash and sweet parsnips—and, if you're lucky, meaty chanterelle mushrooms—or apples, pears, firm peaches, and Fuyu persimmons. Almost any seasonal vegetable or fruit can be grilled or roasted with pleasing results. Some, like asparagus and zucchini, can be grilled without being blanched. Others, especially thick or dense veggies like winter squash, root vegetables, and artichokes, should be blanched before being grilled. Their dense flesh will prevent them from being cooked through before their exteriors become charred by the high direct heat. This also applies if you are roasting these vegetables, though you may also slice them thinner for roasting, without worrying they will fall through the grill grids or break apart from being turned and moved on the grill.

Here is an overview of some of the produce that finds its way onto our grill and into our oven at Millennium. Some are perennial favorites that are available all year long, like button mushrooms and red onions; others, like fiddlehead ferns and strawberry daikon, are with us for a very brief period of time (these may also be hard to find in many areas).

SUMMER

Most of the obvious choices for grilling vegetables are the summer staples: corn, zucchini and other summer squash, eggplant, and peppers. None of these require any blanching, though some varieties of eggplant should be salted, allowed to "sweat," and rinsed to remove some of their bitter acids. A slightly less obvious choice is tomatoes; they will fall apart if sliced thin, but cut them in half or leave them whole (if they're small), sear them quickly on the grill or broil them, and they are not to be missed. Or try grilling slices of firm peaches or plum halves. At the restaurant we grill firm purple-fleshed elephant heart plums with our Sesame-Black Bean Marinade and serve them with slightly underripe O'Henry peaches grilled with our Madras Paste for a truly outrageous flavor combination.

FALL

The coming of the equinox brings us hard squashes, root vegetables, bitter greens like endive, radicchio, and broccoli rabe, green beans, broccoli, and cauliflower, as well as apples and pears and, in our area, the start of wild mushroom season (coinciding with the beginning of

the rainy season). We've had great results grilling most (if not all) varieties of hard squashes. We usually slice 1- to 2-inch wedges of pumpkins and butternut, kuri, and kabocha squashes (to name a few) and blanch them just until the flesh is al dente before grilling. Try smearing rounds of thin-skinned Delicata squash with our Madras Paste and throwing them directly onto the grill without blanching.

Sear stalks of Belgian endive and halved heads of radicchio with our Citrus-Thyme Marinade or Millennium Mojo for no more than a minute or so, so the exterior is charred and caramelized while leaving the interior crunchy and bitter. Try the same technique with blanched broccoli rabe and broccoli spears, using our Sesame-Black Bean Marinade.

Grill or broil slices of most varieties of apples or pears, or the firm-fleshed Fuyu persimmon, with our Rum and Allspice Glaze for a sweet and savory combination that would work as well on an antipasto platter as it would with a scoop of vanilla ice cream.

Mushrooms, wild and domestic, are a year-round favorite on our grill. Besides the common buttons, cremini, and portobellos, do not pass up the opportunity to grill wild species like lobster mushrooms, chanterelles, and porcini, among others, as well as domestic shiitakes. Even the thin-fleshed oyster mushrooms are fantastic grilled—just keep a watchful eye on them to prevent overcooking. Try some of our lighter marinades with the wild mushrooms so as not to mask their delicate flavors (though we really do like lobster mushrooms with Madras Paste or with Millennium Mojo made with chipotle paste).

WINTER

Winter brings more of the same. Look for quality root vegetables, beets, fennel bulbs, leeks, and even daikon radish in addition to the fall vegetables above. Try grilling or roasting blanched slices of parsnip, carrot, celery root, and rutabaga with our Moroccan Marinade. Blanch quartered fennel bulb and beets and grill with our Citrus-Thyme Marinade, then toss with segments of orange and ruby grapefruit for a winter salad. Let's not forget potatoes. We usually blanch ours before we grill them, about 5 to 7 minutes for 1/2-inch pieces. Don't pass up purple Peruvian or other specialty potatoes if they present themselves. We grill slices of tropical pineapple or firm, underripe mango with our Millennium Mojo or Sesame Marinade for intriguing flavor and texture combinations.

SPRING

Spring is also a great time for grilling vegetables. There are lots of young vegetables that can go right on the grill without blanching: baby artichokes, baby bulbs of fennel, and spring garlic shoots without cloves or young garlic with barely developed, tender cloves. Look for baby leeks and onions, as well as sweet Walla Walla and Maui onions.

Foraged fiddlehead ferns and ramps (wild leeks) make a brief appearance in the spring and are great seared on the grill or broiled for a minute or so to caramelize the marinade and slightly char the exterior. Try roasting morel mushrooms and toss with roasted fiddleheads and spring onions drizzled with our Citrus-Thyme Marinade. Sweet peas, fava beans, and other young shelling legumes can be marinated and grilled in the pod until the pod is charred. The beans inside will be steamed al dente and subtly infused with the grill smoke and marinade. Serve them to your guests in the shell for an understated treat. And don't forget asparagus. Grill medium (pencil-thick) stalks with any of the marinades for our favorite treat of the spring market. Blanch older, thicker stalks until al dente before grilling.

Grilled Vegetables

MAKES 6 SERVINGS

1½ pounds vegetables, sliced and/or blanched
    as needed

1 to 1½ cups marinade (recipes follow)

To grill: Make sure the grill grids are clean of burned-on food and carbon deposits, which may stick to the food being grilled and add undesirable burned flavors. It's best to clean the grill grates in between batches as you grill to prevent build-up.

The cooking rack should be preheated and very hot, especially if you are grilling without oil. Sufficiently hot grills will sear a crust on whatever you are grilling, preventing the food from sticking.

Marinate the vegetables by immersing them in the marinade for 4 to 5 minutes or up to 15 minutes for mushrooms, eggplants, and winter squashes before grilling. Drain and place on the hot cooking rack. Turn the vegetables often at a 90-degree angle. Brush on some of the marinade each time you turn the vegetables, to keep them moist and infuse them with flavor.

Cook until the vegetables are done to your personal preference. Some people prefer zucchini and asparagus very crunchy, with few grill marks. Some vegetables, like most wild mushrooms, potatoes, and winter squashes, need to be cooked through to be digestible or appealing to the palate. They may need to spend a bit more time on the grill or be blanched before grilling.

To oven roast or broil: Preheat the oven or broiler to 400° to 450°. Especially for roasting, try to make sure the vegetables or vegetable slices are of relatively uniform size to ensure that they cook evenly.

Place the vegetables on a baking sheet in a single layer without overcrowding. Roast or broil in the center of the oven, turning the vegetables often. Brush with more marinade when you turn the vegetables.

Moroccan Marinade

MAKES 2½ CUPS

The Millennium Standard, this marinade is always on hand—we use it on everything! Try sautéing blanched baby artichokes with it, and see our Moroccan Crepe recipe for other inspirations.

1½ cups tomato sauce or tomato purée

½ cup fresh orange juice

½ cup fresh lemon juice

¼ cup tamari soy sauce

4 cloves garlic

¼ cup honey or sweetener of choice

½ teaspoon red pepper flakes

1 teaspoon ground coriander

½ teaspoon ground cinnamon

2 teaspoons ground cumin

1 teaspoon fennel seeds, ground

2 teaspoons minced fresh ginger

1 tablespoon balsamic vinegar

Combine all the ingredients in a blender and blend until smooth. Store in an airtight container in the refrigerator for up to 2 weeks.

NUTRITIONAL INFORMATION PER
¼ CUP MARINADE:

63 Calories (0% from fat), 1 g Protein, 14 g Carbohydrate, 0 g Fat, 0 mg Cholesterol, 548 mg Sodium, 1 g Fiber

Sesame-Black Bean Marinade

MAKES 2 CUPS

This Asian marinade's pungent quality comes from Chinese fermented black beans. Combine them with spicy ginger, sweet Sucanat, and toasted sesame seeds, and you can't go wrong.

3 tablespoons Sucanat or honey or rice syrup

2 teaspoons fermented black beans, minced

2 or 3 cloves garlic, minced

1 tablespoon minced fresh ginger

1 serrano chile, minced, or $1/2$ teaspoon
   red pepper flakes

2 tablespoons sesame seeds, toasted (see page 234)

$1/2$ cup tamari soy sauce

$2/3$ cup water

2 tablespoons ketchup

$1/4$ cup balsamic vinegar

2 to 3 tablespoons Asian sesame oil (optional)

Combine all of the ingredients in a medium bowl and whisk until incorporated. Store in an airtight container in the refrigerator for up to 2 weeks.

NUTRITIONAL INFORMATION PER
$1/4$ CUP MARINADE:

(with oil) 89 Calories (51% from fat), 2 g Protein, 9 g Carbohydrate, 5 g Fat, 0 mg Cholesterol, 814 mg Sodium, 0.6 g Fiber

(without oil) 53 Calories (17% from fat), 2 g Protein, 9 g Carbohydrate, 1 g Fat, 0 mg Cholesterol, 814 mg Sodium, 0.6 g Fiber

Citrus and Thyme Marinade

MAKES 2 CUPS

This simple marinade is a bit more delicate than our other marinades. If you wish, add minced garlic and substitute fresh tarragon for the rosemary, or add ginger and sesame seeds, or minced chile and chopped cilantro.

$1/2$ cup fresh lemon juice

$2/3$ cup fresh orange, grapefruit, or lime juice

$1/2$ cup olive oil (optional)

1 teaspoon minced lemon zest

$1/2$ teaspoon minced orange zest

2 tablespoons tamari soy sauce

1 tablespoon minced fresh thyme or lemon thyme

1 teaspoon minced fresh rosemary

$1/2$ teaspoon sea salt

Freshly ground black pepper to taste

Combine all of the ingredients in a medium bowl and whisk until incorporated. Store in an airtight container in the refrigerator for up to 1 week.

NUTRITIONAL INFORMATION PER
$1/4$ CUP MARINADE:

(with oil) 146 Calories (86% from fat), 1 g Protein, 4 g Carbohydrate, 14 g Fat, 0 mg Cholesterol, 360 mg Sodium, 0.2 g Fiber

(without oil) 20 Calories (0% from fat), 1 g Protein, 4 g Carbohydrate, 0 g Fat, 0 mg Cholesterol, 360 mg Sodium, 0.2 g Fiber

Mojo Marinade

MAKES 1 1/2 CUPS

Mojos, of Latin-American origin, are somewhere between a marinade, a dipping sauce, a salad dressing, and a salad. The variations are endless (there are probably books devoted exclusively to mojos). The starting point for our mojos is sautéed or toasted garlic (dry toasting it imparts a darker garlic flavor), citrus juice, and usually, cumin. After that, you can go off in a number of different directions. A personal favorite is mojo blended with chipotle chile paste and fresh mango. Use mojos to marinate vegetables, fruits, tofu, tempeh, and seitan. Serve the remaining mojo as a dipping sauce.

4 cloves garlic, minced
2 tablespoons olive oil (optional)
2 teaspoons ground cumin
1/2 cup fresh orange juice
1/4 cup fresh lime juice
2 teaspoons Sucanat or 1 tablespoon honey
1/2 to 1 serrano or jalapeno chile, seeded and minced
1/4 cup canola oil (optional)
Sea salt to taste

In a small sauté pan or skillet over medium heat, sauté the garlic in the olive oil until the garlic is lightly browned. Or toast the garlic in a dry pan. Add the cumin and remove from the heat. In a blender, combine the garlic with the remaining ingredients and blend until smooth. Store in an airtight container in the refrigerator for up to 1 week.

NUTRITIONAL INFORMATION PER 1/4 CUP MARINADE:

(with oil) 101 Calories (80% from fat), 0 g Protein, 5 g Carbohydrate, 9 g Fat, 0 mg Cholesterol, 26 mg Sodium, 0.2 g Fiber

(without oil) 20 Calories (0% from fat), 0 g Protein, 5 g Carbohydrate, 0 g Fat, 0 mg Cholesterol, 26 mg Sodium, 0.2 g Fiber

VARIATIONS

- Add cubes of orange, grapefruit, lemon, and lime to the finished mojo recipe, along with chopped fresh cilantro and/or mint, and serve as a dipping sauce or salsa.

- When blending the mojo, add 2 to 3 tablespoons chopped fresh cilantro, mint, basil (especially lemon basil), or parsley. Note: this will hold only for 2 or 3 days.

- Substitute 2 teaspoons to 1 tablespoon Chipotle Paste (page 174) for the serrano chile. Try blending in the flesh of half a ripe mango along with the chipotle for a sweet, hot, and smoky mojo—addictive!

- Add 1 tablespoon chopped fresh rosemary, 1 tablespoon chopped fresh thyme, and 1 teaspoon chopped fresh sage to the basic mojo when blending—especially with added grapefruit juice or 1 cup cubed fresh pineapple.

Rum, Allspice, and Black Pepper Glaze

MAKES 2/3 CUP

We like to use this on broiled fruit: The glaze really caramelizes onto the fruit. Try it with apples, pears, Fuyu persimmons, peaches, firm bananas, and ripe plantains for starters. Serve the glazed fruit as a dessert with non-dairy ice cream.

1/2 cup dark rum
2 teaspoons orange liqueur (optional)
3 tablespoons Sucanat, or 2 tablespoons maple syrup
1 teaspoon ground allspice
1/2 teaspoon coarsely ground pepper
Salt to taste

In a small bowl, whisk together all the ingredients until well combined. Store in an airtight container in the refrigerator for up to 2 weeks.

NUTRITIONAL INFORMATION PER TABLESPOON GLAZE:

43 Calories (0% from fat), 0 g Protein, 4 g Carbohydrate, 0 g Fat, 0 mg Cholesterol, 10 mg Sodium, 0 g Fiber

Tandoori Marinade

MAKES 3 CUPS

Besides being used on our Madras tofu entrée (page 118), this paste-like marinade is unbeatable on vegetables and on fruits like peaches or pears. It's a little more complex than some of our other marinades, but well worth the effort.

3 tablespoons paprika
1 teaspoon fennel seeds, toasted and ground (see page 234)
1 1/4 teaspoons cardamom seeds, toasted and ground (see page 234)
1 tablespoon coriander seeds, toasted and ground (see page 234)
2 teaspoons cumin seeds, toasted and ground (see page 234)
1/4 teaspoons cayenne pepper
1/2 teaspoon ground pepper
1 teaspoon sea salt
1/2 yellow onion, finely diced
1/4 cup canola oil (optional)
2 cloves garlic
5 ounces silken tofu
1 1/2 cups soy milk or water
1 teaspoon minced lime zest
1/4 cup fresh lime juice

In a dry skillet, combine the paprika, fennel, cardamom, coriander, and cumin. Heat over medium heat. Stir the mixture and toast until the mixture smells fragrant and is slightly darker, approximately 3 minutes.

In a blender, blend the spices and all the remaining ingredients together. Store in an airtight container in the refrigerator for up to 2 weeks.

NUTRITIONAL INFORMATION PER 1/4 CUP MARINADE:

(with oil) 78 Calories (69% from fat), 2 g Protein, 4 g Carbohydrate, 6 g Fat, 0 mg Cholesterol, 184 mg Sodium, 1 g Fiber

(without oil) 33 Calories (27% from fat), 2 g Protein, 4 g Carbohydrate, 1 g Fat, 0 mg Cholesterol, 201 mg Sodium, 1 g Fiber

Cabbage and Shiitake-Filled Spring Rolls with Plum Sauce

MAKES 12 ROLLS; SERVES 6

Next to the plantain torte, this is probably the most popular appetizer to grace our menu. Crisp baked sesame-crusted spring rolls are set over lightly dressed, mint-spiked Napa cabbage in a pool of sweet, pungent, and tangy homemade plum sauce. Yum!

FILLING

2 ounces dry rice stick noodles

1 red onion, cut lengthwise into 1/2-inch crescents

2 teaspoons minced garlic

2 tablespoons canola oil

1/2 teaspoon red pepper flakes

1 tablespoon minced fresh ginger

8 cups shredded red cabbage (about 1 head)

4 ounces shiitake mushrooms, stemmed and thinly sliced

1 teaspoon sea salt

1 tablespoon tamari soy sauce

2 tablespoons finely shredded fresh mint

2 tablespoons finely shredded fresh basil

1 tablespoon chopped fresh cilantro

1/4 cup canola oil

1 tablespoon Asian sesame oil

1 tablespoon Sucanat or fructose

1 16-ounce package filo dough, thawed

1 tablespoon sesame seeds

Marinated Napa Cabbage (recipe follows)

1 1/2 cups Plum Sauce (recipe follows)

3 tablespoons julienned Pickled Ginger (page 19), plus more for garnish

Sesame seeds and minced scallions for garnish

To make the filling: Place the noodles in a mixing bowl. Pour over boiling water to cover. Let sit for 10 minutes, drain the noodles, and set them aside.

In a large sauté pan or skillet, sauté the onion and garlic in the canola oil over medium heat until slightly softened. Add the pepper flakes and ginger and sauté for 2 minutes. Add the cabbage, mushrooms, and salt. Sauté until the cabbage is softened, about 10 minutes. Add the tamari and remove from the heat. Let cool to room temperature. Mix in the noodles, mint, basil, and cilantro, and set aside.

Preheat the oven to 400°. Line a baking sheet with parchment paper.

To assemble: In a small bowl, combine the canola oil, sesame oil, and Sucanat. On a clean, dry surface, lay 1 sheet of filo dough. (Cover the remaining dough with a towel to keep it moist.) Brush some of the oil mixture over the filo. Place 2 more sheets on top, brushing each with oil.

Place a 1-inch-wide by 1-inch-thick layer of filling across the bottom of the filo. Roll the filo into a cylinder, starting from the filling end of the dough. Repeat with remaining filling and sheets of filo.

Slice each roll crosswise into 4 equal pieces and place on the prepared baking sheet. Brush the tops of the rolls with the remaining oil mixture and sprinkle with the sesame seeds. Bake for 15 minutes, or until lightly browned. Let cool for a few minutes before serving.

To serve: mound a 1/3-cup portion of the Marinated Napa Cabbage in the center of each of 6 serving plates. Place 2 of the spring rolls on the cabbage and spoon 4 tablespoons of the Plum Sauce around the plate. Garnish with julienne Pickled Ginger, sesame seeds, and minced scallions.

NUTRITIONAL INFORMATION PER 2-ROLL SERVING:

492 Calories (29% from fat), 11 g Protein, 76 g Carbohydrate, 16 g Fat, 0 mg Cholesterol, 823 Sodium, 7 g Fiber

Marinated Napa Cabbage

MAKES 2 CUPS

4 cups shredded Napa cabbage (about 1/2 head)

1 carrot, peeled and shredded

2 scallions, diced

1/4 cup fresh lemon juice

1 teaspoon sea salt

2 tablespoons finely shredded fresh mint

2 tablespoons minced fresh cilantro

In a large bowl, combine all the ingredients. Salad will keep for up to 2 days if refrigerated in an airtight container, though it will lose its crunchy texture.

NUTRITIONAL INFORMATION PER 1/3 CUP MARINATED NAPA CABBAGE:

28 Calories (0% from fat), 1 g Protein, 6 g Carbohydrate, 0 g Fat, 0 mg Cholesterol, 372 mg Sodium, 1 g Fiber

Plum Sauce

MAKES 3 CUPS

1 tablespoon minced garlic

1 jalapeno chile, minced and seeded

1 tablespoon sesame seeds

2 teaspoons fermented black beans

2 teaspoons minced fresh ginger

1 cup Millennium Ponzu (page 87), or
1/3 cup tamari soy sauce mixed with 3 tablespoons Sucanat or honey, 1/3 teaspoon red pepper flakes, and 2/3 cup vegetable stock or water

1/2 cup vegetable stock or water

1/4 cup fresh lemon juice

1 teaspoon minced lemon zest

1 tablespoon Sucanat

4 to 6 dark-fleshed plums, such as Santa Rosa or elephant heart, pitted and sliced into 1-inch cubes

In a small saucepan, combine the garlic, chile, and sesame seeds. Cook over high heat, stirring constantly, for 2 minutes, or until the seeds and garlic brown slightly. Add all the remaining ingredients. Reduce heat and simmer for 30 minutes, or until the plums are very soft. Transfer to a blender and blend until very smooth. Let cool to room temperature before using. Store in an airtight container for up to 1 week.

NUTRITIONAL INFORMATION PER 4 TABLESPOONS SAUCE:

52 Calories (0% from fat), 1 g Protein, 12 g Carbohydrate, 0 g Fat, 0 mg Cholesterol, 320 mg Sodium, 1 g Fiber

Pickled Ginger

MAKES 1 CUP

1 3-inch piece young fresh ginger, peeled

1/2 cup rice vinegar

1/2 cup water

3 tablespoons fructose or unrefined sugar

1 tablespoon sea salt

Using a vegetable peeler, cut the ginger into long, very thin ribbons. In a small saucepan, combine the ginger and the remaining ingredients. Bring to a boil and cook for 10 minutes.

Remove from heat and let the ginger cool in the brine. Store in an airtight container in the refrigerator for up to 2 weeks.

VARIATION:

Add 1 small sliced beet to the ginger as it boils so the ginger takes on a red hue.

NUTRITIONAL INFORMATION PER 1 OUNCE SERVING GINGER:

16 Calories (0% from fat), 0 g Protein, 4 g Carbohydrate, 0 g Fat, 0 mg Cholesterol, 105 mg Sodium, 0 g Fiber

RICE PAPER SPRING ROLLS WITH CITRUS VINAIGRETTE

MAKES 12 ROLLS; SERVES 6

This light and flavorful appetizer has no added fat. Asian rice paper wrappers are simple to master and are found in the Asian food section of many supermarkets.

12 8-inch round rice paper sheets

1 red onion, cut crosswise into very thin slices

1 carrot, peeled and shredded

1 fennel bulb, cut crosswise into very thin slices

4 cups shredded red cabbage ($1/2$ small head)

3 tablespoons rice vinegar

1 tablespoon umeboshi vinegar or tamari soy sauce

2 tablespoons minced fresh cilantro

3 tablespoons finely shredded fresh mint leaves

3 tablespoons finely shredded fresh Thai basil or sweet basil leaves

1 mango, peeled and cut into $1/4$-inch slices

3 tablespoons unsalted roasted peanuts, coarsely chopped (optional)

$1^1/2$ cups Citrus Vinaigrette (page 35)

Pour some warm water into a medium mixing bowl. Soak 1 paper towel in the water and lay it on a clean, flat surface. Place 1 rice paper wrapper on the wet paper towel and cover it with another wet paper towel. Repeat the processes until all the rice wrappers are covered with damp paper towels. Set aside.

In a large bowl, combine the onion, carrot, fennel, and cabbage with the rice and umeboshi vinegars. Let sit for 15 minutes, or until the cabbage softens. Stir in the cilantro, mint, and basil.

Lay 1 rice paper wrapper on a dry surface and place 2 tablespoons of the cabbage filling in the center of the wrapper. Top with a few slices of the mango and some of the chopped peanuts. Fold two sides of the wrapper over the filling, then roll the wrapper into a tight cylinder starting at the bottom. Repeat the process to use all the rice wrappers. Serve 2 rolls per person with a small bowl of the vinaigrette.

NUTRITIONAL INFORMATION PER 2-ROLL SERVING:

117 Calories (8% from fat), 3 g Protein, 24 g Carbohydrate, 1 g Fat, 0 mg Cholesterol, 278 mg Sodium, 3 g Fiber

JASMINE RICE CAKES WITH OYSTER MUSHROOM-LEEK RAGOUT AND QUINCE CHUTNEY

MAKES 6 SERVINGS

This is not as "out there" as it sounds. The flavors are actually very straightforward and clean. The oyster mushroom ragout owes a debt to the many Chinese seafood preparations that combine ginger and fermented black beans. The quince chutney is a surprising complement to this dish.

JASMINE RICE CAKES

1 yellow onion, cut into small dice

1 teaspoon minced garlic

1 tablespoon sesame seeds

2 cups jasmine rice or brown basmati rice

1 teaspoon minced lime zest

1 teaspoon minced lemongrass, white part only (optional)

$1^1/2$ teaspoons sea salt

$3^1/2$ cups water

$1/4$ cup fresh lime juice

MUSHROOM-LEEK RAGOUT

2 leeks, washed well and cut into $^1/_2$-inch-thick crosswise slices

2 teaspoons minced garlic

$^1/_2$ cup dry white wine, nonalcoholic white wine, or vegetable stock

$^1/_2$ teaspoon red pepper flakes

1 teaspoon minced fresh ginger

2 teaspoons fermented black beans, rinsed

1 pound oyster mushrooms

2 tablespoons tamari soy sauce

1 cup vegetable stock

Sea salt to taste

1 teaspoon cornstarch mixed with 2 tablespoons cold water

6 tablespoons Quince Chutney (recipe follows)

2 scallions, cut into thin diagonal slices

Sesame seeds

1 lemon, cut into 6 wedges

To make the rice cakes: In a large saucepan over high heat, toast the onion, garlic, and sesame seeds, stirring constantly, for 1 minute. Add the rice, lime zest, lemongrass, and salt, and stir to toast the rice for 1 minute. Add the water and lime juice. Bring to a boil, reduce heat, cover, and simmer for 15 minutes if using jasmine rice, 25 minutes if using brown basmati.

Turn the rice out onto a baking sheet and spread out. Let cool to room temperature. Preheat the oven to 400°. Line a baking sheet with parchment paper.

Blend 1 cup of the rice mixture in a blender or food processor until smooth. In a medium bowl, combine the rice purée and remaining rice. Mix well. Form the rice mixture into twelve 2-inch-round by 1-inch-thick cakes and bake on the prepared pan for 15 minutes, or until dry and crisp on top, while still moist in the center.

Meanwhile, make the ragout: In a medium saucepan, cook the leeks and garlic in the wine over medium heat until the liquid evaporates,

about 15 minutes. Add the pepper flakes, ginger, black beans, mushrooms, tamari, and stock and simmer for 15 minutes. Add the salt, stir in the cornstarch mixture to thicken, and remove from heat.

To serve, place $^2/_3$ cup ragout on each of 6 serving plates. Stack 2 rice cakes on top and top with 1 tablespoon of the chutney. Garnish with chopped scallion, sesame seeds, and a lemon wedge.

NUTRITIONAL INFORMATION PER 2-CAKE SERVING:

322 Calories (6% from fat), 8 g Protein, 68 g Carbohydrate, 2 g Fat, 0 mg Cholesterol, 935 mg Sodium, 3 g Fiber

Quince Chutney

MAKES 2 CUPS

$^1/_3$ cup rice vinegar or champagne vinegar

2 tablespoons fructose or Sucanat

1 teaspoon red pepper flakes

1 teaspoon ground coriander

1 red bell pepper, seeded, deribbed, and cut into $^1/_3$-inch dice

2 quince, peeled, pitted, and cut into $^1/_3$-inch dice (about 2$^1/_2$ cups)

$^1/_2$ teaspoon sea salt

2 teaspoons minced fresh ginger

In a medium nonreactive saucepan, heat the vinegar and fructose over medium heat until the sweetener dissolves. Stir in the pepper flakes, coriander, bell pepper, quince, salt, and ginger. Cook for 15 minutes, or until the quince is tender but still retains its shape. Remove from heat and let cool to room temperature. Store in an airtight container in the refrigerator for up to 1 week.

NUTRITIONAL INFORMATION PER 1 TABLESPOON SERVING CHUTNEY:

9 Calories (0% from fat), 0.1 g Protein, 2 g Carbohydrate, 0 g Fat, 0 mg Cholesterol, 36 mg Sodium, 0.2 g Fiber

HEIRLOOM TOMATO AND WHITE BEAN PESTO TORTE

MAKES 6 SERVINGS

We prepared this one for one of our aphrodisiac dinners during the summer, at the height of the tomato and basil season. This dish is visually appealing, especially if you have a variety of tomatoes to use: seek out Marvel Stripes, Evergreen, Green Zebra, Brandywine, or Golden Jubilee tomatoes. The oven drying really intensifies the tomato flavor, though using slices of raw tomato also works well.

OVEN-DRIED TOMATOES

6 large heirloom tomatoes, cut into $1/3$-inch slices
$1/4$ teaspoon sea salt

WHITE BEAN PESTO

1 cup cooked white beans
$1/2$ cup Millennium Braised Garlic (page 230) (equivalent of 1 head)
2 teaspoons minced garlic
$1/2$ bunch fresh basil, stemmed
$1/3$ cup water
1 teaspoon ground pepper
1 teaspoon sea salt

BEAN SALAD

1 cup cooked white beans
$1/2$ cup chopped fresh tomato
1 scallion, sliced thin
$1/4$ cup minced fresh parsley
1 teaspoon minced lemon zest
$1/4$ cup fresh lemon juice
$1/2$ teaspoon sea salt
$1/2$ teaspoon ground pepper
1 bunch arugula, stemmed
$1/3$ cup Citrus Vinaigrette (page 35) or dressing of choice

To prepare the tomatoes: Preheat the oven to 250°. Place the tomato slices on a rack set over a parchment lined baking sheet. Sprinkle with the salt. Bake for 30 minutes, then gently turn the tomatoes over and bake for another 20 to 30 minutes. The tomatoes should be fairly dry. Let cool to room temperature.

To make the pesto: In a blender or food processor, combine the beans, the braised garlic, minced garlic, basil, water, pepper, and salt and blend until smooth. Set aside.

To make the salad: In a medium bowl, toss the beans, tomato, scallion, parsley, lemon zest, lemon juice, salt, and pepper together.

In a medium bowl, toss the arugula with the vinaigrette, then divide the arugula among 6 serving plates. Place a dried tomato slice over each mound of arugula, then top the tomato with 1 tablespoon of the pesto, followed by tablespoon of the bean salad. Repeat the procedure 2 more times until you have 3 layers of filling between 4 tomato slices. Serve immediately.

NUTRITIONAL INFORMATION PER SERVING TORTE:

177 Calories (5% from fat), 8 g Protein, 34 g Carbohydrate, 1 g Fat, 0 mg Cholesterol, 757 mg Sodium, 6 g Fiber

BARLEY RISOTTO CAKES WITH SMOKED ONION-CHIPOTLE SAUCE

MAKES 6 SERVINGS

This one's always a big hit. It's both crunchy and creamy in texture, as well as sweet, spicy and smoky in flavor. For the cakes, we start with a barley risotto, which is chilled so that the creamy element firms up before the risotto is breaded and sautéed.

BARLEY RISOTTO CAKES

1 yellow onion, cut into small dice

2 teaspoons minced garlic

1/4 cup dry sherry or nonalcoholic wine

1 tablespoon canola oil (optional)

1 red bell pepper, seeded, deribbed, and cut into small dice

1 teaspoon dried oregano

1 teaspoon dried thyme

2 cups barley

4 to 5 cups vegetable stock

Kernels cut from 2 ears fresh corn

3 ounces low-fat silken tofu

1 1/2 cups water

1 teaspoon sea salt

1 teaspoon ground pepper

1 1/2 cups all-purpose flour or corn flour

1/2 cup polenta

1/2 teaspoon dried oregano

1 teaspoon dried thyme

1 teaspoon paprika

1 teaspoon ground pepper

2 cups Smoked Onion-Chipotle Sauce

1/2 cup Lime-Pickled Onions (see page 42)

Fresh cilantro leaves

To make the risotto: In a large sauté pan or skillet, sauté the onion and garlic in the sherry and oil over medium heat until the onion is softened, about 5 minutes. Add the bell pepper, oregano, and thyme, and sauté for 2 minutes. Add the barley and stir into the onion mixture. Stir in 4 cups vegetable stock.

Partially cover and simmer until the barley absorbs all the stock, about 20 to 30 minutes. The barley should be cooked through but still al dente. If the barley is still firm, add the remaining 1 cup vegetable stock and cook until it is absorbed. In a blender, purée half the corn kernels with the tofu and water until smooth. Add to the barley with the remaining corn kernels and the salt and pepper. Mix well and pour onto a baking sheet. Refrigerate until cool and firm, about 1 hour.

In a shallow bowl, combine the flour, polenta, oregano, thyme, paprika, and pepper. Set aside. Form the chilled barley risotto into twelve 2-inch-round by 1/2-inch-thick cakes. Dredge in the flour mixture, coating well. In a nonstick sauté pan or skillet brushed with canola oil, cook the cakes for 3 minutes on each side, or until lightly browned. Or bake the cakes on a parchment-lined baking sheet pan in a preheated 450° oven for 10 minutes per side, or until lightly browned.

On each of 6 serving plates, place 1/4 cup warm Smoked Onion-Chipotle Sauce. Place 2 cakes in the sauce on each plate and garnish, if desired, with Lime-Pickled Onions and cilantro.

NUTRITIONAL INFORMATION PER 2-CAKE SERVING:

(with oil) 457 Calories (10% from fat), 11 g Protein, 92 g Carbohydrate, 5 g Fat, 0 mg Cholesterol, 1091 mg Sodium, 10 g Fiber

(without oil) 439 Calories (6% from fat), 11 g Protein, 92 g Carbohydrate, 3 g Fat, 0 mg Cholesterol, 1092 mg Sodium, 10 g Fiber

Smoked Onion-Chipotle Sauce

MAKES 3 CUPS
(¹/4 CUP PER SERVING)

2 red onions, halved and smoked (see page 233)

¹/4 cup dry sherry or nonalcoholic red wine

1 tablespoon canola oil (optional)

1 teaspoon ground cumin

1 teaspoon ground oregano

2 tablespoons honey

1 tablespoon balsamic vinegar

2 cups fresh or canned tomato purée

¹/4 cup Millennium Chipotle Paste (page 174) or
   canned chipotles in adobo

1 cup vegetable stock or water

2 teaspoons sea salt

Sauté the onions in the sherry and oil over medium heat until softened, about 15 minutes. Add the cumin and oregano, and sauté for 2 more minutes. Add the honey, vinegar, tomato purée, chipotle paste, stock, and salt. Simmer for 15 to 20 minutes. Serve warm.

NUTRITIONAL INFORMATION PER
¹/4 CUP SAUCE:

(with oil) 60 Calories (20% from fat), 1 g Protein, 11 g Carbohydrate, 1.3 g Fat, 0 mg Cholesterol, 433 mg Sodium, 1 g Fiber

(without oil) 49 Calories (2% from fat), 1 g Protein, 11 g Carbohydrate, 0.1 g Fat, 0 mg Cholesterol, 433 mg Sodium, 1 g Fiber

ROASTED TOMATO AND WHITE BEAN GALETTES

MAKES 4 SERVINGS

This is a great summer lunch or dinner entrée. It is as good served at room temperature, with a bed of lightly dressed greens, as it is hot. A variety of different-colored heirloom tomatoes makes this both visually pleasing and enjoyable to eat.

ROASTED TOMATOES

4 tomatoes, preferably different heirloom varieties
   of different colors

1 teaspoon extra virgin olive oil (optional)

¹/4 teaspoon sea salt

WHITE BEAN HUMMUS

4 cloves garlic, minced

1 tablespoon extra virgin olive oil (optional)

1¹/2 teaspoons ground cumin

2 teaspoons minced fresh sage or
   1¹/2 teaspoons dried sage

1 cup cooked white beans

1 teaspoon minced lemon zest

¹/4 cup fresh lemon juice

¹/4 cup water

1 teaspoon sea salt

Black pepper or dried chile flakes to taste

GALETTE DOUGH

1¹/2 cups unbleached all-purpose flour

¹/2 cup whole-wheat pastry flour

¹/4 teaspoon sea salt

¹/4 teaspoon ground pepper

¹/4 teaspoon dried thyme

3 tablespoons canola oil

¹/4 cup water

(recipe continues on next page)

TOPPING

1 tablespoon extra virgin olive oil (optional)
1 tablespoon mixed chopped fresh rosemary, oregano, and thyme

To roast the tomatoes: Preheat the oven to 300°. Cut the tomatoes into halves or thirds. Oil a parchment-lined sided baking sheet with the oil, place the tomato slices on the pan, and sprinkle with the salt. Bake for 30 minutes, or until the tomatoes are soft and release their liquid. Let cool. Using a slotted spatula, remove the tomatoes from the pan, reserving the excess liquid.

To make the hummus: In a small sauté pan or skillet, sauté the garlic in the oil over medium heat until just starting to brown, about 5 minutes. Add the cumin and sage and sauté for 1 minute. Remove to a medium bowl. Add the beans, lemon zest and juice, salt, and pepper. In a blender or food processor, purée until fairly smooth. Set aside.

To make the galette dough: In a medium bowl, combine the all-purpose flour, whole-wheat flour, salt, pepper, and thyme. Drizzle the oil into the flour mixture. Work the oil into flour with your hands until incorporated. Drizzle the water into the mixture, working it into the dough with your hands until you can form the dough into a ball that holds together. Cover in plastic wrap and refrigerate for 20 minutes. Dough can be made in advance and refrigerated up to 1 day.

Preheat the oven to 400°. Line a baking sheet with parchment paper. Divide the dough into 4 equal pieces. To roll out, place a piece of dough between 2 pieces of floured waxed or parchment paper. Roll the dough out to an 8- to 9-inch round. Repeat with the remaining dough.

Place 2 tablespoons hummus in the center of each circle of the dough and top with 4 pieces roasted tomato. Fold the sides of the dough over but not covering the filling to make a square shape. Place the galette on the prepared pan. Repeat with the remaining dough and fillings.

Drizzle the tomatoes on the galettes with the olive oil and sprinkle with the chopped herbs. Bake for 15 to 20 minutes, or until the dough is light brown and firm. Serve hot or at room temperature.

VARIATION:

For an oil-free version, delete the sautéing procedure in the hummus by substituting 1/4 cup Millennium Braised Garlic (page 230) and toasting the cumin (page 234).

NUTRITIONAL INFORMATION PER GALETTE:

385 Calories (30% from fat), 9 g Protein, 58 g Carbohydrate, 13 g Fat, 0 mg Cholesterol, 559 mg Sodium, 5 g Fiber

NUTRITIONAL INFORMATION PER 2 TABLESPOONS HUMMUS:

(with oil) 41 Calories (22% from fat), 2 g Protein, 6 g Carbohydrate, 1 g Fat, 0 mg Cholesterol, 232 mg Sodium, 1 g Fiber

(without oil) 32 Calories (0% from fat), 2 g Protein, 6 g Carbohydrate, 0 g Fat, 0 mg Cholesterol, 232 mg Sodium, 1 g Fiber

PLANTAIN TORTE

MAKES 1 TEN-INCH TORTE; SERVES 8

*This torte and our Smoked Portobello Mush-
rooms are our signature appetizers. The plantain torte has been a hit from day one. The
origins date back to the Milly's crew of Steve
Mclaine and Tiffany Puffert, though it has gone
through various permutations through the years.
We serve it with either a mango- or
papaya-enhanced tomato salsa, and our version
of Romescu sauce. For a completely oil-free
version, use oil-free whole-wheat tortillas from
your local natural foods store.*

PLANTAIN FILLING

1 yellow onion, cut lengthwise into thin crescents

1 teaspoon minced garlic

1/4 cup dry sherry, nonalcoholic red wine, or
    vegetable stock

1 tablespoon ground cumin

1 teaspoon ground coriander

1 teaspoon dried oregano

1 teaspoon red pepper flakes

2 ripe plantains or bananas, sliced 1/2 inch thick

1 cup water

1 teaspoon sea salt

CILANTRO-TOFU FILLING

8 ounces firm tofu

1 bunch cilantro, stemmed and coarsely chopped

1/2 teaspoon sea salt

2 tablespoons champagne vinegar

1 tablespoon light miso

2 or 3 tablespoons water as needed

5 eight-inch oil-free whole wheat tortillas

1 cup Mango Salsa (page 178)

1/2 cup Romesco Sauce (page 173), optional

To make the plantain filling: in a large sauté
pan or skillet, sauté the onion and garlic in the
sherry over medium heat until the onions are
soft, about 5 minutes. Add the cumin, coriander,
oregano, and pepper flakes, then the plantains,
water, and salt. Reduce heat to low and cook
until the plantains are soft and the liquid evaporates, about 15 minutes. Remove from heat and
let cool to room temperature. In a blender or
food processor, purée the plantain filling until
smooth. Set aside.

To make the cilantro-tofu filling: combine the
tofu, cilantro, 1/2 teaspoon salt, vinegar, and miso
in a blender or food processor and blend until
mixture is the texture of blended cream cheese.
Add water as needed to thin. Set aside

Preheat oven to 400°. Spread half the plantain
filling evenly over one tortilla and place it on a
parchment-lined 8-inch baking sheet. Spread half
the cilantro-tofu filling evenly over a second tortilla and place it on top of the first tortilla. Repeat
the procedure, until there is one more layer each
of plantain and cilantro-tofu filling. Top with the
remaining tortilla. Slice the torte into 8 pieces.
Bake for 15 minutes, or until edges are golden.
Serve warm, with 2 tablespoons of Mango Salsa
and 1 tablespoon of Romesco Sauce, if using.

NUTRITIONAL INFORMATION PER
SERVING TORTE:

158 Calories (11% from fat), 5 g Protein, 30 g Carbohydrate, 2 g Fat, 0 mg Cholesterol, 786 mg Sodium,
3 g Fiber

GRILLED PORTOBELLOS WITH HERB-TOFU AIOLI AND RED ONION MARMALADE

MAKES 6 SERVINGS

You may wish to sauté or smoke the mushrooms rather than grilling them. For smoking instructions, see page 233. If you do grill them, we recommend that you steam them beforehand to ensure they cook through, and to reduce cooking time.

6 medium-sized portobello mushrooms, stemmed
1 cup Moroccan Marinade (page 13)
1^1/2 cups Garlic-Herb Aioli (page 173)
1^1/2 cups Red Onion Marmalade (recipe follows)
1 baguette, cut into ^{1}/3-inch-thick diagonal slices and toasted or grilled

To grill the mushrooms: light a fire in a charcoal or gas grill. In a large sauté pan or skillet, heat ^{1}/4 inch water until boiling, add the mushrooms, cover, and steam for 10 minutes. Put the mushrooms in a mixing bowl and toss with the marinade. Let sit for 15 minutes. Grill over a medium fire for 3 to 4 minutes each side, or until the mushrooms are soft, with charred grill marks on the tops of the caps.

To sauté the mushrooms: in a large sauté pan or skillet heat ^{1}/2 cup of the marinade over high heat. Add the mushrooms and cook for 2 minutes on each side. Remove from the pan.

Cut the mushrooms into thin diagonal slices and fan onto each of 6 serving plates. Brush on a little reserved marinade and serve with a dollop of aioli and marmalade. Fan 3 slices of bread at the top of each plate and serve.

NUTRITIONAL INFORMATION PER SERVING MUSHROOMS:

259 Calories (10% from fat), 9 g Protein, 49 g Carbohydrate, 3 g Fat, 0 mg Cholesterol, 790 mg Sodium, 4 g Fiber

Red Onion Marmalade

MAKES 2^1/2 CUPS

4 red onions, cut lengthwise into thin crescents
1 cup dry red wine or nonalcoholic red wine
^{1}/4 cup Sucanat, unrefined sugar, or brown sugar
1 tablespoon balsamic vinegar
Juice of 1 orange
^{1}/2 teaspoon minced orange zest (optional)
^{1}/2 cup fresh cranberries (optional), or 1 tablespoon dried cranberries
2 teaspoons minced fresh ginger
1^1/2 teaspoons sea salt
^{1}/2 teaspoon ground pepper

In a large sauté pan or skillet, combine all the ingredients. Cover and cook over medium-high heat for 10 minutes. Remove the cover and cook until all the liquid evaporates, stirring to prevent scorching. Once the liquid evaporates, turn heat to medium-low and continue to cook, stirring often, until the mixture is caramelized, 15 to 20 minutes. Let cool to room temperature before serving. Store in an airtight container in the refrigerator for up to 1 week.

NUTRITIONAL INFORMATION PER 2 TABLESPOONS MARMALADE:

28 Calories (0% from fat), 0 g Protein, 7 g Carbohydrate, 0 g Fat, 0 mg Cholesterol, 169 mg Sodium, 1 g Fiber

SALADS

Sometimes, salads at Millennium start off as a whim sparked by the produce we see at the local farmers market. When you look at these recipes, let the season guide you in your choice of which to prepare. And don't feel compelled to hold these recipes as gospel: let a visit to you local market help define the salad's composition.

Even if you are not interested in oil-free cookery, try some of these oil-free dressings. You'll be surprised at how vibrant and balanced they are, and what a far cry they are from most bottled dressings full of vegetable gums, emulsifiers, and powdered herbs and spices.

MILLENNIUM CAESAR SALAD

MAKES 6 SERVINGS

This is our version of the classic. The combination of capers and nutritional yeast gives this dressing the pungent bite and body that eludes many vegetarian Caesar dressings. If nutritional yeast is unavailable, add $1/4$ cup bread that has been soaked in water. This will help keep the dressing emulsified and thick.

3 heads romaine lettuce (all but the very
    outermost leaves)
$1^{1}/_{2}$ cups Oil-Free Croutons (recipe follows)
$1^{1}/_{2}$ cups Caesar Dressing (recipe follows) or
    Oil-Free Caesar Dressing (recipes follows)
1 carrot, peeled and shredded

Tear the lettuce leaves into bite-sized pieces. In a large bowl, toss the lettuce and croutons with the dressing. Dividing among 6 salad plates and top with the shredded carrot.

NUTRITIONAL INFORMATION PER
SERVING OF DRESSED SALAD:

(with oil) 512 Calories (84% from fat), 4 g Protein, 16 g Carbohydrate, 48 g Fat, 0 mg Cholesterol, 270 mg Sodium, 3 g Fiber

(without oil) 114 Calories (16% from fat), 7 g Protein, 17 g Carbohydrate, 2 g Fat, 0 mg Cholesterol, 531 mg Sodium, 3 g Fiber

Caesar Dressing

MAKES $1^{3}/_{4}$ CUPS

1 cup fresh lemon juice
2 cloves garlic, minced
2 teaspoons capers, drained
1 tablespoon Dijon mustard
2 teaspoons nutritional yeast
$1/_{2}$ teaspoons ground pepper
$1/_{2}$ cup extra virgin olive oil
1 cup canola oil or light olive oil
Sea salt to taste

In a blender, combine the lemon juice, garlic, capers, mustard, yeast, pepper, and extra virgin olive oil. Blend until smooth. With the machine running, gradually add the canola oil in a thin stream until incorporated. Add the sea salt. Store in an airtight container in the refrigerator for up to 1 week.

NUTRITIONAL INFORMATION PER
$1/4$ CUP DRESSING:

443 Calories (95% from fat), 1 g Protein, 4 g Carbohydrate, 47 g Fat, 0 mg Cholesterol, 86 mg Sodium, 0.2 g Fiber

Oil-Free Caesar Dressing

MAKES 2 CUPS

One 12.3-ounce package low-fat silken tofu

3/4 cup fresh lemon juice

1 clove garlic, minced, or more to taste

3 tablespoons capers, drained

1/4 cup nutritional yeast

2 tablespoons Dijon mustard

1/4 teaspoon ground pepper

1 cup water

Sea salt to taste

In a blender, purée all the ingredients until smooth. Taste and adjust the seasoning. Thin with more water if needed to reach the desired consistency. Store in an airtight container in the refrigerator for up to 1 week.

NUTRITIONAL INFORMATION PER
1/4 CUP DRESSING:

41 Calories (22% from fat), 4 g Protein, 4 g Carbohydrate, 1 g Fat, 0 mg Cholesterol, 302 mg Sodium, 0.1 g Fiber

Oil-Free Croutons

MAKES 4 CUPS

2 cups slightly stale bread cubes

1/4 cup water

1/2 teaspoon dried oregano

1/2 teaspoon dried thyme

1/2 teaspoon dried basil

1/2 teaspoon paprika

1/2 teaspoon sea salt

Preheat the oven to 350°. In a medium bowl, combine all the ingredients and toss well. Spread the bread cubes on a baking sheet and bake, turning every 5 minutes, for 15 minutes, or until the bread cubes are crisp and dry. Let cool to room temperature. Store in an airtight container for up to 1 week.

NUTRITIONAL INFORMATION PER
1/4 CUP CROUTONS:

53 Calories (17% from fat), 2 g Protein, 9 g Carbohydrate, 1 g Fat, 0 mg Cholesterol, 216 mg Sodium, 0.5 g Fiber

MILLENNIUM WARM SPINACH SALAD

SERVES 6

This salad is simple, straightforward, and always a hit. Smoked tofu replaces the bacon and gives the salad an unmistakable smoky quality.

3 cloves garlic, minced

1 red onion, cut into thin slices

6 cremini or button mushrooms, sliced thin

4 ounces Millennium Smoked Tofu (page 235) or packaged smoked tofu

1/4 cup extra virgin olive oil

1 teaspoon sea salt

1/2 teaspoon ground pepper

1 pound spinach, well washed and stemmed

1/3 cup balsamic vinegar

Shredded carrot or beets (optional)

Oil-Free Croutons (page 33) and toasted walnuts

In a large sauté pan or skillet, sauté the garlic, onion, mushrooms, and smoked tofu in the oil until the onions and mushrooms soften, about 5 to 7 minutes. Add the salt and pepper. While the onion mixture sautés, combine the spinach and balsamic vinegar in a large bowl. Add the sautéed mixture to the spinach. Toss to wilt the spinach. Transfer the spinach to the hot pan and toss for a few seconds. Divide among salad plates and top with the shredded carrot and beets. Sprinkle with the croutons and walnuts.

NUTRITIONAL INFORMATION PER SALAD SERVING:

176 Calories (61% from fat), 5 g Protein, 12 g Carbohydrate, 12 g Fat, 0 mg Cholesterol, 575 mg Sodium, 3 g Fiber

MIXED GREENS WITH CITRUS VINAIGRETTE

MAKES 6 SERVINGS

A light, refreshing salad with the coolness of mint and the slight sting of chile tossed with an oil-free vinaigrette. Try this salad with any of the following oil-free dressings, as well.

16 ounces baby lettuce mix

2 cups Citrus Vinaigrette (recipe follows)

1 carrot, peeled and shredded

1 cucumber, seeded and cut into julienne

3 radishes, thinly sliced, for garnish (optional)

Toss the lettuce with the dressing and arrange it on serving plates. Top with the carrots and cucumber and, if you like garnish with thinly sliced radish.

NUTRITIONAL INFORMATION PER SERVING DRESSED SALAD:

52 Calories (0% from fat), 2 g Protein, 12 g Carbohydrate, 0 g Fat, 0 mg Cholesterol, 394 mg Sodium, 2 g Fiber

Citrus Vinaigrette

MAKES 2¹/2 CUPS

1 cup water

¹/4 cup fresh lemon juice

2 tablespoons unrefined sugar or fructose

¹/2 cup fresh orange juice

¹/4 cup champagne or rice vinegar

3 tablespoons tamari soy sauce

1 clove garlic, minced

¹/4 teaspoon red pepper flakes, plus more to taste

1 tablespoon minced fresh mint

1 tablespoon minced fresh tarragon (optional)

2 tablespoons minced red bell pepper (optional)

1 teaspoon grated fresh ginger

Sea salt and freshly ground pepper to taste

¹/2 teaspoon guar gum (optional)

In a bowl or a jar with a tight-fitting lid, whisk or shake the water, lemon juice, and sweetener until well blended. Add the remaining ingredients and whisk or shake until incorporated. Taste and adjust the seasonings. Store in an airtight container for up to 2 weeks.

NUTRITIONAL INFORMATION PER 2¹/2-OUNCE SERVING VINAIGRETTE:

32 Calories (0% from fat), 1 g Protein, 7 g Carbohydrate, 0 g Fat, 0 mg Cholesterol, 378 mg Sodium, 0.2 g Fiber

GOLDEN PEPPER AND FENNEL SEED DRESSING

MAKES 2 CUPS

This dressing was created towards the end of summer when there was an overabundance of amazing local sweet peppers at the farmer's market. Try it on all sorts of summer vegetables. We've served it with braised leeks, chickpeas, shaved fresh fennel, and green olives.

2 yellow bell peppers, roasted and peeled (see page 235)

¹/2 cup fresh orange juice

³/4 cup fresh lemon juice

2 tablespoons white miso

1 teaspoons fennel seed, toasted and ground (see page 234)

1 cup water

¹/4 teaspoon cayenne pepper, or ¹/2 teaspoon minced serrano chile (optional)

¹/2 teaspoon sea salt

In a blender, purée all of the ingredients. Store in an airtight container in the refrigerator for up to 1 week.

NUTRITIONAL INFORMATION PER 2 TABLESPOONS DRESSING:

16 Calories (0% from fat), 0 g Protein, 4 g Carbohydrate, 0 g Fat, 0 mg Cholesterol, 146 mg Sodium, 0 g Fiber

APRICOT DRESSING

MAKES 2¹/₂ CUPS

This sweet and spicy dressing is perfect for crunchy greens like romaine, Napa cabbage, and even iceberg lettuce. You can also make this dressing with fresh stone fruit like peach, nectarines, and apricots.

1 cup water

¹/₃ cup dried apricots

¹/₂ cup fresh lime juice

3 tablespoons champagne vinegar or other light vinegar

¹/₂ serrano chile, seeded and minced

1 teaspoon minced fresh ginger

2 tablespoons honey

¹/₂ teaspoon sea salt

In a small saucepan, heat the water to a simmer. Remove from heat and add the apricots. Let set for 15 minutes, or until soft. Drain and cool. In a blender, combine the apricots with all the remaining ingredients and blend until smooth. Store in an airtight container in the refrigerator for up to 1 week.

NUTRITIONAL INFORMATION PER 2 TABLESPOONS DRESSING:

16 Calories (0% from fat), 0 g Protein, 4 g Carbohydrate, 0 g Fat, 0 mg Cholesterol, 54 mg Sodium, 0 g Fiber

CARAMELIZED SHALLOT DRESSING

MAKES 2 CUPS

This dressing has an earthy flavor that is suited for a fall salad of roasted parsnips and beets with citrus.

12 shallots, peeled and diced

2 teaspoons Sucanat or unrefined sugar

2 tablespoons dry sherry or nonalcoholic red wine

¹/₄ teaspoon sea salt

¹/₄ cup balsamic vinegar, or 3 tablespoons sherry vinegar

2 tablespoons white miso

¹/₂ teaspoon grated lemon zest

¹/₂ cup fresh lemon juice

¹/₂ cup fresh orange juice

2 teaspoons fresh lemon thyme or regular thyme

¹/₄ teaspoon ground pepper

¹/₂ cup water or cold vegetable stock, plus more as needed

Sea salt to taste

In a small sauté pan or skillet, combine the shallots, Sucanat, sherry, and salt. Sauté over medium heat until the shallots are soft and caramel brown, about 15 minutes. Stir in the balsamic vinegar and remove from heat. Let cool to room temperature.

In a blender combine the shallot mixture with the miso, lemon zest and juice, orange juice, thyme, pepper, and water. Blend until smooth, adding more water if needed. Add the salt. Store in an airtight container in the refrigerator for up to 1 week.

NUTRITIONAL INFORMATION PER 2 TABLESPOONS DRESSING:

20 Calories (0% from fat), 0 g Protein, 5 g Carbohydrate, 0 g Fat, 0 mg Cholesterol, 120 mg Sodium, 0 g Fiber

CRANBERRY-GINGER DRESSING

MAKES 2 CUPS

Another fall dressing of the sweet, pungent, and spicy variety.

1/2 cup fresh cranberries
1 cup fresh orange juice
3 tablespoons honey
1/4 cup balsamic vinegar
2 tablespoons light miso
1 tablespoons minced fresh ginger
1 cup water
Sea salt to taste

In a small saucepan, bring the cranberries and orange juice to a boil, reduce to a simmer, cover, and cook until the cranberries are very soft, about 20 minutes. Let cool to room temperature. In a blender, purée the cranberries, honey, vinegar, miso, ginger, and water until smooth. Add more water if necessary to achieve the desired consistency. Add sea salt to taste. Store in an airtight container in the refrigerator for up to 2 weeks.

NUTRITIONAL INFORMATION PER
2 TABLESPOONS DRESSING:

24 Calories (0% from fat), 0 g Protein, 6 g Carbohydrate, 0 g Fat, 0 mg Cholesterol, 80 mg Sodium, 0.3 g Fiber

CREAMY GREEN PEPPERCORN AND DILL DRESSING

MAKES 2 CUPS

This creamy oil-free dressing has the kick of green peppercorns, fresh ginger, and a bit of garlic. The miso and honey help to balance and tame it. Green peppercorns, whether packed in brine or dried, are more pungent, with slightly less heat than black or white peppercorns. Try this with our Strawberry-Asparagus Salad (page 48).

3/4 cup fresh lemon juice
6 ounces silken tofu
1 small clove garlic, minced
1 tablespoon light miso
1 teaspoon nutritional yeast
2 tablespoons honey
1 teaspoon minced fresh ginger
2 tablespoons chopped fresh dill
1 cup rice milk or soy milk
1 teaspoons green peppercorns, preferably packed in brine
1 teaspoon capers, drained (optional)
Sea salt to taste

In a blender, combine all the ingredients except the peppercorns, capers, and salt. Blend until smooth. Add the peppercorns and capers and pulse the blender to crush but not purée the peppercorns and capers into the dressing. Stir in the salt. Store in an airtight container in the refrigerator for up to 1 week.

NUTRITIONAL INFORMATION PER
2 TABLESPOONS DRESSING:

25 Calories (18% from fat), 1 g Protein, 4 g Carbohydrate, 0.5 g Fat, 0 mg Cholesterol, 56 mg Sodium, 0.4 g Fiber

BITTER GREENS, FIGS, BUTTERNUT SQUASH, AND BEETS WITH CURRIED ALMOND DRESSING

MAKES 6 SERVINGS

Try this dressing over other roasted vegetables besides the butternut squash.

1/2 butternut squash, peeled, seeded, and cut into 1-inch cubes (about 2 cups)

1 teaspoon canola oil

1 teaspoon balsamic vinegar

1/4 teaspoon sea salt

1/4 teaspoon ground fennel (optional)

12 ounces mixed bitter greens, such as arugula, frisée, and watercress

1 1/2 cups Curried Almond Dressing (recipe follows)

2 Belgian endive

18 Mission figs

1 red beet, peeled and shredded, for garnish (optional)

Preheat oven to 350°. In a large bowl, toss the squash with oil, balsamic vinegar, salt, and fennel. Spread on a baking pan and bake, for 15 to 20 minutes, or until tender but firm, stirring halfway through cooking. Let cool to room temperature.

Toss the greens with enough dressing to coat, and place a portion on each serving plate. If using Belgian endive, fan the endive spears out around the plate. Slice the figs in quarters lengthwise, but not all the way through. Peel back the quarters, so that the fig lies open like a flower. Place three quartered figs around each plate. Place the cubed squash around the salad. Top the greens with a tuft of shredded beets and top with an opened-up fig. Drizzle the salad with more dressing.

NUTRITIONAL INFORMATION PER SERVING DRESSED GREENS:

268 Calories (19% from fat), 6 g Protein, 52 g Carbohydrate, 6 g Fat, 0 mg Cholesterol, 465 mg Sodium, 9 g Fiber

Curried Almond Dressing

MAKES 2 CUPS

1/2 cup slivered almonds, toasted (see page 234)

4 ounces silken tofu

1/2 cup fresh orange juice

1/4 cup maple syrup

1/2 cup water

2 shallots or 1/4 red onion, coarsely chopped

2 tablespoons mild curry powder

1/4 teaspoon ground pepper or cayenne pepper

3 tablespoons minced fresh cilantro

1 tablespoon minced fresh mint

1 teaspoon sea salt

In a blender, combine all the ingredients and blend until smooth. Add more water if needed to thin out. This dressing will have a slightly grainy texture due to the almonds. Excess dressing will keep up to 1 week in the refrigerator.

NUTRITIONAL INFORMATION PER 2 TABLESPOONS DRESSING:

46 Calories (39% from fat), 1 g Protein, 6 g Carbohydrate, 2 g Fat, 0 mg Cholesterol, 164 mg Sodium, 1 g Fiber

Satsuma Mandarin-Spinach Salad with Fennel, Beets, and Toasted Walnuts

MAKES 6 SERVINGS

Satsuma mandarins appear fresh in our Bay Area farmer's market close to Thanksgiving. This salad with its delicate sweet-sour balance is an obvious choice for the beginning of a lavish Thanksgiving meal at Millennium.

12 shallots, cut into 1/4-inch slices

SATSUMA MANDARIN DRESSING

2 Satsuma mandarins, peeled and segmented

2 shallots, minced

1 teaspoon fennel seeds, toasted and ground (see page 234)

1 teaspoon minced fresh lemon thyme or regular thyme

2 teaspoons minced fresh cilantro

1/4 cup champagne vinegar

1/2 cup fresh orange juice

1/4 cup walnuts, toasted (see page 234)

4 ounces silken tofu

1/4 cup water

1/2 teaspoon sea salt

1/4 teaspoon ground pepper

SALAD

12 ounces baby spinach leaves

3 to 4 Satsuma mandarins or any variety of tangerine, peeled and segmented

1 fennel bulb, cut into paper-thin slices

12 Curry and Fennel Marinated Beets (page 182)

1 cup walnuts, toasted (see page 234)

Preheat oven to 300°. Place the sliced shallots on a baking sheet lined with parchment paper. Roast for 20 to 30 minutes, or until lightly browned, checking and turning the pan, if necessary, every 5 minutes after the first 15 minutes. Set aside.

To make the dressing: In a blender, blend all the ingredients together until smooth. Taste and adjust the seasoning.

Toss the spinach with half the dressing. Arrange on 6 chilled plates. Scatter the mandarin segments, fennel, beets, and walnuts on top of the spinach. Spoon more of the dressing over each salad. Top with the toasted shallots.

NUTRITIONAL INFORMATION PER SERVING SALAD:

280 Calories (51% from fat), 6 g Protein, 28 g Carbohydrate, 16 g Fat, 0 mg Cholesterol, 277 mg Sodium, 5 g Fiber

Ruby Grapefruit, Avocado, and Pickled Red Onions with Baby Spinach and Grapefruit Mojo Dressing

MAKES 6 SERVINGS

This salad's inspiration is from Latin America. The dressing is a variation of a Cuban mojo, which we use as a marinade for vegetables and seitan. Try other tropical fruit with the salad. Don't forget the chile-lime toasted almonds—they add a delightful texture to the salad.

GRAPEFRUIT MOJO DRESSING

2 cloves garlic, minced

6 tablespoons extra virgin olive oil

1 teaspoon ground cumin

1 cup fresh grapefruit juice

1/2 cup fresh lemon juice

1 tablespoon light miso

1/2 jalapeno chile, seeded and minced

2 teaspoons Sucanat, or 1 tablespoon honey

3 tablespoons chopped fresh mint

1/4 cup canola oil

Sea salt to taste

1 tablespoon thinly shredded lemon basil or
    Italian basil (optional)

12 ounces baby spinach leaves

2 ruby grapefruit

2 ripe but firm avocados, pitted, and cut into
    thin slices

Lime-Pickled Red Onions (recipe follows)

Chile-Lime Toasted Almonds (recipe follows)

Julienned fresh mint, cilantro, or basil leaves,
    for garnish (optional)

To make the dressing: In a small sauté pan or skilled, sauté the garlic in 2 tablespoons of the olive oil over medium heat until the garlic browns, about 5 minutes. Remove from heat, add the cumin, and stir well. Transfer the mixture to a bowl and let cool.

In a blender, combine the garlic mixture with the grapefruit juice, lemon juice, miso, chile, Sucanat, and mint. Blend until incorporated. With the machine running, gradually add the remaining 4 tablespoons olive oil and the canola oil until all the oil is incorporated and the dressing thickens. Pour the dressing into a bowl or other container and add the salt. Mix the basil into the finished dressing.

Toss the spinach leaves with enough dressing to coat, about 1/2 cup. Place equal portions of spinach in the center of each serving plate. Fan the grapefruit and avocado around the spinach and drizzle with dressing. Top the spinach with pickled onions and sprinkle with toasted almonds. Garnish with julienned mint, cilantro, or basil.

VARIATION:

For an oil-free version of the dressing, delete the olive oil and the canola oil, substitute 4 ounces of silken tofu, and dry-sauté the garlic.

NUTRITIONAL INFORMATION PER
SERVING DRESSED SALAD:

349 Calories (64% from fat), 5 g Protein, 26 g Carbohydrate, 25 g Fat, 0 mg Cholesterol, 540 mg Sodium, 7 g Fiber

NUTRITIONAL INFORMATION PER
2 OUNCE SERVING DRESSING:

(with oil) 177 Calories (86% from fat), 1 g Protein, 5 g Carbohydrate, 17 g Fat, 0 mg Cholesterol, 82 mg Sodium, 0.2 g Fiber

(without oil) 51 Calories (52% from fat), 1 g Protein, 5 g Carbohydrate, 3 g Fat, 0 mg Cholesterol, 82 mg Sodium, 0.2 g Fiber

(recipe continues on next page)

Lime-Pickled Red Onions

MAKES 1 1/2 CUPS

1 teaspoon minced lime zest

1/2 cup fresh lime juice

1 1/2 teaspoons sea salt

2 red onions, cut into very thin rounds

In a medium bowl, combine all the ingredients and let sit for at least 30 minutes before serving. Store in an airtight container in the refrigerator for up to 2 weeks.

NUTRITIONAL INFORMATION PER
1/4 CUP ONIONS:

36 Calories (0% from fat), 1 g Protein, 8 g Carbohydrate, 0 g Fat, 0 mg Cholesterol, 535 mg Sodium, 1 g Fiber

Chile-Lime Toasted Almonds

MAKES 3/4 CUP (SERVES 6)

3/4 cup slivered almonds

1/4 cup fresh lime juice

1 teaspoon mild chile powder

1/4 teaspoon cayenne pepper

1/4 teaspoon sea salt

Preheat the oven to 350°. In a small bowl, combine all the ingredients and toss. Spread the almonds on a baking sheet and bake for 10 to 15 minutes, stirring the almonds every 5 minutes so they brown evenly. Let cool before using.

NUTRITIONAL INFORMATION PER SERVING:

113 Calories (72% from fat), 3 g Protein, 5 g Carbohydrate, 9 g Fat, 0 mg Cholesterol, 96 mg Sodium, 2 g Fiber

BUTTERBALL LETTUCE WITH FENNEL, NECTARINES, TOASTED ALMONDS AND ROSE GERANIUM DRESSING

MAKES 6 SERVINGS

This is an exquisite salad. It reminds us of how lucky we are to live in San Francisco and shop at its bountiful farmer's markets. Perfect sweet-tart white nectarines, crisp, crunchy little heads of butterball lettuce, and the fragrant perfume of rose geraniums are worth the airfare alone. We prepared this salad to feature some of the specialty produce from Green Gulch Farm in Marin County.

1 or 2 fennel bulbs, cut into paper-thin slices
2 or 3 white nectarines, pitted and cut into
    $1/3$-inch-thick slices
1 cup Rose Geranium Dressing (recipe follows)
Leaves from 6 small heads butterball lettuce
$3/4$ cup Chile-Lime Toasted Almonds (page 42)

Toss the fennel and nectarine slices in the dressing and arrange over the butter lettuce. Top with the almonds and serve.

NUTRITIONAL INFORMATION PER SERVING DRESSED SALAD:

118 Calories (46% from fat), 3 g Protein, 13 g Carbohydrate, 6 g Fat, 0 mg Cholesterol, 448 mg Sodium, 3 g Fiber

Rose Geranium Dressing

MAKES 1 CUP

$1/2$ cup champagne vinegar
$1/3$ cup fructose
1 teaspoon sea salt
$1/2$ teaspoon minced jalapeno
$1/4$ teaspoon ground pepper
$1/2$ teaspoon ground fennel
$1/2$ teaspoon ground coriander
2 teaspoons minced rose geranium flowers, or
    1 teaspoon rose water

In a small saucepan, bring the vinegar and fructose to a boil. Stir until the fructose is dissolved, then remove from heat. Stir in the remaining ingredients and let the dressing cool.

NUTRITIONAL INFORMATION PER 2 TABLESPOONS DRESSING:

32 Calories (0% from fat), 0 g Protein, 8 g Carbohydrate, 0 g Fat, 0 mg Cholesterol, 316 mg Sodium, 0 g Fiber

HEIRLOOM TOMATO AND ARUGULA SALAD WITH ORANGE-CHIPOTLE DRESSING

SERVES 6

While quality heirloom tomatoes really need very little help from flavorful dressings, this dressing is very complementary to the acid of the tomato, the bitter of the arugula, and the sweet of the corn. This makes a great main course salad with the addition of grain like quinoa or nutty wild rice. There is a lot of variation in the heat of chipotles, so we recommend that you start with 1 teaspoon and add more to your desired heat level.

MARINATED BLACK BEANS

1 cup cooked black beans

1/4 cup minced red onion

1 teaspoon minced fresh oregano, or
    1/2 teaspoon dried oregano

1 tablespoon minced fresh basil or cilantro

1/4 cup fresh lime juice

Sea salt to taste

2 bunches arugula, stemmed and cleaned

3/4 cup Orange-Chipotle Dressing (recipe follows)

4 assorted heirloom tomatoes, sliced

Kernels cut from 2 ears sweet corn

Julienned fresh basil or cilantro leaves for garnish

To make the marinated beans: In a bowl, toss together the black beans, red onion, oregano, basil or cilantro, lemon juice, and salt to taste.

Toss the arugula with enough of the dressing to lightly coat (about 3/4 to 1 cup). Divide among 6 plates. Arrange the slices of tomato around the plate. Drizzle with some of the remaining dressing. Sprinkle on the corn, beans, and basil.

NUTRITIONAL INFORMATION PER SERVING DRESSED SALAD:

206 Calories (9% from fat), 9 g Protein, 38 g Carbohydrate, 2 g Fat, 0 mg Cholesterol, 202 mg Sodium, 7 g Fiber

Orange-Chipotle Dressing

MAKES 2 CUPS

1 tablespoon grated orange zest

1 cup fresh orange juice

5 ounces silken tofu

3 tablespoons honey

2 tablespoons light miso

1/4 cup balsamic vinegar

1 clove garlic, minced

1 teaspoon Chipotle Paste (page 174) or canned chipotle in adobo

1/2 cup water

Sea salt and freshly ground pepper to taste

In a blender, combine all the ingredients and blend until smooth. Store in an airtight container for up to 1 week.

VARIATION:

For a simple oil and vinegar vinaigrette, delete the tofu and the water and gradually blend 1/2 cup extra virgin olive oil into the other ingredients.

NUTRITIONAL INFORMATION PER 2 TABLESPOONS DRESSING:

33 Calories (15% from fat), 1 g Protein, 6 g Carbohydrate, 0.6 g Fat, 0 mg Cholesterol, 90 mg Sodium, 0 g Fiber

CHILLED SOBA NOODLE SALAD

MAKES 6 SERVINGS

This is a favorite on our summer lunch menu. The addition of fresh peach and arame sea vegetable make it unique.

DRESSING

1 cup fresh lemon juice

1/3 cup tamari soy sauce

1 tablespoon Sucanat or 2 tablespoons honey

1 tablespoon ketchup

1/2 cup water or vegetable stock

1/4 cup sesame seeds, toasted (see page 234)

3 tablespoons minced fresh ginger

1/4 teaspoon red pepper flakes

1 teaspoon fermented black beans, minced (optional)

2 kaffir lime leaves, minced or finely shredded (optional)

2 tablespoons Asian sesame oil (optional)

6 ounces soba noodles

Kernels cut from 2 ears of sweet corn

1 peach, peeled, pitted, and cut into thin slices

4 to 6 snow peas, cut into julienne

4 ounces Millennium Smoked or Baked Tofu (page 235), or packaged smoked tofu

2 tablespoons arame sea vegetables, soaked and drained

1 1/2 cups shredded romaine lettuce, or 6 ounces mixed baby greens

3 tablespoons julienned scallion, white part only

3 tablespoons julienned Thai basil or Italian basil leaves

12 to 18 Sweet 100 or cherry tomatoes

To make the dressing: In a small bowl, whisk all the ingredients together. Store in an airtight container in the refrigerator for up to 2 weeks.

Cook the noodles in boiling, salted water for 6 to 8 minutes, until they are al dente. Drain and set aside to cool.

Toss the noodles, corn, peach, snowpeas, tofu, and arame sea vegetable with dressing. Divide the shredded romaine or mixed greens among 6 salad plates. Top with a mound of the noodle mixture. Top the salads with scallion and basil, arrange the tomatoes around the plates.

NUTRITIONAL INFORMATION PER SERVING:

(with oil) 208 Calories (35% from fat), 7 g Protein, 27 g Carbohydrate, 8 g Fat, 0 mg Cholesterol, 781 mg Sodium, 3 g Fiber

(without oil) 172 Calories (21% from fat), 7 g Protein, 27 g Carbohydrate, 4 g Fat, 0 mg Cholesterol, 781 mg Sodium, 3 g Fiber

ASIAN ROMAINE SPRING ROLLS WITH SESAME-LIME DRESSING

MAKES 6 SERVINGS

This is always a favorite when it goes onto the menu. The dressing features the herbal trinity of many Southeast Asian cuisines: mint, cilantro, and basil.

1 large head romaine lettuce

1 papaya, peeled, seeded, and cut into thin slices

1 red bell pepper, seeded, deribbed, and cut into thin slices

Kernels cut from 1 ear fresh corn

1 small jicama, peeled and cut into thin buttons

6 kumquats, cut into thin slices

1 tablespoon finely shredded fresh mint leaves

1 tablespoon minced fresh cilantro

2$^{1}/_{2}$ cups Sesame Lime Dressing (recipe follows)

Saffron-Lotus Root Pickles (page 181)

Sesame seeds for garnish

Bring a large pot of water to a boil. Prepare a large bowl of ice water. Separate 12 of the largest romaine leaves from the head. Trim off the thick parts of the romaine stems. Blanch the romaine leaves for 10 seconds in the boiling water, then drain. Immediately immerse in the ice water to stop the blanching. Drain and pat dry with paper towels. Set aside.

Shred the remaining lettuce to make 2 cups. In a medium bowl, combine the shredded lettuce, papaya, bell pepper, corn, jicama, kumquats, mint, and cilantro with $^{1}/_{2}$ cup dressing.

On a flat work surface, place 2 romaine leaves, overlapping the stem of one next to the leaf of the other. Place 1 cup filling on the bottom of the leaves. Fold over the sides of the leaves, then roll

them from the bottom into a cylinder. Repeat with the remaining leaves.

To serve, cover the bottom of each plate with $^{1}/_{4}$ cup dressing. Cut the rolls in half crosswise on the diagonal. Place half a roll on each plate, with the other half standing up or leaning against it. Garnish with a slice of Quick Pickled Lotus Root and sesame seeds.

NUTRITIONAL INFORMATION PER ROLL:

172 Calories (21% from fat), 4 g Protein, 30 g Carbohydrate, 4 g Fat, 0 mg Cholesterol, 854 mg Sodium, 5 g Fiber

Sesame-Lime Dressing

MAKES 2$^{1}/_{2}$ CUPS

1 cup fresh lime juice

1 clove garlic, minced

2 teaspoons minced fresh ginger

3 tablespoons honey, or 2 tablespoons maple syrup

$^{1}/_{4}$ bunch cilantro, stemmed

$^{1}/_{2}$ bunch mint, stemmed

$^{1}/_{2}$ bunch Thai or Italian basil, stemmed

1 kaffir lime leaf (optional)

1 Thai bird's-eye chile, seeded, or 1 serrano chile

$^{1}/_{2}$ cup plus 1 tablespoon sesame seeds, toasted (see page 234)

3 tablespoons light miso

1$^{1}/_{2}$ cups water

1 teaspoon minced lime zest

In a blender, combine the lime juice, garlic, ginger, honey, cilantro, mint, basil, kaffir lime leaf, chile, $^{1}/_{2}$ cup of the sesame seeds, miso, and water and blend until smooth. Transfer the dressing to a bowl or other container and add the 1 tablespoon sesame seeds and the lime zest. Store in an airtight container in the refrigerator for up to 1 week.

NUTRITIONAL INFORMATION PER 2 TABLESPOONS DRESSING:

46 Calories (39% from fat), 1 g Protein, 6 g Carbohydrate, 2 g Fat, 0 mg Cholesterol, 98 mg Sodium, 0 g Fiber

STRAWBERRY-ASPARAGUS SALAD WITH MINT-DILL DRESSING

MAKES 6 SERVINGS

This salad is a winner! Lightly blanched aspara-gus, fresh strawberries, and caramelized baby beets are served on caraway-marinated red cab-bage and greens tossed with a sweet dill and mint dressing and sprinkled with toasted almonds.

1/2 head red cabbage, thinly shredded
1/4 cup champagne vinegar
1 teaspoon sea salt, plus a pinch
1 teaspoon caraway seeds, toasted (see page 234)

18 baby beets, assorted varieties (optional)
1/3 teaspoon canola oil
1/2 teaspoon Sucanat or unrefined sugar
1 teaspoon balsamic vinegar

Leaves from 1 head butter lettuce
24 small asparagus spears, blanched until crisp-tender
18 strawberries, sliced thin or sliced and fanned
Mint-Dill Dressing (recipe follows)
1/2 cup chopped toasted almonds (see page 234)

To cook the cabbage: Heat a dry saute pan over medium heat until very hot. In a medium bowl, combine the cabbage, champagne vinegar, and the 1 teaspoon sea salt and mix well. Add the caraway seeds. With a fork or tongs, turn half of the cabbage into the hot pan to wilt. Mix the wilted cabbage with the rest of the cabbage. Let marinate for 30 minutes.

To cook the beets: Preheat the oven to 350°. Bring a medium saucepan of water to a boil and blanch the beets for 5 minutes. Drain the beets, peel them, halve them, and toss them with the oil, Sucanat, balsamic vinegar, and the pinch of sea salt. Place in a baking pan and bake for 15 to 20 minutes, or until the beets are tender and caramelized. Let cool.

Line each salad plate with the lettuce and mound 1 cup of the cabbage on one end of the plate. Fan 4 asparagus spears on the other end and add 3 sliced strawberries and 6 caramelized beet halves. Drizzle 1/4 cup of the dressing over each salad and sprinkle with the chopped almonds.

NUTRITIONAL INFORMATION PER SERVING DRESSED SALAD:

384 Calories (75% from fat), 4 g Protein, 20 g Carbo-hydrate, 32 g Fat, 0 mg Cholesterol, 659 mg Sodium, 5 g Fiber

Mint-Dill Dressing

MAKES 1 1/2 CUPS

2 fresh strawberries, stems removed, thinly sliced
1 tablespoon chopped fresh dill
1 tablespoon chopped fresh mint
1 teaspoon Dijon mustard
3 tablespoons raspberry vinegar
2 tablespoons champagne vinegar
1/4 teaspoon ground pepper
1/2 teaspoon sea salt
1/4 cup water
3/4 cup canola oil
2 tablespoons Sucanat or maple syrup

In a blender, combine all of the ingredients except the oil and blend until smooth. With the machine running, gradually add the oil until it is thoroughly incorporated. Taste and adjust the seasoning.

NUTRITIONAL INFORMATION PER 2 TABLESPOONS DRESSING:

138 Calories (91% from fat), 0 g Protein, 3 g Carbo-hydrate, 14 g Fat, 0 mg Cholesterol, 117 mg Sodium, 0 g Fiber

MOROCCAN EGGPLANT SALAD

MAKES 6 SERVINGS

This recipe is reason enough to have preserved lemons on hand. If you substitute Japanese eggplants, delete the soaking step. (If you use globe eggplant, peel it.)

2 Italian eggplants, cut into $1/3$-inch matchsticks
2 tomatoes, cut into $1/3$-inch cubes
1 cup cooked chickpeas or any firm-textured bean
1 bunch scallions, white part only, chopped
$1/2$ cup preserved lemons (page 180), chopped
$1^1/2$ cups Moroccan Dressing (recipe follows)
1 bunch cilantro, stemmed and chopped
$1/3$ bunch mint, stemmed and chopped
Leaves from 1 head romaine lettuce, shredded

Soak the eggplant in warm salted water for 15 minutes. Drain, then blanch in boiling water until just tender, about 5 minutes. Drain and transfer to an ice water bath. When cool, drain well. In a medium bowl, combine the eggplant with all the remaining ingredients except for the shredded romaine. Serve over the shredded romaine lettuce.

NUTRITIONAL INFORMATION PER SERVING DRESSED SALAD:

(with oil) 274 Calories (46% from fat), 7 g Protein, 30 g Carbohydrate, 14 g Fat, 0 mg Cholesterol, 585 mg Sodium, 9 g Fiber

(without oil) 196 Calories (18% from fat), 8 g Protein, 32 g Carbohydrate, 4 g Fat, 0 mg Cholesterol, 665 mg Sodium, 9 g Fiber

Moroccan Dressing

MAKES $2^1/2$ CUPS

2 teaspoons ground cumin
1 teaspoon ground coriander
2 teaspoons Spanish paprika
$1/2$ cup fresh lemon juice (about 4 lemons)
1 tablespoons balsamic vinegar
2 teaspoons minced fresh ginger
2 teaspoons minced garlic
$1/3$ cup chopped fresh cilantro
$1/2$ cup light olive oil
$1/3$ cup water
2 teaspoons sea salt
1 teaspoon ground pepper

In a dry, small sauté pan or skillet, toast the cumin, coriander, and paprika over medium heat until the spices become fragrant and the color slightly darkens, about 1 minute. In a blender, combine the toasted spices with the lemon juice, vinegar, ginger, garlic, and cilantro. With the machine running, gradually add the oil, then the water, salt, and pepper. Leftover dressing will keep in the refrigerator for up to a week.

VARIATION:

For an oil-free version, replace the oil with $1/2$ cup (4 ounces) low-fat silken tofu plus 1 tablespoon of light miso. Increase the water to $1/2$ cup.

NUTRITIONAL INFORMATION PER TABLESPOON DRESSING:

(with oil) 58 Calories (93% from fat), 0 g Protein, 2 g Carbohydrate, 6 g Fat, 0 mg Cholesterol, 214 mg Sodium, 0 g Fiber

(without oil) 25 Calories (36% from fat), 1 g Protein, 3 g Carbohydrate, 1 g Fat, 0 mg Cholesterol, 254 mg Sodium, 0 g Fiber

CHESTNUT LIMA BEAN AND POTATO SALAD WITH BLACK OLIVE DRESSING

MAKES 4 SERVINGS

This is a favorite salad that becomes one of our more popular entrées when served warm and topped with sautéed cornmeal-crusted portobello mushroom. On its own, it is substantial and satisfying enough to make a light entrée over a bed of greens.

1/2 cup dried chestnut lima beans, or substitute dried lima beans or butter beans

2 Yellow Finn potatoes, cut into 1/2-inch dice

2 purple Peruvian potatoes, cut into 1/2-inch dice

1 clove garlic, minced

1 tablespoon olive oil or canola oil (optional)

1/2 teaspoon sea salt

Freshly ground pepper to taste

1 cup Black Olive Dressing (recipe follows)

Lettuce leaves (optional)

1 medium tomato, seeded and cut into small cubes

Chopped fresh parsley or basil for garnish

Quick-soak the beans in a saucepan for 1 hour (see page 236). Add water to cover if necessary, then simmer for 45 minutes. Drain and set aside to cool.

Preheat the oven to 400°. In a small bowl, toss the potatoes with the garlic, oil, salt, and pepper. Spread the potatoes on a baking sheet and roast in the oven until cooked through and crisp, about 30 minutes, turning the potatoes after the first 15 minutes. Let cool to room temperature or use while hot.

Toss the potatoes with the beans and olive dressing. Serve on a platter or on individual plates lined with lettuce. Top with the tomato cubes and the chopped parsley.

NUTRITIONAL INFORMATION PER SERVING DRESSED SALAD:

(with oil) 396 Calories (45% from fat), 7 g Protein, 47 g Carbohydrate, 34 g Fat, 0 mg Cholesterol, 548 mg Sodium, 6 g Fiber

(without oil) 247 Calories (11% from fat), 8 g Protein, 47 g Carbohydrate, 3 g Fat, 0 mg Cholesterol, 548 mg Sodium, 6 g Fiber

Black Olive Dressing

MAKES 2 CUPS

1/2 cup black kalamata olives, pitted

1/4 cup olive brine (drained from the olives)

1 teaspoon minced lemon zest

1/2 cup fresh lemon juice

2 teaspoons minced fresh oregano, or 1 teaspoon dried oregano

1 or 2 garlic cloves, minced

2 teaspoons Dijon mustard

1 teaspoon nutritional yeast (optional)

1/2 teaspoon ground pepper

1/4 cup extra-virgin olive oil

1/4 cup canola oil or light olive oil

In a blender, combine the olives, brine, lemon zest and juice, oregano, garlic, mustard, yeast, pepper, and extra virgin olive oil. Blend until smooth. With the machine running, gradually add the canola oil in a thin stream until incorporated. Store in an airtight container in the refrigerator for up to 2 weeks.

VARIATION:

To make an oil-free variation of this dressing, omit the oil and substitute $1/2$ cup of silken tofu, added at once to all the other ingredients.

NUTRITIONAL INFORMATION PER
2 TABLESPOONS DRESSING:

(with oil) 80 Calories (65% from fat), 0 g Protein, 2 g Carbohydrate, 8 g Fat, 0 mg Cholesterol, 110 mg Sodium, 0.2 g Fiber

(without oil) 21 Calories (43% from fat), 1 g Protein, 2 g Carbohydrate, 1 g Fat, 0 mg Cholesterol, 110 mg Sodium, 0.3 g Fiber

CALYPSO BEAN AND ROASTED PEPPER SALAD WITH MANGO MOJO

MAKES 6 SERVINGS

This is a flavorful bean salad for the summer. We used calypso beans as much for the calypso association to Caribbean music as for their bright tan color and firm texture; almost any bean will work. The dressing is a variation on our mojo with puréed mango added.

2 cups cooked calypso beans

1 large red bell pepper or pimiento, roasted, peeled, and cut into strips (see page 235)

1 yellow bell pepper, roasted, peeled, and cut into strips (see page 235)

2 scallions, including green parts, sliced thin

1 mango, peeled, cut from the pit, and cut into cubes

Kernels cut from 1 ear fresh corn

$1/2$ bunch cilantro, stemmed and chopped (optional)

1 cup Mango Mojo (recipe follows)

In a medium bowl, toss all of the ingredients together. Serve immediately.

NUTRITIONAL INFORMATION PER SERVING:

278 Calories (45% from fat), 7 g Protein, 31 g Carbohydrate, 14 g Fat, 0 mg Cholesterol, 49 mg Sodium, 7 g Fiber

Mango Mojo

MAKES 1 $1/2$ CUPS

2 cloves garlic, minced

2 tablespoons olive oil

1 teaspoon ground cumin

$1/4$ cup fresh orange juice

$1/2$ cup fresh lime juice

$1/2$ mango, peeled and cut from the pit

$1/2$ to 1 serrano or jalapeno chile, seeded and minced

$1/4$ cup canola oil

Sea salt to taste

In a medium sauté pan or skillet, sauté the garlic in the oil until lightly browned. Add the cumin to the pan and remove from heat. In a blender, combine the garlic mixture with the remaining ingredients and blend until smooth. Store in an airtight container in the refrigerator for up to 1 week.

NUTRITIONAL INFORMATION PER
2 TABLESPOONS:

80 Calories (90% from fat), 0 g Protein, 4 g Carbohydrate, 8 g Fat, 0 mg Cholesterol, 2 mg Sodium, 0.2 g Fiber

WILD RICE AND BARLEY SALAD WITH WILD MUSHROOMS AND PERSIMMONS

MAKES 6 SERVINGS

This hearty salad combines the earthy and complementary flavors of chanterelle mushrooms, celery root, and nutty wild rice with toasted nuts. We add the sweet crunch of Fuyu persimmons, but citrus such as mandarins would work quite well. To serve this as a light entrée, add some French lentils.

2 leeks, washed well and cut into
   1/2-inch crosswise slices

1 clove garlic, minced

1 bulb fennel, cut into 1/4-inch dice

4 ounces chanterelle mushrooms, halved

4 ounces cremini or button mushrooms,
   cut into quarters

1/4 cup dry sherry, nonalcoholic red wine,
   or vegetable stock

2 teaspoons minced fresh thyme or lemon thyme

1 teaspoon sea salt

2 Fuyu persimmons, cut into small cubes

1 celery root, peeled, cut into small cubes,
   blanched until crisp-tender, and cooled

2 cups cooked wild rice

2 cups cooked pearl barley

1/2 cup hazelnuts, toasted and coarsely chopped
   (see page 234)

1 1/2 cup Tarragon-Dijon Dressing or Oil Free
   Tarragon-Dijon Dressing (recipe follows)

Sea salt and freshly ground pepper to taste

2 tablespoons chopped fresh parsley

Fresh tarragon leaves and chopped fresh parsley
   for garnish

In a large sauté pan or skillet, combine the leeks, garlic, fennel, mushrooms, sherry, thyme, and salt and cook uncovered over medium heat until the mushrooms are just tender, about 5 minutes. The leeks and fennel will still be fairly firm. Let cool to room temperature.

In a large bowl, combine the mushroom mixture, 1 1/2 of the persimmons, celery root, grains, and nuts. Fold in the dressing, mixing well. Add the salt, pepper, and parsley. Pour onto a serving platter or individual plates and garnish with the tarragon, parsley, leeks, and the reserved 1/2 persimmon.

NUTRITIONAL INFORMATION PER SERVING DRESSED SALAD:

(with oil) 437 Calories (51% from fat), 7 g Protein, 46 g Carbohydrate, 25 g Fat, 0 mg Cholesterol, 865 mg Sodium, 7 g Fiber

(without oil) 288 Calories (25% from fat), 8 g Protein, 46 g Carbohydrate, 8 g Fat, 0 mg Cholesterol, 865 mg Sodium, 7 g Fiber

Tarragon-Dijon Dressing

MAKES 2 CUPS

1/2 bunch fresh tarragon, stemmed

1 teaspoon minced garlic

1 1/2 tablespoons Dijon mustard

1/2 teaspoon minced lemon zest

1/2 cup fresh lemon juice

1 teaspoon ground pepper

1/2 teaspoon green or pink peppercorns

2 teaspoons nutritional yeast

1 teaspoon sea salt

1/2 cup light olive oil or 1/4 cup canola oil and
   1/4 cup extra virgin olive oil

1/4 cup walnut or hazelnut oil

In a blender, combine all the ingredients except the oils. Add half the olive oil and blend. With the machine running, gradually add the remaining olive oil and the nut oil.

Oil-Free Tarragon-Dijon Dressing

Delete the salt and oils from the preceding recipe. Substitute 1 tablespoon light miso, 1/2 cup (6 ounces) silken tofu, and 1/2 cup water.

NUTRITIONAL INFORMATION PER 2 TABLESPOONS DRESSING:

(with oil) 98 Calories (92% from fat), 0 g Protein, 2 g Carbohydrate, 10 g Fat, 0 mg Cholesterol, 170 mg Sodium, 0 g Fiber

(without oil) 21 Calories (43% from fat), 1 g Protein, 2 g Carbohydrate, 1 g Fat, 0 mg Cholesterol, 210 mg Sodium, 0 g Fiber

QUINOA PILAF

MAKES 4 CUPS

2 cups quinoa

1/2 yellow onion, finely diced

1/2 red bell pepper, seeded, deribbed, and cut into small dice

2 teaspoons olive oil

1 teaspoon sea salt

2 tablespoons minced fresh cilantro

1 tablespoon minced fresh mint

1 orange, pith removed, segmented, and finely diced (optional)

Bring 4 cups of water to boil in a saucepan. Add the quinoa, lower heat to simmer, cover and cook for 7 minutes. Remove from heat and let sit for 5 minutes. Drain in a colander and let cool.

In a medium sauté pan or skillet, sauté the onions and bell pepper in the oil over high heat until tender. In a large bowl, toss with the remaining ingredients and the quinoa.

VARIATION:

For an oil-free version, substitute 2 tablespoons vegetable stock for the olive oil.

NUTRITIONAL INFORMATION PER 1/2 CUP SERVING:

(without oil) 76 Calories (0% from fat), 4 g Protein, 15 g Carbohydrate, 0 g Fat, 0 mg Cholesterol, 216 mg Sodium, 2 g Fiber

(with oil) 94 Calories (19% from fat), 4 g Protein, 15 g Carbohydrate, 2 g Fat, 0 mg Cholesterol, 216 mg Sodium, 2 g Fiber

APRICOT AND FENNEL SALAD WITH BEETS

MAKES 4 SERVINGS

This salad often appears on our antipasto platter. Simple, light, and very clean on the palate, it's a contrast to the earthy, smoky flavors of the grilled vegetables. Try this in the winter with segments of orange and grapefruit. Also try substituting fresh jicama for the fennel.

2 ripe yet firm apricots, pitted and cut into 1/4-inch-thick slices

1 fennel bulb, cut into paper-thin slices

1 golden beet, peeled and shaved or sliced paper thin

1 red or Chioga beet, peeled and shaved or sliced paper thin

1/2 cup fresh lemon juice

1 teaspoon fructose or unrefined sugar

1/2 teaspoon each fennel seeds and coriander seeds, toasted (see page 234)

Sea salt and ground pepper to taste

In a large bowl, mix the apricot, fennel, and beet slices together. In a separate bowl, mix the lemon juice, fructose, fennel seeds, and coriander seeds together and pour over the apricot mixture. Add salt and pepper.

NUTRITIONAL INFORMATION PER SERVING SALAD:

47 Calories (6% from fat), 1 g Protein, 10 g Carbohydrate, 0.3 g Fat, 0 mg Cholesterol, 37 mg Sodium, 1 g Fiber

SAFFRON BASMATI RICE SALAD WITH CURRIED APRICOT DRESSING

MAKES 6 SERVINGS

This salad utilizes our saffron basmati rice pilaf, though plain basmati or long-grain brown rice works just as well. What makes it "winter" are chunks of winter squash or root vegetables and apple. The dressing comes courtesy of our lunch chef Rob Wesely. One day he needed a dressing for a pasta salad, so he threw a bunch of stuff in a blender and out came this marvelous dressing. The whole process of recipe development can't have taken more than a minute and a half— probably the land speed record! Give it a try with a pasta salad.

2 cups Saffron Basmati Pilaf (page 104) or cooked basmati or brown rice

2 cups cubed winter squash or root vegetables, blanched and cooled

1 apple, peeled, cored, and sliced in 1/2-inch cubes

2 scallions, white part only, sliced thin

1/4 cup pine nuts, toasted (see page 234)

Curried Apricot Dressing (recipe follows)

1 beet, peeled and grated or cut into thin julienne, for garnish

2 tablespoons finely shredded fresh mint leaves, for garnish

In a large bowl, toss the pilaf, squash, apple, scallions, and pine nuts with the dressing. Arrange on a serving platter. Garnish with a mound of grated beet and sprinkle with the mint.

NUTRITIONAL INFORMATION PER SERVING DRESSED SALAD:

(with oil) 315 Calories (43% from fat), 5 g Protein, 40 g Carbohydrate, 15 g Fat, 0 mg Cholesterol, 207 mg Sodium, 5 g Fiber

(without oil) 238 Calories (23% from fat), 6 g Protein, 40 g Carbohydrate, 6 g Fat, 0 mg Cholesterol, 213 mg Sodium, 5 g Fiber

Curried Apricot Dressing

MAKES 1 CUP

1/4 cup apricot preserves

1/2 cup rice vinegar or champagne vinegar

1 tablespoon mild curry powder, toasted (see page 234)

1/4 teaspoon ground cardamom

1/4 teaspoon cayenne pepper

1/3 cup water

1/4 cup canola oil

Sea salt to taste

In a blender, combine all the ingredients together and blend until emulsified. Taste and adjust the seasonings. Serve or refrigerate for up to 1 week.

VARIATION:

For an oil-free version, substitute 1/4 cup silken tofu for the oil.

NUTRITIONAL INFORMATION PER 1/4 CUP SERVING:

(with oil) 190 Calories (66% from fat), 0 g Protein, 16 g Carbohydrate, 14 g Fat, 0 mg Cholesterol, 10 mg Sodium, 0.7 g Fiber

(without oil) 77 Calories (12% from fat), 1 g Protein, 16 g Carbohydrate, 1 g Fat, 0 mg Cholesterol, 20 mg Sodium, 1 g Fiber

S O U P S

Soups are not an afterthought at Millennium; in fact, they are one of our favorite courses to prepare. With soups, you can improvise and personalize without much risk of ruining the final result. While we have a number of standard recipes, we're constantly changing elements of a soup based on variations in raw ingredients, combinations of seasonings, and garnishes. Try these recipes, learn what they're about, then try some again, varying an ingredient or two. Make these recipes your own.

HOT SOUPS

LEMONGRASS MISO SOUP WITH ENOKI MUSHROOM AND BASIL RELISH

MAKES 6 SERVINGS

Some folks consider miso soup to be the "vegetarian chicken soup"—and with good reason. They are simple, quick, and nourishing. But miso soup can also be exciting and elegant. This recipe and the two that follow are all variations on Asian themes borrowing from Thai, Japanese, and Chinese cuisine. The relish adds wonderfully bright, sour, and herbal flavors.

4 leeks, white part only, washed well and cut into 1/4-inch crosswise slices

2 carrots, peeled and cut into 1/4-inch matchsticks

4 ounces shiitake mushrooms, stemmed and cut into thin slices

8 cups Asian stock (page 228) or vegetable stock

2 tablespoons dried arame or kombu strips

2 stalks fresh lemongrass, coarsely chopped and tied in a cheesecloth square

2 tablespoons minced fresh ginger

1/2 cup white miso

Sea salt to taste

Cayenne pepper or ground white pepper to taste

1 cup cooked bean thread noodles

4 snow peas, julienned

1 cup fresh corn kernels

4 ounces firm silken tofu, cut into 1/2-inch dice

Enoki Mushroom and Basil Relish (recipe follows) or 2 minced scallions

1 tablespoon sesame seeds, toasted (see page 234)

In a soup pot, combine the leeks, carrots, mushrooms, and 1/2 cup of the stock. Cook over high heat until the liquid evaporates. Add the remaining stock, arame, and lemongrass. Lower the heat and simmer for 20 minutes. Remove the lemongrass, add the ginger, and whisk in the miso. Add salt and cayenne.

Divide the noodles, snow peas, corn, and tofu among the serving bowls. Ladle the soup over the vegetables. Top each with 1 tablespoon relish and sprinkle with sesame seeds.

NUTRITIONAL INFORMATION PER SERVING OF SOUP:

232 Calories (12% from fat), 8 g Protein, 43 g Carbohydrate, 3 g Fat, 0 mg Cholesterol, 560 mg Sodium, 6 g Fiber

Enoki Mushroom and Basil Relish

One 2-ounce package enoki mushrooms, bottom part of stem trimmed

1/2 red bell pepper, seeded, deribbed, and cut into 1/4-inch cubes (optional)

1/2 cup 1/4-inch-diced English cucumber

2 scallions, cut into thin diagonal slices

1/4 cup fresh Thai basil or Italian basil leaves, cut into julienne

1/4 cup fresh lemon juice

2 teaspoons tamari soy sauce (optional)

1/3 teaspoon ground white pepper or cayenne pepper (optional)

Toss all the ingredients together right before serving so the relish remains crisp.

NUTRITIONAL INFORMATION PER TABLESPOON RELISH:

4 Calories (0% from fat), 0 g Protein, 1 g Carbohydrate, 0 g Fat, 0 mg Cholesterol, 5 mg Sodium, 0.1 g Fiber

CORN, GINGER, AND KAFFIR LIME SOUP

MAKES 6 SERVINGS

A descendent of Lemongrass Miso Soup, this thick and creamy chowder has the elusive floral aroma and flavor of fresh kaffir lime leaves. If fat is not a concern, try a little coconut milk swirled into each bowl.

2 white or yellow onions, cut in half crosswise
    then cut into lengthwise slices

1 carrot, peeled and finely diced

2 stalks celery, finely diced

8 cups Asian Stock (page 228) or vegetable stock

4 cups fresh corn kernels (about 6 ears)

2 stalks fresh lemongrass, coarsely chopped and
    tied in a cheesecloth or sliced in half and tied
    together with baker's string

3 tablespoons minced fresh ginger

$1/3$ cup light miso

4 kaffir lime leaves, cut into fine julienne

$1/4$ cup fresh lime juice

$1/3$ teaspoon ground pepper

Sea salt to taste

1 lime, cut into very thin crosswise slices

$1/3$ bunch cilantro, stemmed

In a soup pot, combine the onions, carrot, celery, and $1/2$ cup stock. Cook over high heat until the liquid evaporates. Add the remaining stock, corn, and lemongrass. Lower heat and simmer for 30 minutes. Remove the lemongrass, add the ginger, and whisk in the miso. In a blender, purée half of the soup. Return the purée to the soup in the pot. Add the kaffir lime leaf and the lime juice. Add the salt and pepper. Divide among the serving bowls and top with lime slices and cilantro leaves.

NUTRITIONAL INFORMATION PER
SERVING OF SOUP·

195 Calories (14% from fat), 7 g Protein, 35 g Carbohydrate, 3 g Fat, 0 mg Cholesterol, 616 mg Sodium, 6 g Fiber

HOT AND SOUR ASIAN CABBAGE SOUP

MAKES 6 SERVINGS

This combines the sweet and herbal flavors of Thai tom yum goon soup and the peppery-sour notes of Chinese-style hot and sour soup. This soup will probably require a visit to an Asian market for the tiger lily buds, lemongrass, Thai basil, and dried tree fungus. Garnish with Thai basil and give it some crunch with some fresh bean sprouts sprinkled over the top.

2 leeks, white part only, mashed well and cut into $1/4$-inch slices

2 teaspoons minced garlic

2 carrots, sliced into $1/4$-inch matchsticks

1 cup shredded red cabbage

1 cup thin-sliced shiitake mushrooms (4 to 6 medium), or cremini or oyster mushrooms

1 tablespoon dried tree ear fungus, soaked in hot water, drained, and sliced thin

6 cups Asian Stock (page 228) or vegetable stock

1 cup fresh or canned tomato purée

1 tablespoon tiger lily buds, soaked in warm water for 10 minutes, drained, and sliced open

$1 1/2$ cups cubed fresh pineapple

4 kaffir lime leaves (optional)

2 stalks lemongrass, sliced in half and tied together with bakers string

2 tablespoons grated ginger

$1/4$ cup white miso

1 teaspoon black pepper or white pepper

$1/3$ to $1/2$ teaspoon minced Thai chile (optional)

2 tablespoons tamari soy sauce

2 tablespoons rice vinegar plus more to taste

Sucanat or sugar to taste

3 tablespoons julienned Thai basil, for garnish

$1/2$ cup fresh bean sprouts, for garnish

1 tablespoon sesame seeds, toasted, for garnish (see page 234)

In a large saucepan over medium heat, sweat together the leeks, garlic, carrots, cabbage, mushrooms, and tree ear fungus with $1/2$ cup of the vegetable stock until the liquid evaporates, about 10 minutes. Add the stock, tomato purée, tiger lily buds, pineapple, kaffir lime leaves, and lemongrass. Bring to a boil, lower heat, and simmer for 30 minutes.

Remove the lemongrass, add the ginger, and whisk in the miso. Add the pepper and Thai chile, the tamari, vinegar, and sweetener. Adjust the sweetener and vinegar to your liking.

Top each bowl of soup with the julienned basil, bean sprouts, and sesame seeds.

NUTRITIONAL INFORMATION PER SERVING OF SOUP:

199 Calories (14% from fat), 6 g Protein, 37 g Carbohydrate, 3 g Fat, 0 mg Cholesterol, 829 mg Sodium, 7 g Fiber

Sharlyn Melon Soup with Cucumber-Chile Ice (page 74), Hot and Sour Asian Cabbage Soup

ONION AND APPLE SOUP WITH APPLE, SESAME, AND GINGER RELISH

MAKES 6 SERVINGS

Another onion soup that takes on an Asian flavor with the addition of fresh ginger. Try this soup with pears instead of apples.

4 large yellow onions cut into thin slices (6 cups)
2 cups dry red wine or nonalcoholic red wine
3 apples, peeled and cut into thin slices (4 cups)
¼ cup minced fresh ginger
2 teaspoons Sucanat or unrefined sugar
2 teaspoons minced fresh tarragon
1 teaspoon minced fresh thyme
½ teaspoon ground pepper
8 cups vegetable stock
⅓ cup dark miso
1 tablespoon balsamic vinegar
½ cup wild rice, cooked (1 cup when cooked)
Sea salt to taste

Apple, Sesame, and Ginger Relish (recipe follows)

In a soup pot, combine the onions and red wine. Cook, covered, over medium heat until the onions soften, about 15 minutes. Add the apples, ginger, Sucanat, tarragon, thyme, and pepper. Cook another 5 minutes, then add the vegetable stock. Reduce heat and simmer for 40 minutes to 1 hour.

Whisk in the miso and add the balsamic vinegar and wild rice. Add salt. Serve each bowl of soup topped with 1 tablespoon of the apple relish.

NUTRITIONAL INFORMATION PER SERVING OF SOUP:

227 Calories (12% from fat), 5 g Protein, 45 g Carbohydrate, 3 g Fat, 0 mg Cholesterol, 560 mg Sodium, 5 g Fiber

Apple, Sesame, and Ginger Relish

MAKES 1 CUP

1 apple, peeled, cored, and finely diced
2 scallions, finely diced
¼ cup fresh lemon juice
1 tablespoon sesame seeds, toasted (see page 234)
1 tablespoon minced fresh ginger
½ teaspoon ground black pepper

Toss all the ingredients together in a bowl.

NUTRITIONAL INFORMATION PER TABLESPOON RELISH:

10 Calories (18% from fat), 0.1 g Protein, 2 g Carbohydrate, 0.2 g Fat, 0 mg Cholesterol, 1 mg Sodium, 0.2 g Fiber

CARAMELIZED ONION SOUP

MAKES 6 SERVINGS

Here is our oil-free version of French onion soup. Try it with our flavorful oil-free croutons (page 33) and swirl in a little Dill-Tofu Sour Cream (page 69).

6 red onions, cut into thin slices

1/2 teaspoon sea salt

2 teaspoons Sucanat or unrefined sugar

2 cups Cabernet, Rhone, or other dry red wine, or nonalcoholic red wine

2 cloves garlic, minced

2 cups finely diced carrot

1 cup finely diced celery

2 teaspoon minced fresh thyme

1 teaspoon minced fresh rosemary

2 bay leaves

2 quarts Dark Vegetable Stock (page 228)

1/3 cup dark miso or red miso

1/2 teaspoon ground pepper

In a large saucepan, combine the onions, salt, Sucanat, and wine. Cook over medium heat until the wine evaporates, about 10 minutes, stirring occasionally. Continue to cook, stirring constantly, for another 5 minutes, or until the onions are very soft and caramel brown.

Add the garlic, carrots, celery, thyme, rosemary, and bay leaves, and stir. Add the vegetable stock, cover, and simmer for 40 minutes.

Whisk in the miso. Add the pepper and serve.

NUTRITIONAL INFORMATION PER SERVING OF SOUP:

210 Calories (9% from fat), 5 g Protein, 43 g Carbohydrate, 2 g Fat, 0 mg Cholesterol, 827 mg Sodium, 5 g Fiber

CARROT AND PARSNIP SOUPS WITH TARRAGON-CASHEW SOUR CREAM

SERVES 6

Nope, that is not a misprint in the recipe title. This recipe is for two soups served in a single bowl. Both soups have a similar viscosity, so when poured simultaneously from two ladles into one bowl, they remain separate in the bowl. This lends itself to a striking presentation: half the bowl is a striking red-orange and the other half white-gold, garnished with the light green tarragon cream. When you prepare the tarragon cream, make sure it is thinner in consistency than the soup.

CARROT AND RED PEPPER SOUP

2 yellow onions, cut lengthwise into
   $1/2$-inch-thick crescents

2 or 3 carrots, peeled and cut into $1/2$-inch-thick
   slices (3 cups)

$1/3$ cup dry sherry, dry white wine, or
   nonalcoholic white wine

$1/4$ teaspoon sea salt

2 red bell peppers, roasted, peeled, and
   cut into $1/2$-inch dice (see page 235)

1 teaspoon dried thyme

$1/3$ teaspoon dried dill

3 cups vegetable stock or Asian Stock (page 228)

$1/3$ cup white miso

2 cups soy milk or rice milk

Sea salt to taste

$1/4$ teaspoon cayenne pepper

PARSNIP SOUP

2 yellow onions, cut lengthwise into
   $1/2$-inch-thick crescents

2 or 3 parsnips, cut into $1/2$-inch-thick slices (3 cups)

$1/3$ cup dry sherry or white wine or
   nonalcoholic white wine

$1/4$ teaspoon sea salt

1 teaspoon dried thyme

1 teaspoon dried tarragon

$1/3$ teaspoon ground nutmeg

2 cups vegetable stock

$1/3$ cup white miso

4 cups soy milk or rice milk

Sea salt and freshly ground pepper to taste

$1/2$ cup Tarragon-Cashew Sour Cream (page 175)

To make the carrot and red pepper soup: In a soup pot, combine the onions, carrots, sherry, and sea salt. Cook over medium heat for 10 minutes, or until the liquid evaporates. Add the red peppers, thyme, dill, and stock. Cover and simmer for 30 to 40 minutes, or until the carrots are tender. Transfer to a blender. Add the miso and blend until smooth. Return to the pot and stir in the soy milk. Add the sea salt and cayenne.

To make the parsnip soup: In a soup pot, combine the onions, parsnips, sherry, and salt. Cook over medium heat for 10 minutes, or until the liquid evaporates. Add the thyme, tarragon, nutmeg, and stock. Cover and simmer covered for 30 to 40 minutes, or until the parsnips are tender. Transfer to a blender and add the miso. Blend until smooth. Return to the soup pot and stir in the soy milk. Add the salt and pepper.

Rewarm the soups if necessary. Into each serving bowl, simultaneously ladle both soups, keeping the ladles close to the bowl. Drizzle on the Tarragon-Cashew Sour Cream in an artistic pattern.

NUTRITIONAL INFORMATION PER SERVING OF SOUP:

282 Calories (19% from fat), 13 g Protein, 44 g Carbohydrate, 6 g Fat, 0 mg Cholesterol, 710 mg Sodium, 10 g Fiber

YELLOW SPLIT PEA SOUP WITH SAGE AND SMOKED DULSE GREMOLATA

MAKES 6 SERVINGS

Our version of a classic split pea soup, complete with the kind of warm, smoky nuances usually provided by a ham hock. We achieved this by smoking and toasting dulse, a sea vegetable, which is then minced with parsley, dill, and lemon zest to garnish the soup.

3 yellow onions, cut into 1/2-inch dice

6 cloves garlic, minced

2 carrots, peeled and cut into small dice

4 stalks celery, cut into small dice

2 tablespoons olive oil, or 1 cup dry sherry or nonalcoholic wine

1 tablespoons dried sage

1 teaspoon dried thyme

1 teaspoon dried dill

8 cups vegetable stock

1 cup dried yellow or green split peas, rinsed

3 tablespoons light miso

1 teaspoon ground pepper

1/4 cup fresh lemon juice

2 teaspoons sea salt

In a soup pot, cook the onions, garlic, carrots, and celery in the oil over medium heat until the liquid has evaporated and the onions are soft, about 10 minutes. Add the dried herbs and sauté for 2 minutes. Add the stock and peas. Cover and simmer for 1 hour, or until the peas are very soft. Watch out for the soup boiling over if the heat is too high. In a blender or food processor, purée the soup until smooth, in batches if necessary. Whisk in the miso, pepper, lemon juice, and salt. Top each serving with 1 teaspoon gremolata (please note that the gremolata is salty).

NUTRITIONAL INFORMATION PER 10-OUNCE SERVING:

(with oil) 346 Calories (16% from fat), 14 g Protein, 59 g Carbohydrate, 6 g Fat, 0 mg Cholesterol, 816 mg Sodium, 9 g Fiber

(without oil) 319 Calories (8% from fat), 14 g Protein, 59 g Carbohydrate, 3 g Fat, 0 mg Cholesterol, 816 mg Sodium, 12 g Fiber

Smoked Dulse Gremolata

MAKES 1/2 CUP

1 ounce dried dulse, preferably smoked (see Note)

Minced zest of 1 lemon

1/2 bunch parsley, stemmed and minced

1 tablespoon minced fresh dill

In a large sauté pan or skillet, toast the dulse over high heat, stirring constantly, for approximately 2 minutes, or until crisp. Transfer to a plate and let cool.

Either crumble the dulse with your hand or pulse it in a food processor until reduced to small flakes. Toss the lemon zest, parsley, and dill with the crumbled dulse.

NOTE:

Look for smoked dulse from Maine Coast Sea Vegetable in natural food stores.

NUTRITIONAL INFORMATION PER TEASPOON GREMOLATA:

4 Calories (0% from fat), 0 g Protein, 1 g Carbohydrate, 0 g Fat, 0 mg Cholesterol, 65 mg Sodium, 0 g Fiber

BRAZILIAN BLACK BEAN SOUP WITH COFFEE AND ORANGE

MAKES 6 SERVINGS

Black bean soups are a perennial favorite here at Millennium. We have probably come up with a dozen variations on this theme, ranging from Asian style with fermented black beans used as a seasoning to smoking the black beans. This variation on a Brazilian theme includes finely ground coffee, orange juice, a little smoked chipotle chile, and cumin, giving the soup a warm, complex, and elusive quality.

4 yellow onions, cut lengthwise into
   1/2-inch-thick crescents

1 tablespoon minced garlic

2 celery stalks, diced small

1 carrot, peeled and finely diced

1/2 cup dry sherry, dry white wine, or
   nonalcoholic white wine

11/2 tablespoons ground cumin

11/2 teaspoons dried oregano

2 bay leaves

1 tablespoon Chipotle Paste (page 174)

1 tablespoon finely ground dark-roast coffee or
   a coffee substitute like Cafix

3 cups black beans, soaked and drained (see page 236)

2 cups fresh orange juice

8 cups unsalted vegetable stock

2 teaspoons sea salt

Tamari soy sauce to taste (optional)

Cilantro-Tofu Cream (page 127) or Chipotle-Cashew
   Sour Cream (page 175)

Minced orange zest for garnish

In a soup pot, cook the onions, garlic, celery, carrot, and sherry over medium heat for 10 minutes. In a small sauté pan or skillet, toast the cumin, oregano, and bay leaves over high heat, stirring constantly, for 1 minute, or until aromatic and slightly darker in color. Add this mixture to the soup pot along with the Chipotle Paste, coffee, black beans, orange juice, and vegetable stock. Cover and simmer until the beans are tender, 1 to 11/2 hours. Add the salt and tamari. Remove the bay leaves. In a blender or food processor, blend one quarter to all of the soup, depending on the desired texture. Serve in soup bowls, topped with 1 tablespoon Cilantro Cream or Chipotle Cream and sprinkle with orange zest.

NUTRITIONAL INFORMATION PER SERVING OF SOUP:

387 Calories (7% from fat), 18 g Protein, 72 g Carbohydrate, 3 g Fat, 0 mg Cholesterol, 843 mg Sodium, 16 g Fiber

CHANTERELLE, LOBSTER, AND OYSTER MUSHROOM BISQUE

MAKES 4 SERVINGS

We prepared this for our first wild-mushroom-tasting dinner and it was absolutely sinful: rich and creamy, with more than a subtle shellfish-like taste (they don't call them oyster and lobster mushrooms for nothing). This version is definitely not for the low-fat contingent, though you could easily omit the oil and replace the cashew cream with blended low-fat tofu and stock. The chanterelles and lobster mushrooms are not the easiest to find, and they usually cost a pretty penny, so when you do find them, create a special occasion to serve this soup.

2 leeks, white part only, washed well and thinly sliced (3 cups)

$^2/_3$ cup finely diced carrot

1 teaspoon minced garlic

1 cup finely diced celery root or celery

2 tablespoons light olive oil

$^1/_2$ teaspoon sea salt

4 ounces chanterelle mushrooms, washed and thinly sliced

4 ounces lobster mushrooms, washed and thinly sliced

4 ounces oyster mushrooms, cleaned and halved, or left whole if small

2 teaspoons minced fresh thyme

1 teaspoon Spanish paprika

$^1/_3$ teaspoon ground nutmeg

$^1/_3$ cup dry sherry or nonalcoholic wine

6 cups vegetable stock

$^2/_3$ cups unsalted cashews

1 tablespoon fresh lemon juice

1 tablespoon white miso

Sea salt to taste

$^1/_2$ teaspoon ground pepper

Dry sherry for garnish (optional)

1 tablespoon chopped fresh chives

In a soup pot, sauté the leeks, carrot, garlic, and celery root in the oil for 10 minutes. Add the salt and mushrooms and cook for 5 minutes. Stir in the thyme, paprika, and nutmeg and sauté another few minutes. Stir in the sherry, then 4 cups of the vegetable stock. Cover and simmer for 20 minutes.

In a blender, combine the remaining cashews, 2 cups stock, lemon juice, and miso. Blend until thoroughly smooth, adding more stock if needed to achieve the consistency of heavy cream. Whisk the mixture into the soup until completely blended. Let simmer for 5 to 10 minutes to thicken the soup. Add the sea salt and pepper. Serve with a few drops of dry sherry and chopped chives.

NUTRITIONAL INFORMATION PER 1 CUP SERVING:

(with oil) 322 Calories (50% from fat), 8 g Protein, 32 g Carbohydrate, 18 g Fat, 0 mg Cholesterol, 642 mg Sodium, 6 g Fiber

(without oil, and low-fat version—tofu replacing cashews) 146 Calories (12% from fat), 7 g Protein, 25 g Carbohydrate, 2 g Fat, 0 mg Cholesterol, 695 mg Sodium, 5 g Fiber

GOLDEN BEET SOUP WITH DILL-TOFU "SOUR CREAM"

SERVES 6

A simple yet elegant variation on traditional borscht. The dill-tofu sour cream makes the dish.

2 yellow onions, thinly sliced

2 carrots, thinly sliced

$1/2$ cup dry sherry, dry white wine, or nonalcoholic white wine

Four 2-inch-diameter yellow beets, peeled and thinly sliced

2 bay leaves

1 teaspoon dried thyme

$1/2$ teaspoon toasted ground caraway seeds

8 cups vegetable stock

$1/2$ cup white miso

2 tablespoons minced fresh tarragon (optional)

1 tablespoon balsamic vinegar (optional)

Sea salt and freshly ground pepper to taste

Dill-Tofu Sour Cream (recipe follows)

In a soup pot, cook the onions, carrots, and sherry until the onions are soft, about 15 minutes. Add the beets, bay leaves, thyme, caraway, and stock. Cover and simmer for 40 minutes, or until the beets are very soft. Remove from heat and whisk in the miso. Add the tarragon and vinegar. In a blender, blend the soup in batches until smoothly puréed. Add the salt and pepper.

Serve the soup with 2 tablespoons of the dill-tofu sour cream per serving.

NUTRITIONAL INFORMATION PER SERVING OF SOUP:

146 Calories (12% from fat), 4 g Protein, 28 g Carbohydrate, 2 g Fat, 0 mg Cholesterol, 971 mg Sodium, 3 g Fiber

Dill-Tofu "Sour Cream"

MAKES 1 CUP

3 ounces low-fat silken tofu

1 tablespoon white miso

$1/2$ cup fresh lemon juice

3 tablespoons minced fresh dill or 1 tablespoon dried dill

$1/4$ teaspoon ground nutmeg

$1/2$ cup water, plus more as needed

In a blender or food processor, blend all the ingredients together until smooth. Thin out with additional water if needed.

NUTRITIONAL INFORMATION PER 2 TABLESPOONS:

12 Calories (0% from fat), 1 g Protein, 2 g Carbohydrate, 0 g Fat, 0 mg Cholesterol, 78 mg Sodium, 0 g Fiber

No-Cream of Mushroom Soup

Serves 6

Here is a very low-fat cream-style soup that can be as simple or as elegant as you want it to be. Low-fat silken tofu gives this soup its creamy texture. Add some cooked barley to the finished soup to serve as a light main meal. To make this a little richer, swirl in a bit of Cashew Sour Cream (page 175).

4 red onions, cut lengthwise into
   1/2-inch-thick crescents

2 teaspoons minced garlic

1 cup dry red wine or nonalcoholic red wine

2 teaspoons Sucanat or unrefined sugar (optional)

2 pounds button or cremini mushrooms, sliced
   (try with fresh shiitake mushrooms mixed in)

1 ounce dried porcini mushrooms, soaked
   in warm stock (optional)

1/2 teaspoon dried sage

1 teaspoon dried thyme

1 teaspoon dried tarragon

1/3 teaspoon ground nutmeg

8 cups vegetable stock

2 tablespoons tamari soy sauce

1 tablespoon balsamic vinegar

8 ounces low-fat silken tofu or low-fat firm tofu

Sea salt and freshly ground pepper to taste

In a soup pot, combine the onions, garlic, wine, and Sucanat. Cook over medium heat, stirring often, until the onions are reddish brown, about 15 minutes. Add the mushrooms, including the porcini and their soaking liquid (except the very bottom where the sand and grit have accumulated). Stir and cook for 10 minutes. Add the herbs, nutmeg, and stock. Simmer the soup for 40 minutes. The mushrooms will be very soft. Add the tamari and vinegar. In a blender or food processor, blend the soup and tofu, in batches if necessary, until smooth. Add salt and pepper and serve.

Nutritional information per serving of soup:

118 Calories (15% from fat), 7 g Protein, 18 g Carbohydrate, 2 g Fat, 0 mg Cholesterol, 294 mg Sodium, 3 g Fiber

Golden Tomato Soup

Serves 6

The key to this soup is to use the most flavorful vine-ripened tomatoes you can find and then highlight their flavor. This recipe marries restrained amounts of fresh rosemary, a pinch of orange zest, a very slight sting of jalapeno, and a hint of fresh mint with sweet, low-acid golden tomatoes. We use Golden Jubilee or Valencias. A low-acid red tomato such as Celebrity or Brandywine will work just as well and if you ever run across large green ripe tomatoes called "Evergreen," snatch them up, prepare them in this recipe, and serve the soup chilled.

2 yellow onions, thinly sliced

1/2 cup dry white wine

1 teaspoon sea salt

8 to 10 golden tomatoes, cut into quarters
   (about 6 cups)

1 teaspoon minced fresh rosemary

1 teaspoon minced orange zest

1/2 teaspoon minced jalapeno chile

4 cups light vegetable stock

Sea salt to taste

1 lemon, cut lengthwise into thin crescents

6 tablespoons finely shredded fresh mint

In a soup pot, cook the onions in white wine and salt over medium heat until the onions are tender, about 15 minutes. Add the tomatoes, rosemary, orange zest, jalapeno, and stock. Bring to a boil, then reduce heat and simmer for 15 minutes. Transfer to a blender in batches and blend until smooth. Add the salt. Serve hot or chilled with a slice of lemon and sprinkled with mint.

NUTRITIONAL INFORMATION PER SERVING OF SOUP:

101 Calories (9% from fat), 3 g Protein, 20 g Carbohydrate, 1 g Fat, 0 mg Cholesterol, 420 mg Sodium, 3 g Fiber

TOMATO, ROOT VEGETABLE, AND WILD RICE SOUP

MAKES 6 SERVINGS

This is definitely not a light, summery tomato soup. We prepare this soup in the fall with either fresh tomatoes or organic canned tomatoes. Basil-Garlic Cashew Sour Cream (page 175) is the perfect complement to the big hearty flavors of this soup. Try a variety of root vegetables, including beets. Add them in greater proportion to turn this soup into a winter stew.

2 cups finely diced yellow onions

8 cloves garlic, minced

1/2 cup dry sherry or nonalcoholic wine

2 cups finely diced root vegetables, such as celery root, parsnips, and turnips

1 cup cremini or stemmed shiitake mushrooms, thinly sliced

1/2 cup wild rice

1 teaspoon dried thyme

1/2 teaspoon dried rosemary

1 teaspoon dried oregano

1 teaspoon fennel seeds, ground

6 cups vegetable stock, plus more if needed

3 pounds fresh tomatoes, finely diced, or 32 ounces canned tomatoes, drained and finely diced (juice reserved)

2 teaspoons sea salt

1/2 teaspoon ground pepper

2 tablespoons balsamic vinegar (optional)

In a soup pot, cook the onions, garlic, and sherry over high heat until the liquid evaporates. Add the root vegetables, mushrooms, wild rice, thyme, rosemary, oregano, and ground fennel to the pot. Toss with the onions. Add the 6 cups vegetable stock, bring to a boil, then reduce heat. Cover and simmer for 30 minutes.

Add the tomatoes (and their juice) and cook, uncovered, for 20 to 30 minutes, or until the root vegetables and wild rice are tender. Add more stock if the soup becomes too thick. Add the salt, pepper, and balsamic vinegar and serve.

NUTRITIONAL INFORMATION PER SERVING OF SOUP:

182 Calories (10% from fat), 5 g Protein, 36 g Carbohydrate, 2 g Fat, 0 mg Cholesterol, 834 mg Sodium, 6 g Fiber

Celery Root and Chestnut Soup

Serves 6

This soup is ideal for holiday entertaining or any cold winter's night. The dried chestnuts are worth the search. Look for them in Asian markets and specialty foods stores. They impart a velvety smooth texture and a nutty, slightly smoky flavor to the soup and, although chestnuts give food a creamy quality, they are in reality low in fat.

2 leeks, washed, halved lengthwise, and thinly sliced

2 cloves garlic, minced

$1/4$ teaspoon sea salt

$1/2$ cup dry sherry, dry white wine, nonalcoholic white wine, or vegetable stock

2 teaspoons dried thyme

4 bay leaves

2 celery roots, peeled and cut into 1-inch cubes

8 cups light vegetable stock

4 ounces dried chestnuts, rinsed

1 teaspoons minced lemon zest

$1/2$ teaspoon ground nutmeg

1 tablespoon minced fresh tarragon leaves

$1/4$ teaspoon ground pepper

2 tablespoons white miso

$1/2$ teaspoon sea salt

Rice milk or soy milk to thin soup, if needed

1 lemon, cut into thin wheels, for garnish

Chopped fresh tarragon, for garnish

In a large soup pot, cook the leeks, garlic, salt, and sherry over medium heat, stirring often, for 10 minutes, or until the leeks are very tender and starting to caramelize. Add the thyme, bay, celery root, stock, and chestnuts.

Cover and simmer for 40 minutes, or until the celery root and chestnuts are soft. Add the lemon zest, nutmeg, tarragon, pepper, miso, and salt. Remove from heat and discard the bay leaves. In a blender, blend the soup in batches until smooth. Add rice milk to thin soup to the desired consistency. Taste and adjust the seasoning. Garnish each serving with a few drops of dry sherry, a lemon wheel, and some chopped tarragon.

Nutritional information per serving of soup:

191 Calories (14% from fat), 5 g Protein, 36 g Carbohydrate, 3 g Fat, 0 mg Cholesterol, 582 mg Sodium, 5 g Fiber

GOLDEN GAZPACHO WITH AVOCADO-CILANTRO SORBET

MAKES 6 SERVINGS

We have come up with a number of gazpacho variations at Millennium. This one, using yellow peppers, golden tomatoes, and lemon cucumbers, is completely golden in hue. Lemon cucumbers are small yellow colored globes with a pale yellow-white flesh.

GAZPACHO

1 yellow onion, finely diced

4 yellow bell peppers, roasted and peeled (see page 235)

1 or 2 pale green Anaheim or yellow Hungarian chiles, roasted and peeled (see page 235)

6 golden tomatoes, cut into quarters

2 lemon cucumbers, cut into quarters, or peeled English cucumber, chopped

1/2 teaspoon minced garlic

3/4 cup fresh lime juice

1 teaspoon minced fresh oregano

6 cups vegetable stock

2 teaspoons sea salt

1/2 teaspoon ground pepper

GOLDEN TOMATO SALSA

2 scallions, finely diced

1 yellow bell pepper, finely diced

2 golden tomatoes, thinly diced (substitute golden sweet 100's or cherry tomatoes)

1 lemon cucumber, finely diced

1 golden zucchini, seeded and finely diced (optional)

2 to 3 tablespoons extra virgin olive oil (optional)

Avocado-Cilantro Sorbet (recipe follows)

In a blender, purée all the ingredients for the gazpacho until smooth. In a small serving bowl, combine all the salsa ingredients. Pour the soup into bowl and stir in the salsa. Refrigerate for at least 1 hour before serving. Add 1 scoop sorbet to each bowl of soup and serve.

NUTRITIONAL INFORMATION PER SERVING OF SOUP:

146 Calories (12% from fat), 4 g Protein, 28 g Carbohydrate, 2 g Fat, 0 mg Cholesterol, 373 mg Sodium, 7 g Fiber

Avocado-Cilantro Sorbet

MAKES 1 1/2 CUPS

1 avocado, peeled and chopped

1/4 cup fresh lime juice

1/2 bunch cilantro, stemmed

1/2 serrano chile, seeded

1/2 cup water

1 1/2 teaspoons sea salt

4 to 6 green olives, pitted (optional)

In a blender, purée all the ingredients together. Freeze in an ice cream maker according to the manufacturer's directions.

NUTRITIONAL INFORMATION PER 2 TABLESPOONS SORBET:

36 Calories (75% from fat), 0.4 g Protein, 2 g Carbohydrate, 3 g Fat, 0 mg Cholesterol, 318 mg Sodium, 0.5 g Fiber

SHARLYN MELON SOUP WITH CUCUMBER-CHILE ICE

MAKES 6 SERVINGS

Next to our golden gazpacho, this is our most asked-for cold soup. It is light and refreshing, with a little zip and zing provided by the accompanying Cucumber-Chile Ice. The ice is easy. You don't even need an ice cream maker. Try this with other varieties of melon besides Sharlyn, which is similar to honeydew.

1 small Sharlyn melon, seeded and flesh scooped out (about 6 cups)

5 ounces silken tofu

1/4 cup fresh lime juice

1 cup lemon juice

4 tablespoons Sucanat or fructose

5 cups cold water

1 tablespoon light miso (optional)

1 bunch mint, stemmed, plus fresh mint sprigs for garnish

1/2 teaspoon sea salt

1/4 teaspoon cayenne pepper

Cucumber-Chile Ice (recipe follows), or lemon and/or lime slices, for garnish

6 fresh mint sprigs, for garnish

In a large bowl, combine all the ingredients except the garnish and mix with a fork to break up and distribute the tofu. In a blender, blend the mixture in batches until smooth. Serve immediately or refrigerate until needed.

Top each serving with a small scoop of Cucumber-Chile Ice or slices of lemon and mint sprigs.

NUTRITIONAL INFORMATION PER SERVING OF SOUP:

153 Calories (6% from fat), 3 g Protein, 33 g Carbohydrate, 1 g Fat, 0 mg Cholesterol, 560 mg Sodium, 4 g Fiber

Cucumber-Chile Ice

MAKES 1 1/2 CUPS

1 cucumber, peeled, seeded, and coarsely chopped (about 1 cup)

1/2 serrano chile, seeded

1/2 cup fresh lime juice

2 scallions, white part only, chopped (optional)

1/2 bunch cilantro, stemmed

1 teaspoon sea salt

1 cup water

In a blender, blend all the ingredients together until smooth, adding more water if necessary to achieve the consistency of thin soup or cream rather than a thick purée. Pour the mixture into a sheet tray that will fit in your freezer and freeze for a minimum of 2 hours.

At serving time, remove the tray from the freezer and scrape the ice with the tines of a fork to flake off the ice crystals. Place the ice in a bowl and serve immediately. Store any leftover ice in an airtight container in the freezer.

NUTRITIONAL INFORMATION PER 1/8 CUP (1 OZ. SCOOP):

14 Calories (0% from fat), 0.5 g Protein, 3 g Carbohydrate, 0 g Fat, 0 mg Cholesterol, 421 mg Sodium, 0.5 g Fiber

CHILLED APRICOT SOUP WITH LEMON-GINGER ICE

SERVES 6

Don't scoff at the idea of a chilled fruit soup served as a first course. Our fruit soups are light, palate cleansing, and appetite stimulating. This apricot soup is simple, slightly tart, and infused with a bit of citrus and lemongrass. The accompanying ice does not need an ice cream maker.

1 pound fresh apricots

1 cup fresh lemon juice

3 cups water

4 tablespoons Sucanat or fructose

1 teaspoon lemon zest

1 stalk lemongrass, halved and crushed

1/4 teaspoon cayenne pepper

4 ounces soft low-fat silken tofu

1 teaspoon sea salt

Lemon-Ginger Ice (recipe follows)

In a large saucepan, combine the apricots, lemon juice, water, Sucanat, zest, lemongrass, and cayenne and simmer, covered, for 20 minutes, or until the apricots are soft. Remove the lemongrass. Transfer to a blender in batches and purée with the tofu. Add the salt and refrigerate for at least 2 hours. Serve with the Lemon-Ginger Ice.

NUTRITIONAL INFORMATION PER SERVING OF SOUP:

177 Calories (3% from fat), 2 g Protein, 41 g Carbohydrate, 0.6 g Fat, 0 mg Cholesterol, 385 mg Sodium, 2 g Fiber

Lemon-Ginger Ice

MAKES 1 CUP

1/3 cup fresh lemon juice

2 tablespoons unrefined sugar or fructose

2 teaspoons grated fresh ginger

2/3 cup water

In a medium bowl, whisk all the ingredients together. Pour into an 8-inch baking pan and freeze until frozen solid. At serving time, scrape the ice into small granules with the tines of a fork.

NUTRITIONAL INFORMATION PER 1/8 CUP (1 OZ. SCOOP):

16 Calories (0% from fat), 0 g Protein, 4 g Carbohydrate, 0 g Fat, 0 mg Cholesterol, 0 mg Sodium, 0 g Fiber

CHILLED CREAMY CUCUMBER-MINT SOUP

SERVES 6

This is a simple and refreshing soup for the dog days of summer.

2 large English cucumbers, seeded and chopped

5 ounces silken tofu

2 scallions, coarsely chopped

$1/4$ cup fresh lime juice

$1/4$ cup fresh lemon juice

1 tablespoon fructose or Sucanat

4 cups cold water

2 tablespoons white miso

$1/2$ bunch mint, stemmed

$1/2$ teaspoon sea salt

$1/4$ teaspoon cayenne pepper

Roasted-Pepper Harissa (page 176) or thin slices lemon or lime for garnish

In a large bowl, combine all the ingredients except the harissa and mix with a fork to break up and distribute the tofu. In a blender, blend the mixture in batches until smooth. Serve immediately or refrigerate until needed. Top each serving with $1/2$ teaspoon of Roasted Pepper Harissa or slices of lemon or lime.

NUTRITIONAL INFORMATION PER SERVING OF SOUP:

81 Calories (11% from fat), 3 g Protein, 15 g Carbohydrate, 1 g Fat, 0 mg Cholesterol, 401 mg Sodium, 1 g Fiber

PASTA AND PIZZA

For both pasta and pizza, the same rules apply: either keep it simple or give it the works. We have a selection of pasta sauces and serving suggestions on what type of pasta and what additional ingredients to pair them with. Like soups, many of these pasta sauces are a good starting point for you to add your creative spin to.

Even if you do not follow a lower fat diet, give some of our oil-free "cream sauces" a try. Because we purée them with braised garlic, or other vegetable purées in addition to silken tofu, they have an appealing texture and mouth feel. You won't miss the fat.

Don't let some of our unconventional pizza toppings intimidate you, nor the fact that we grill our pizzas. Try them. You will like them.

MILLENNIUM PASTA "CARBONARA"

MAKES 6 SERVINGS

This version of traditional carbonara sauce is easy and flavorful. Its creamy texture thickens when heated, and I think it works best on heartier pastas like penne, rotelli, or fettuccini. Try adding some sun-dried tomatoes, capers, and fresh peas.

CARBONARA SAUCE

3 cups light soy milk

1 cup Millennium Braised Garlic (page 230)

2 tablespoons nutritional yeast

2 tablespoons white miso (optional)

1 teaspoon dried oregano

1/2 teaspoon ground pepper

1/2 teaspoon ground nutmeg

1 teaspoon fennel seeds, ground

2 teaspoons Spanish paprika

1 chipotle chile, or 2 teaspoons Chipotle Paste, (page 174) or 1/3 teaspoon cayenne pepper (optional)

3/4 pound pasta

To make the sauce: In a blender, combine all the ingredients and blend until smooth. Set aside and keep warm.

In a large pot of salted boiling water, cook the pasta until al dente. Drain and toss with the sauce. Serve at once.

NUTRITIONAL INFORMATION PER SERVING:

290 Calories (6% from fat), 13 g Protein, 55 g Carbohydrate, 2 g Fat, 0 mg Cholesterol, 250 mg Sodium, 3 g Fiber

PASTA WITH MINT AND CUMIN CREAM, SMOKED EGGPLANT, AND TOMATOES

MAKES 6 SERVINGS

MINT AND CUMIN CREAM

1/4 cup fresh mint leaves

2 teaspoons ground cumin

Cayenne and freshly ground pepper to taste

Braised Garlic Cream (page 81)

1 globe eggplant, smoked and cut into 1/2-inch dice (see page 235)

2 cloves garlic, minced

1/2 cup vegetable stock or water

3/4 pound fusilli

2 tomatoes, finely diced

1 tablespoon fresh whole oregano leaves

Chopped green olives and fresh mint leaves for garnish

To make the cream sauce: In a blender, combine the mint leaves, cumin, cayenne, pepper, and garlic cream. Blend until smooth. In a large sauté pan or skillet, combine the eggplant, garlic, and stock. Cook over medium-high heat until the eggplant is softened, about 10 minutes. Add the cream sauce and heat. Set aside and keep warm.

In a large pot of salted boiling water, cook the fusilli until al dente. Drain. Add the fusilli to the sauce in the pan and toss to coat. Toss with the tomatoes and oregano. Serve garnished with the olives and mint.

NUTRITIONAL INFORMATION PER SERVING:

291 Calories (9% from fat), 8 g Protein, 58 g Carbohydrate, 3 g Fat, 0 mg Cholesterol, 638 mg Sodium, 3 g Fiber

80

FETTUCINE WITH BRAISED GARLIC CREAM

MAKES 6 SERVINGS

This dish is simple and quick if you already have braised garlic on hand. It is creamy and very flavorful. This recipe is a starting point for an endless number of variations, several of which follow. If you don't like or cannot have garlic, substitute an equal amount of caramelized onions (page 229), boiled potatoes, roasted eggplant, or butternut squash.

BRAISED GARLIC CREAM

3 cups light soy milk
1 1/2 cups Braised Garlic (page 230)
2 tablespoons nutritional yeast
2 tablespoons white miso
1/2 teaspoon ground nutmeg
1/2 teaspoon sea salt

3/4 pound fettucine

To make the garlic cream: In a blender, combine all ingredients and blend until smooth. Set aside and keep warm.

In a large pot of salted boiling water, cook the fettucine until al dente. Drain and toss with the garlic cream. Serve at once.

NUTRITIONAL INFORMATION PER SERVING:

302 Calories (6% from fat), 12 g Protein, 59 g Carbohydrate, 2 g Fat, 0 mg Cholesterol, 434 mg Sodium, 3 g Fiber

Roasted Pepper Cream

Blend 2 or 3 roasted and peeled bell peppers or pimiento (see page 235). Try adding 2 teaspoons fresh oregano or 1/2 bunch chopped fresh cilantro or 2 teaspoons cumin or fennel seeds along with other ingredients in the main recipe.

NUTRITIONAL INFORMATION PER SERVING:

310 Calories (6% from fat), 12 g Protein, 61 g Carbohydrate, 2 g Fat, 0 mg Cholesterol, 434 mg Sodium, 4 g Fiber

Pesto Cream

Stem 1 large bunch of fresh basil and blend the leaves along with the other ingredients in the main recipe.

NUTRITIONAL INFORMATION PER SERVING:

302 Calories (6% from fat), 12 g Protein, 59 g Carbohydrate, 2 g Fat, 0 mg Cholesterol, 434 mg Sodium, 4 g Fiber

Lemon, Black Pepper, and Caper Cream

Blend the grated zest of 1 lemon, 1 1/2 teaspoons coarsely ground pepper, and 1 teaspoon drained capers along with the other ingredients in the main recipe. Add 1/2 cup fresh lemon juice and 1 teaspoon drained capers to the tossed pasta. Garnish with a little more grated zest.

NUTRITIONAL INFORMATION PER SERVING:

310 Calories (6% from fat), 12 g Protein, 61 g Carbohydrate, 2 g Fat, 0 mg Cholesterol, 454 mg Sodium, 4 g Fiber

PASTA WITH WHITE WINE-MARINATED TOMATOES AND BASIL

MAKES 6 SERVINGS

We make this quintessential summer pasta with a variety of vine-ripened tomatoes of all shapes, sizes, colors, and flavors. The presentation is as stunning as it is flavorful. We cook the marinated tomatoes and basil over high heat for a few minutes to reduce the liquid, cook out the alcohol, and soften the tomatoes before we add the pasta. The braised garlic enhances the flavor and thickens the sauce.

WHITE WINE-MARINATED TOMATO AND BASIL SAUCE

1½ pounds vine-ripened tomatoes of choice, cut into 1-inch cubes

4 cups dry Chardonnay or nonalcoholic white wine

1 cup Millennium Braised Garlic (page 230)

2 to 4 cloves garlic, minced

1 bunch basil, stemmed (try half green and half purple basil)

2 teaspoons capers, drained

1½ teaspoons sea salt

Freshly ground pepper to taste

3/4 pound capellini, linguine, or fettuccine

4 tablespoons extra virgin olive oil (optional)

Finely shredded fresh basil for garnish

To make the sauce: In a large bowl, combine all the sauce ingredients. Let sit for at least 30 minutes or up to 2 hours. In a large sauté pan or skillet, cook the mixture over high heat for about 10 minutes, or until the liquid reduces, the tomatoes soften, and the alcohol is cooked out. Add the olive oil. Set aside and keep warm.

In a large pot of salted boiling water, cook the pasta until al dente. Drain. In a large bowl, toss the pasta with the sauce. Garnish with basil and serve.

NUTRITIONAL INFORMATION PER SERVING:

(with oil) 367 Calories (27% from fat), 10 g Protein, 57 g Carbohydrate, 11 g Fat, 0 mg Cholesterol, 655 mg Sodium, 3 g Fiber

(without oil) 277 Calories (3% from fat), 10 g Protein, 57 g Carbohydrate, 1 g Fat, 0 mg Cholesterol, 655 mg Sodium, 3 g Fiber

RED LENTIL, LEMON, AND ROSEMARY ORECCHIETTE

MAKES 6 SERVINGS

Another simple, oil-free pasta sauce. The red lentils cook quickly and have a slightly nutty flavor that complements Mediterranean flavors. Wilted spinach, arugula, or mustard is a good addition to this pasta.

RED LENTIL, LEMON, AND ROSEMARY SAUCE

1 yellow onion, cut into 1/2-inch cubes

4 cloves garlic, minced

2 ripe tomatoes, cubed, or 1 cup canned tomatoes

2/3 cups dried red lentils, rinsed and picked over

3 cups vegetable stock or water

1 tablespoon minced fresh rosemary

1/4 teaspoon red pepper flakes

2 teaspoons minced lemon zest

1/2 cup fresh lemon juice

2 teaspoons sea salt

Freshly ground black pepper

3/4 pound orecchiette

1 cup finely diced tomatoes (optional)

2 cups loosely packed spinach, arugula, or mustard greens (optional)

1 or 2 teaspoons capers, drained, for garnish (optional)

Chopped fresh parsley, for garnish

To make the sauce: In a medium saucepan, cook the onions, garlic, and tomatoes over medium-high heat for 10 minutes, or until the onions start to soften and the tomatoes break down. Add the lentils, then the stock. Add the rosemary and pepper flakes. Cover and simmer for 20 minutes, or until the lentils are soft. Add the lemon zest and juice, salt, and pepper. Set aside and keep warm.

In a large pot of salted boiling water, cook the pasta until al dente. Drain. Toss with the pasta sauce and tomatoes and greens. Serve at once, garnished with the capers and parsley.

NUTRITIONAL INFORMATION PER SERVING:

330 Calories (5% from fat), 15 g Protein, 63 g Carbohydrate, 2 g Fat, 0 mg Cholesterol, 885 mg Sodium, 6 g Fiber

LINGUINE WITH ARUGULA PESTO

MAKES 6 SERVINGS

Arugula pesto is a mainstay of our pasta sauce repertoire, especially during the fall when local arugula is so prevalent. This version is a favorite of one of our chefs, Marilyn Nauss.

ARUGULA PESTO

2 bunches arugula, stemmed

4 cloves garlic

1/2 cup pine nuts, toasted (see page 234)

3 tablespoons extra virgin olive oil, plus more to cover pesto if needed

Water as needed (up to 1/2 cup)

1/2 teaspoon sea salt

Freshly ground pepper to taste

1 teaspoon capers, drained

3/4 pound linguine

To make the pesto: In a blender, combine the arugula, garlic, and pine nuts. Blend until finely chopped. With the machine running, drizzle in the 3 tablespoons oil and water to achieve a smooth paste, about the consistency of smooth peanut butter. Add more water if needed. Add the salt, pepper, and capers. Set aside and keep warm. To make ahead, pour into an airtight container, pour over a thin layer of olive oil, cover, and refrigerate for up to 1 week. Rewarm before using.

In a large pot of salted boiling water, cook the pasta until al dente. Drain. Toss with the pesto and serve.

VARIATIONS:

Add sautéed bell peppers, tomatoes, and spinach or broccoli rabe to the cooked pasta along with the pesto. Garnish with minced lemon zest.

For a lower-fat pesto, substitute silken tofu for the nuts and oil.

NUTRITIONAL INFORMATION PER SERVING:

(with oil and pine nuts) 314 Calories (29% from fat), 11 g Protein, 45 g Carbohydrate, 10 g Fat, 0 mg Cholesterol, 233 mg Sodium, 2 g Fiber

(without oil or pine nuts) 225 Calories (6% from fat), 9 g Protein, 44 g Carbohydrate, 1.4 g Fat, 0 mg Cholesterol, 245 mg Sodium, 2 g Fiber

FUSILLI WITH ROASTED PEPPER AND KALAMATA OLIVES

MAKES 6 SERVINGS

Olives, cinnamon, and oregano add their perfume to this Greek-inspired pasta.

SAUCE

2 red onions, sliced in thin crescents

1/4 cup olive oil

1/2 teaspoon sea salt

1 teaspoon Sucanat or unrefined sugar

1/2 cup dry red wine or nonalcoholic red wine

3 or 4 red bell peppers or pimientos, roasted, peeled, and cut into 1/2-inch strips (see page 235)

4 cloves garlic, minced

1 teaspoon dried oregano

1 teaspoon cumin seeds, toasted (see page 234)

1/4 teaspoon red pepper flakes

1/2 teaspoon ground cinnamon

1 teaspoon minced orange zest

1/2 cup pitted and coarsely chopped Kalamata olives

1 cup vegetable stock

2 tablespoons balsamic vinegar (optional)

Sea salt and freshly ground pepper to taste

3/4 pound fusilli

To make the sauce: In a large sauté pan or skillet, sauté the onion in the oil until tender, about 5 minutes. Add the sea salt, Sucanat, and wine. Sauté until the liquid is evaporated and the onions are browned, about 10 minutes. Add the peppers and garlic and sauté 1 minute. Add the oregano, cumin, pepper flakes, cinnamon, and zest, followed by the olives and stock. Cook to reduce by half. Add the vinegar, salt, and pepper. Set aside and keep warm. To make ahead, let cool, then refrigerate in an airtight container for up to 1 week. Rewarm to serve.

In a large pot of salted boiling water, cook the pasta until al dente. Drain. Toss with sauce and serve at once.

VARIATION:

Sauté 2 cups of sliced zucchini and 2 diced tomatoes, blanch 4 loosely packed cups of broccoli rabe for 2 minutes, and toss all with the pasta before adding the sauce. Finish off by tossing in some fresh mint leaves.

NUTRITIONAL INFORMATION PER SERVING:

369 Calories (32% from fat), 9 g Protein, 54 g Carbohydrate, 13 g Fat, 0 mg Cholesterol, 605 mg Sodium, 3 g Fiber

MUSHROOM, FENNEL, AND DILL CREAM PENNE

MAKES 6 SERVINGS

This sauce's earthy flavors are balanced by the pungent green peppercorns and brightened by fresh dill. If you're a mycophile, this is a great sauce for blewits.

MUSHROOM, FENNEL, AND DILL CREAM

1 fennel bulb, sliced thin

2 leeks, white parts only, washed and thinly sliced

4 cloves garlic, minced

1 tablespoon olive oil

1/2 teaspoon sea salt

10 ounces button, cremini, or wild mushrooms such as blewits or chanterelles

1/2 cup dry sherry, port, or nonalcoholic white wine

1 tablespoon minced fresh thyme or lemon thyme leaves, or 1 teaspoon dried thyme

1 teaspoon minced fresh dill, plus additional for garnish

1/4 teaspoon ground nutmeg

1/2 teaspoon minced lemon zest

2 teaspoons nutritional yeast

2 cups Mushroom Stock (page 228) or 1 tablespoon dried porcini soaked in 2 cups warm vegetable stock, strained

1 cup Cashew Cream (recipe follows)

1 teaspoon brine-packed green peppercorns, drained

1/3 teaspoon pink peppercorns (optional)

1/2 cup fresh lemon juice

3/4 pound penne

To make the sauce: In a large sauté pan or skillet, sauté the fennel, leeks, and garlic in the oil until the leeks are tender, about 10 minutes. Add the sea salt and mushrooms and sauté for 5 minutes. Add the sherry and stir to scrape up all the browned bits from the bottom of the pan. Add the thyme, dill, nutmeg, zest, and yeast and sauté 1 more minute. Add the mushroom stock and simmer to reduce by half. Remove from heat and add the cashew cream, peppercorns, and lemon juice. Set aside and keep warm. To make ahead, let cool and refrigerate in an airtight container for up to 4 days. Rewarm to serve.

In a large pot of salted boiling water, cook the pasta until al dente. Drain. Toss with the mushroom, fennel, and dill cream and serve at once, garnished with additional minced fresh dill.

NUTRITIONAL INFORMATION PER SERVING:

369 Calories (22% from fat), 11 g Protein, 61 g Carbohydrate, 9 g Fat, 0 mg Cholesterol, 330 mg Sodium, 4 g Fiber

Cashew Cream

MAKES 1 CUP

1/2 cup unsalted cashews

1 cup water, plus more as needed

In a blender, combine the cashews and 1/2 cup of the water. Blend until coarsely puréed. Slowly add the remaining 1/2 cup water until smooth. Add additional water if needed to thin the consistency of heavy cream. Store refrigerated in an airtight container for up to 4 days.

NUTRITIONAL INFORMATION PER 1/4 CUP CREAM:

108 Calories (66% from fat), 3 g Protein, 6 g Carbohydrate, 8 g Fat, 0 mg Cholesterol, 3 mg Sodium, 0.5 g Fiber

LINGUINE WITH TEMPEH BOLOGNESE

SERVES 4

Our version of the classic Italian meat sauce is hearty, flavorful, and works well with either fresh or canned tomatoes. This is a good introduction to tempeh for those who are not familiar with it.

TEMPEH BOLOGNESE SAUCE

1 yellow onion, finely diced

1 carrot, peeled and finely diced

2 stalks celery, finely diced

2 to 4 cloves garlic, minced

2 tablespoons olive oil

$1/4$ teaspoon sea salt

$1/2$ teaspoon dried thyme

$1/2$ teaspoon ground fennel seed

$1/2$ teaspoon dried oregano

1 teaspoon minced fresh rosemary

1 bay leaf

8 ounces Baked Marinated Tempeh (page 231) or packaged marinated tempeh, finely crumbled

1 cup dry red wine or nonalcoholic wine

8 to 10 fresh tomatoes, peeled, seeded, and cut into $1/2$-inch dice (see page 235), or 28 ounces canned tomatoes, drained and chopped (juice reserved)

$1/2$ teaspoon ground pepper

Sea salt to taste

$3/4$ pound linguine or fettucine

Chopped fresh parsley or minced fresh basil for garnish

To make the sauce: In a large sauté pan or skillet, sauté the onion, carrot, celery, and garlic in the olive oil until the onion is soft and slightly browned. Add the salt, thyme, fennel, oregano, rosemary, and bay leaf. Stir in the crumbled tempeh and sauté for 5 minutes. Add the wine, tomatoes, and juice. Cover, reduce heat to low, and simmer the sauce, stirring frequently, for 30 to 40 minutes. Uncover and cook a few more minutes to thicken. Add the pepper and salt. Set aside and keep warm.

In a large pot of salted boiling water, cook the pasta until al dente. Drain and toss with the sauce. Serve at once.

VARIATION:

Add $1/2$ pound of chopped button or cremini mushrooms, or wild mushrooms such as porcini, to the onion, carrot, and garlic sauté.

NUTRITIONAL INFORMATION PER SERVING:

547 Calories (18% from fat), 20 g Protein, 92 g Carbohydrate, 11 g Fat, 0 mg Cholesterol, 416 mg Sodium, 7 g Fiber

Asian Noodles with Millennium Ponzu Sauce

Makes 6 servings

This is our Asian mother sauce, which we use as the basis for a number of sauces, marinades, soups, and even salad dressings. An infusion of lemongrass, ginger, garlic, and hot pepper in tamari, sweetened with rice syrup, the flavors are salty, spicy, slightly sweet, and pungent. If you plan on preparing some of the other Asian-inspired recipes in this book, double the sauce recipe.

3/4 pound dried soba or udon noodles

2 cloves garlic, minced

1 tablespoon canola oil (optional)

6 ounces shiitake mushrooms, sliced thin

1 head broccoli sliced into small florets

1 red bell pepper, sliced in thin strips

4 ounces smoked tofu sliced into thin strips

3 cups Ponzu Sauce

3 teaspoons toasted sesame oil (optional)

2 teaspoons toasted sesame seeds

1 1/2 tablespoons Arame Sea Vegetable Salad (page 182)

1 tablespoon each chiffonade of fresh basil and mint (optional)

Cook the pasta in salted water until al dente, 5 to 7 minutes. Drain and cool the pasta (if not using immediately).

In a large sauté pan or preferably a wok, sauté the garlic in the oil for 30 seconds. Add the shiitakes, broccoli, bell pepper, and tofu. Sauté an additional 2 to 3 minutes. Add the ponzu and bring to a boil. Either add the pasta and heat through or toss the pasta with ponzu and vegetables in a large mixing bowl. Toss with the sesame oil and divide among 6 serving bowls. Top with the sesame seeds, arame salad, and basil-mint chiffonade.

Nutritional information per serving:

(with oil) 336 Calories (11% from fat), 10 g Protein, 65 g Carbohydrate, 4 g Fat, 0 mg Cholesterol, 850 mg Sodium, 5 g Fiber

(without oil) 309 Calories (3% from fat), 10 g Protein, 65 g Carbohydrate, 1 g Fat, 0 mg Cholesterol, 850 mg Sodium, 5 g Fiber

Ponzu Sauce

4 cloves garlic

2 tablespoons coarsely chopped fresh ginger

1 1/2 stalks lemongrass, mostly white parts, chopped into 1/2-inch pieces

1/4 teaspoon red pepper flakes

1/4 cup dry sherry, dry white wine, or nonalcoholic wine

2 cups water

1/3 cup tamari soy sauce

1/2 cup brown rice syrup

In a medium saucepan, combine all the ingredients and bring to a boil. Reduce heat and simmer for 20 minutes. Remove from heat and strain through a fine meshed sieve. To make ahead, let cool, then refrigerate in an airtight container for up to 1 month.

YAM AND SAGE GNOCCHI WITH ROASTED TOMATO AND GARLIC BROTH

MAKES 4 SERVINGS

We made this dish for an autumnal equinox dinner that mixed summer and fall produce. The gnocchi are not that difficult but it might take some trial and error to get the proportions of flour right due to variables in moisture content of the potatoes. We bake our yams and russets so the flesh is much drier than if we boiled them.

2 yams
1 russet potato
2 cloves garlic, minced
2 teaspoons olive oil
2 teaspoons minced fresh sage
2/3 cup unbleached all-purpose flour, plus more as needed
1 teaspoon sea salt
Roasted Tomato and Garlic Broth (recipe follows)

Preheat the oven to 400°. Prick the skins of the yams and potato all over with a fork. Bake directly on an oven rack until tender when pierced with a knife, about 40 minutes. Let cool to room temperature. Scrape the flesh out of the yams and potato into a medium bowl.

In a small sauté pan or skillet, sauté the garlic in the oil until it starts to turn golden-brown. Stir in the sage. Add to the potato mixture and stir well. Stir in the 2/3 cup flour and salt. Turn out onto a lightly floured board and knead a few times to form a smooth, cohesive mass, adding a little more flour if needed.

Cut off a quarter of the dough and roll it with your hands into a 1-inch-thick rope. Cut the dough into 1/2-inch-long segments. Pinch in each side of the dough so it looks like a bow tie, or make an indent in the center of each dumpling with your thumb. Place the finished gnocchi on a floured pan. Repeat with the remaining dough. Refrigerate or freeze the gnocchi for at least 1 hour.

To cook, bring at least 1 gallon of salted water to a boil. Add half the gnocchi to the boiling water and cook until the gnocchi float to the surface, about 7 or 8 minutes. Using a slotted spoon, transfer the gnocchi to a plate. Toss with a little oil to prevent sticking. Repeat with the remaining gnocchi. Serve immediately in the broth.

NUTRITIONAL INFORMATION PER SERVING:

287 Calories (9% from fat), 6 g Protein, 59 g Carbohydrate, 3 g Fat, 0 mg Cholesterol, 641 mg Sodium, 4 g Fiber

Roasted Tomato and Garlic Broth

MAKES 4 CUPS

6 ripe tomatoes, halved
6 cloves garlic
6 cups light vegetable stock
2 bay leaves
1/2 teaspoon fennel seeds
1/4 teaspoon saffron threads (optional)
1 sprig rosemary
1-inch square piece lemon zest (peel it off with a vegetable peeler)
Sea salt and freshly ground pepper to taste
2 tablespoons dry sherry (optional)

Preheat the broiler, Put the tomatoes and garlic in a baking pan. Place under the broiler and broil, until the tomato skin and garlic cloves start to char and soften, about 10 minutes, turning frequently.

In a large pot, combine the tomatoes and garlic with the stock, herbs, and zest. Simmer, uncovered, for 30 minutes, or until reduced by 1/3. Strain through a fine-meshed sieve. Add salt and pepper. Add sherry right before serving.

NUTRITIONAL INFORMATION PER
1/2 CUP BROTH:

20 Calories (0% from fat), 0 g Protein, 5 g Carbohydrate, 0 g Fat, 0 mg Cholesterol, 63 mg Sodium,
1 g Fiber

VARIATION:

Sauté the gnocchi in 1 tablespoon olive oil and
serve with Arugula Pesto (page 83) or Pesto
Cream (page 81).

CANNELLINI WITH ROASTED EGGPLANT AND RED PEPPER COULIS

SERVES 6

*Simplicity and the bold flavors of smoky egg-
plant, roasted garlic, and peppers make this sum-
mertime dish special.*

ROASTED EGGPLANT FILLING

2 Italian eggplants

1 teaspoon olive oil

1 teaspoon sea salt

1/4 cup Millennium Braised Garlic (page 230) or
    purée from 1 head roasted garlic

1 teaspoon capers, drained

2 teaspoons minced fresh oregano or
    1 teaspoon dried oregano

1 tablespoon chopped fresh basil or mint (optional)

1 cup toasted bread crumbs (see page 234)

1/4 teaspoon cayenne pepper or ground pepper to taste

Sea salt to taste

2 teaspoons extra virgin olive oil

3/4 pound fresh pasta sheets

Red Pepper Coulis (recipe follows)

Basil Cashew Cream (recipe follows)

To make the filling: Preheat the oven to 400°.
Slice the eggplants in half lengthwise and poke
them all over with the tines of a fork. Rub the cut
surface with the oil and salt, put in baking pan,
and bake until very tender, about 25 minutes. Or,
grill the eggplant over coals until the flesh is tender and the skin is charred, adding some soaked
wood chips to the coals if you want a smoky flavor. Let cool to the touch, then scrape out the flesh
of the eggplant and discard the skin. In a medium
bowl, combine the eggplant, braised garlic, capers,
oregano, basil, bread crumbs, cayenne, salt, and
olive oil, lightly mashing them together with the
back of a fork. Set aside and keep warm.

Cut the pasta sheets into twelve 4-inch
squares. In a large pot of salted boiling water,
cook the pasta squares until al dente. Drain the
squares and lay them out on a work surface.
Spread 1/2 cup filling on the bottom third of the
pasta square and roll the pasta into a cylinder.
Repeat with the other sheets. If not serving immediately, place them on a baking sheet. Brush
with a little water, cover with aluminum foil,
and place in a 200° oven.

For each serving, spoon 1/3 cup coulis in the
center of each plate and shake the plate so the
coulis coats the entire bottom of the plate. Place
2 cannellini on the coulis. Drizzle 2 tablespoons
of basil cashew cream over the cannellini and
coulis.

NUTRITIONAL INFORMATION PER SERVING:

379 Calories (17% from fat), 11 g Protein, 68 g Carbohydrate, 7 g Fat, 0 mg Cholesterol, 564 mg Sodium,
6 g Fiber

VARIATION:

For a lower fat version, substitute 4 ounces
low-fat silken tofu for the cashews.

(recipe continues on next page)

Red Pepper Coulis

MAKES 2 1/2 CUP

4 red bell peppers, roasted, peeled, and seeded
  (see page 235)

1 clove garlic, minced

1/2 cup vegetable stock, plus more as needed

2 teaspoons light miso (optional)

Sea salt and freshly ground pepper to taste

In a blender, combine the pepper, garlic, 1/2 cup stock, and miso. Blend until smooth, adding more stock if needed to reach a smooth sauce consistency. Add the salt and pepper.

NUTRITIONAL INFORMATION PER
1/3 CUP SERVING:

17 Calories (5% from fat), 0.1 g Protein, 4 g Carbohydrate, 0 g Fat, 0 mg Cholesterol, 59 mg Sodium, 1 g Fiber

Basil Cashew Cream

MAKES 1 1/2 CUPS

1/4 cup unsalted cashews

1/2 bunch basil, stemmed

1/4 cup fresh lemon juice

2 teaspoons light miso

1/4 teaspoon ground nutmeg (optional)

1 cup water

Sea salt to taste

In a blender, combine all the ingredients except the salt and blend until smooth. Add the salt.

NUTRITIONAL INFORMATION PER
2 TABLESPOON SERVING:

24 Calories (56% from fat), 0.6 g Protein, 2 g Carbohydrate, 1.5 g Fat, 0 mg Cholesterol, 36 mg Sodium, 0.2 g Fiber

SAFFRON LASAGNETTE WITH WHITE BEAN AND SEITAN SAUSAGE RAGOUT

MAKES 6 SERVINGS

Often, instead of making individual ravioli, which are time-consuming to prepare, we layer sheets of cooked fresh pasta with various fillings. The variations are endless, from butternut squash and smoked bean ragout with lemon-pepper pasta and sage-onion sauce, to roasted Indian-spiced vegetables with curry pasta sheets and cumin dal with pickled figs. Explore different-flavored pasta sheets from a pasta shop. For this version, we've used saffron and red pepper pasta.

WHITE BEAN AND
SEITAN SAUSAGE RAGOUT

1 yellow onion, finely diced

2 tablespoons olive oil, vegetable stock,
  dry white wine, or nonalcoholic white wine

1 carrot, peeled and finely diced

1 parsnip, turnip, celery root, or other
  root vegetable, finely diced (optional)

2 stalks celery, finely diced

2 to 4 cloves garlic, minced

1/4 teaspoon sea salt

1/4 teaspoons minced fresh rosemary

1 tablespoon minced fresh sage or
  1 teaspoon dried sage

1 bay leaf

1/4 teaspoon ground cloves (optional)

1/4 teaspoon ground nutmeg

1/4 cup dry white wine or nonalcoholic white wine

1 teaspoon Dijon mustard

2 cups cooked cannellini or other white beans

2 cups vegetable stock

1 cup Spicy Fennel Seitan Sausage (page 108),
  finely chopped

Freshly ground pepper to taste

1 pound fresh pasta sheets (approximately
   12 x 9 inches per sheet, cut into
   18 3 x 3-inch squares)
Saffron-Garlic Cream Sauce (recipe follows)
Finely diced tomato and finely shredded basil,
   or Sun-Dried Tomato and Roasted Pepper
   Tapenade (recipe follows) for garnish

To make the ragout: In a large sauté pan or skillet, sauté the onion in the oil until lightly browned. Add the carrot, root vegetable, celery, garlic, and salt and sauté for 5 minutes. Add the rosemary, sage, bay leaf, cloves, and nutmeg and sauté for 1 minute. Add the wine and stir to scrape up any browned bits from the bottom of the pan. Stir in the mustard, then the beans and stock. Simmer, uncovered, until most of the moisture has cooked out of the bean mixture. Add the seitan sausage and simmer for 5 minutes. Add the pepper. Keep warm.

Cut the pasta sheets into eighteen 3-inch squares. In a large pot of salted boiling water, cook the pasta until al dente, usually 2 to 3 minutes. Drain. For each serving, ladle 1/4 cup Saffron Garlic Cream sauce onto a dinner plate or into a pasta bowl. Place 1 pasta square on top of the sauce. Layer with 1/4 cup ragout. Top with another pasta square, then another 1/4 cup ragout. Finish with 1 pasta square.

Top with tomato and basil or tapenade.

NUTRITIONAL INFORMATION PER SERVING:

387 Calories (26% from fat), 20 g Protein, 52 g Carbohydrate, 11 g Fat, 0 mg Cholesterol, 663 mg Sodium, 7 g Fiber

Saffron-Garlic Cream Sauce

MAKES 3 CUPS

1/2 cup Millennium Braised Garlic (page 230)
1 clove garlic, minced
1/4 cup cashews, or 2 ounces low-fat silken tofu
1/4 cup fresh lemon juice
1 tablespoon capers, drained
2 teaspoons nutritional yeast
1/2 teaspoon ground pepper
Sea salt to taste
2 cups water

In a blender, combine all the ingredients and blend thoroughly until smooth, adding more water to thin if needed. Taste and adjust the seasoning. Heat until just hot and serve.

NUTRITIONAL INFORMATION PER SERVING:

32 Calories (38% from fat), 1 g Protein, 4 g Carbohydrate, 1.3 g Fat, 0 mg Cholesterol, 28 mg Sodium, 0.3 g Fiber

Sun-Dried Tomato–Roasted Pepper Tapenade

MAKES 1 CUP

1 red bell pepper, roasted and peeled
6–8 sun-dried tomato halves, reconstituted in
   warm water
1 teaspoon lemon zest
2 tablespoons lemon juice
1 tablespoon capers
6–8 Kalamata olives, pitted
Black pepper to taste

Place all ingredients in a food processor and pulse until coarsely chopped. You can also dice the pepper, tomatoes, and olives by hand, and then combine with the other ingredients. Use immediately or store refrigerated for up to a week.

MILLENNIUM PIZZA

MAKES ENOUGH DOUGH FOR
4 INDIVIDUAL PIZZAS

We use this all-purpose dough for lunch pizzas and for focaccia for our sandwiches. The polenta adds a slight crunch.

MILLENNIUM PIZZA DOUGH
1/2 package active dry yeast
1/4 cup warm water (105° to 115°)
1/4 teaspoon Sucanat or unrefined sugar
1 1/2 tablespoons polenta
1/2 teaspoon sea salt
1 clove garlic, minced
1/4 teaspoon dried basil
1/4 teaspoon flaxseeds (optional)
2 cups unbleached all-purpose flour (or bread flour)
Sauce of choice
Toppings of choice

In a large mixing bowl, combine the yeast, water, and Sucanat. Let set for 10 to 15 minutes, or until bubbly. Whisk in the polenta, salt, garlic, basil, and flaxseeds. Gradually whisk in the flour, 1/2 cup at a time until the dough is too thick to whisk. Switch to a wooden spoon and continue to add flour until the dough pulls away from the side of the bowl.

Turn the dough out onto a floured surface and knead for 5 minutes, adding a little more flour if necessary. Put the dough in a large oiled bowl, turn it to coat the top, and let rise in a warm place until doubled, about 1 hour. Punch the dough down. Turn it out on a floured surface. Cut the dough into 4 pieces and form each into a ball. If not using immediately, wrap them in plastic wrap and store on a baking sheet in the refrigerator.

On a floured work surface, roll each ball of dough out to a 10-inch round. Preheat oven to 450°, with a baking stone inside if you have one. Dust a baker's peel or a baking sheet with polenta or flour.

Spread 3 tablespoons sauce over each pizza, leaving a 1/2-inch border. Evenly distribute the toppings over the pizza.

To bake: If using a baking stone, use a baking sheet or peel to transfer 2 of the pizzas directly onto the preheated stone and bake for 5 to 7 minutes or until the bottom is crisp and light brown and the toppings are bubbling and browning. Otherwise, put the pizzas on 2 baking sheets and bake for 10 to 15 minutes. Slice and serve immediately.

Focaccia Dough

Substitute whole-wheat flour for half of the unbleached flour. If you wish, you may also use:

2 tablespoons extra virgin olive oil, optional
1 scallion, sliced thin, optional

Preheat the oven to 450°.
Do not divide the dough.
Lightly oil an 8 x 10 inch baking pan, and dust with polenta. Press the dough into the pan. If desired, brush the dough with oil and press the scallion pieces into it. Bake for 15 to 20 minutes, until the top is golden brown and the bread easily pulls away from the pan, Slice and serve warm.

NUTRITIONAL INFORMATION PER PIZZA:
241 Calories (4% from fat), 7 g Protein, 51 g Carbohydrate, 1 g Fat, 0 mg Cholesterol, 316 mg Sodium, 3 g Fiber

MILLENNIUM GRILLED PIZZA

Yep, grilled pizza. We roll out our dough and place it on our hot grill. The intense heat sears the crust immediately, causing the leavening in the dough to create random small air pockets.

We flip the crust over and sear the other side, then place it on a pizza pan and add the topping. The pizza goes under the broiler just long enough to heat the toppings. If the topping is overly moist, the pizza is returned to the grill to crisp the bottom crust. Now onto a plate and out the kitchen door it goes. The whole process takes a matter of minutes. This process does take a watchful eye, to prevent overcooking and burning the crust.

To grill: Using the peel or baking sheet, transfer the dough to the grill over a hot fire. Sear the crust for 45 seconds to 1 minute, then give the dough a half a turn and sear another 45 seconds to 1 minute. This will create a cross-hatch pattern of grill marks and prevent the dough from burning in any one spot. Flip the dough over and sear another 30 seconds to 1 minute, or until the dough firms up but is softer than on the first side. Transfer the crust to a peel or baking sheet with the side with the cross pattern grill marks on the bottom.

Spread 3 tablespoons sauce over each pizza, leaving a $1/2$-inch border. Evenly distribute the toppings over the pizza. Broil the pizza until the toppings are hot and bubbling or browning, about 1 minute. If the bottom crust appears soggy, place the pizza back on the grill for 30 seconds. Serve immediately.

At home, put the toppings on the crust as the bottom cooks on the grill, then cover the grill to cook the top of the pizza as the bottom sears, about 5 to 7 minutes.

INDIAN PIZZETTE WITH APPLE-CILANTRO CHUTNEY

MAKES 6 PIZZAS; SERVES 6

We serve this as a dinner appetizer. The little pizzas will bring to mind seasoned Indian flat bread like nan or puri. The pizza dough is highly seasoned with toasted aromatic spices topped with saffron-flavored onions, and served with apple-cilantro chutney. Hot out of the oven, few pizzas can top these.

SAFFRON ONIONS

2 yellow onions, sliced in thin crescents
2 tablespoons olive oil (optional)
1/4 cup vegetable stock or water
1/4 teaspoon saffron threads
1 teaspoon sea salt
1/2 teaspoon ground pepper

PIZZA DOUGH

1 1/2 teaspoons fennel seeds
1 1/2 teaspoons cumin seeds
1/2 teaspoon coriander seeds
1/2 teaspoon black mustard seed (optional)
1 package active dry yeast
2 1/2 cups warm water (105°–100°)
1/2 teaspoon Sucanat or unrefined sugar
4 cups unbleached all-purpose flour
1/4 cup polenta
2/3 teaspoon sea salt
1 tablespoon minced garlic

Apple-Cilantro Chutney (recipe follows)

To make the saffron onions: In a medium sauté pan or skillet, sauté the onions in the oil or stock over medium-low heat until soft and translucent, about 20 minutes. Add the saffron threads, salt, and pepper. Sauté until the liquid evaporates. Remove from heat.

To make the pizza dough: Toast the fennel, cumin, coriander seeds, and mustard in a dry sauté pan over high heat for 1 minute, or until they smell fragrant. In a large bowl, combine the yeast, warm water, and Sucanat. Stir to dissolve. Let sit until foamy, 10 to 15 minutes. In another large bowl, combine the flour, polenta, salt, garlic, fennel, cumin, coriander, and mustard seeds. Mix well. Gradually whisk the dry ingredients into the wet until thick enough to require mixing with a wooden spoon. Turn the dough out onto a floured surface and knead for 5 minutes, or until smooth and elastic.

Preheat oven to 400°. Oil a large bowl, add the dough, and turn to coat. Cover the bowl and let the dough rise in a warm place until doubled, about 1 hour. Punch down and divide into 6 pieces. Form each piece into a ball. Let rise for 15 minutes. If not using immediately, wrap and refrigerate on a baking sheet pan for up to 24 hours. Let dough come to room temperature before using.

On a floured surface, roll out each ball of dough approximately 6 to 7 inches in diameter. Top each pizza dough with 1/4 cup of the saffron onions. Bake for 10 to 15 minutes or until crust is lightly browned. Remove the pizzas and cut each into 4 slices. Transfer to serving plates and serve each pizza at once with 1 to 2 tablespoons chutney, placed in the center of the pizza.

NUTRITIONAL INFORMATION PER PIZZA:

(with oil) 447 Calories (14% from fat), 11 g Protein, 85 g Carbohydrate, 7g Fat, 0 mg Cholesterol, 821 mg Sodium, 6 g Fiber

(without oil) 402 Calories (4% from fat), 11 g Protein, 85 g Carbohydrate, 2 g Fat, 0 mg Cholesterol, 821 mg Sodium, 6 g Fiber

Apple-Cilantro Chutney

MAKES 1 1/2 CUPS

1/2 cup fresh lemon juice

1 serrano chile, seeded

1 bunch fresh cilantro, stemmed

3 tablespoons water

1/2 teaspoon sea salt

2 apples, cored, peeled, and cut into 1/3-inch dice

In a blender, purée the lemon juice, chile, cilantro, water, and salt until smooth. In a medium bowl, toss the apples in the purée. Store in an airtight container in the refrigerator for 2 days.

NUTRITIONAL INFORMATION PER TABLESPOON CHUTNEY:

8 Calories (0% from fat), 0 g Protein, 2 g Carbohydrate, 0 g Fat, 0 mg Cholesterol, 45 mg Sodium, 0.2 g Fiber

CORN, ANAHEIM CHILE, AND JAPANESE EGGPLANT PIZZA WITH CILANTRO PESTO

MAKES FOUR 10-INCH PIZZAS

CILANTRO PESTO

1 bunch cilantro, stemmed

2 cloves garlic

1/4 cup pine nuts, toasted (see page 234)

2 tablespoons extra virgin olive oil

1/3 teaspoon sea salt

Freshly ground black pepper

1 teaspoon chopped black olives (optional)

1/4 cup water

Millennium Pizza Dough (page 92)

Kernels cut from 1 ear fresh corn

2 Anaheim chiles, roasted, peeled, and cut into 1/2-inch strips (see page 235)

2 small Japanese eggplants, halved lengthwise, grilled or broiled, and cut into 1/2-inch strips

Sea salt and freshly ground black pepper

Fresh cilantro or fresh oregano leaves for garnish

To make the pesto: In a blender, combine all the ingredients. Add more water if necessary to yield a spreadable consistency.

On a floured surface, roll each ball of dough out to a 10-inch circle. Spread each crust with cilantro paste. Top with the corn, chiles, and eggplant. Sprinkle with salt and pepper. Bake (see page 92). Garnish with the cilantro or oregano leaves. Slice and serve at once.

NUTRITIONAL INFORMATION PER SERVING TOPPING (SEE PAGE 92 FOR NUTRITIONAL INFORMATION FOR CRUST):

165 Calories (65% from fat), 4 g Protein, 10 g Carbohydrate, 12 g Fat, 0 mg Cholesterol, 205 mg Sodium, 4 g Fiber

(full pizza) 408 Calories (29% from fat), 11 g Protein, 61 g Carbohydrate, 13 g Fat, 0 mg Cholesterol, 521 mg Sodium, 7 g Fiber

MARINATED FIG, ONION, AND BLACK OLIVE PIZZAS WITH HERB-TOFU AIOLI

MAKES FOUR 10-INCH PIZZAS

4 fresh mission figs, cut into slices

1 tablespoon balsamic vinegar

1/4 teaspoon sea salt

1/4 teaspoon red pepper flakes

1/3 teaspoon fennel seeds

1/4 teaspoon ground pepper

3/4 cup Herb-Tofu Aioli (page 173)

2 red onions, cut into 1/2-inch-thick slices and grilled
   (see page 10)

8 kalamata olives, pitted and coarsely chopped

Millennium Pizza Dough (page 92)

2 tablespoons finely shredded fresh basil for garnish

In a small bowl, combine the figs, vinegar, salt, pepper flakes, fennel seed, and pepper. Let sit for 10 minutes before using. Spread 3 tablespoons aioli over each pizza. Top with the onions, fig slices, and olives.

Bake as on page 92. Garnish with the chopped basil. Serve at once.

NUTRITIONAL INFORMATION PER SERVING TOPPING (SEE PAGE **92** FOR NUTRITIONAL INFORMATION FOR CRUST):

101 Calories (9% from fat), 2 g Protein, 21 g Carbohydrate, 1 g Fat, 0 mg Cholesterol, 190 mg Sodium, 4 g Fiber

(full pizza) 342 calories (5% from fat), 9 g Protein, 72 g Carbohydrate, 2 g Fat, 0 mg Cholesterol, 506 mg Sodium, 7 g Fiber

From top to bottom: *Marinated Fig, Onion, and Black Olive Pizza; Indian Pizzette with Apple–Cilantro Chutney; Roasted Tomato and White Bean Gallette*

CARAMELIZED GARLIC AND SMOKED PORTOBELLO PIZZAS

MAKES FOUR 10-INCH PIZZAS

16 garlic cloves, halved lengthwise

2 teaspoon extra virgin oil

1/2 cup vegetable stock

1 teaspoon Sucanat or sugar

1 teaspoon balsamic vinegar

1 teaspoon tamari soy sauce

1 teaspoon fresh rosemary, minced

Millennium Pizza Dough (page 92)

3/4 cup Garlic-Herb Aioli (page 173)

2 portobello mushrooms, smoked and thinly sliced
   (see page 233) or 6 cremini mushrooms

2 tablespoons pine nuts

Red pepper flakes to taste

In a small saucepan, combine the garlic, oil, stock, Sucanat, vinegar, tamari, and rosemary. Bring to a boil, then reduce heat and simmer to reduce until brown and syrupy, about 15 minutes. Remove from heat.

On a floured surface, roll each ball of dough out to a 10-inch circle. Spread each crust with 3 tablespoons aioli. Top with the mushrooms, 4 cloves of caramelized garlic, and 1 1/2 teaspoons pine nuts.

Bake as on page 92. Sprinkle with pepper flakes.

NUTRITIONAL INFORMATION PER SERVING TOPPING (SEE PAGE **92** FOR NUTRITIONAL INFORMATION FOR CRUST):

84 Calories (43% from fat), 3 g Protein, 9 g Carbohydrate, 4 g Fat, 0 mg Cholesterol, 195 mg Sodium, 2 g Fiber

(full pizza) 325 Calories (14% from fat), 10 g Protein, 60 g Carbohydrate, 5 g Fat, 0 mg Cholesterol, 511 mg Sodium, 5 g Fiber

TEMPEH PIZZAS WITH PUTTANESCA SAUCE

MAKES FOUR 10-INCH PIZZAS

Admittedly there's more than a little similarity to crumbled Italian sausage. Try this on your carnivorous friends.

1/2 red onion, finely diced

2 garlic cloves, minced

2 teaspoons olive oil or 1/4 cup vegetable stock or water

4 ounces marinated tempeh, smoked tempeh, or seitan sausage, crumbled finely

1 teaspoon dried sage

1/2 teaspoon fennel seeds

1/2 teaspoon ground nutmeg

1/4 teaspoon red pepper flakes

1/4 teaspoon ground pepper

1 teaspoon tamari soy sauce

Millennium Pizza Dough (page 92)

3/4 cup Puttanesca Sauce (page 137)

Finely shredded fresh basil leaves for garnish

In a medium sauté pan or skillet, sauté the onion and garlic in the oil over medium heat until the garlic starts to brown. Add the tempeh, sage, fennel, nutmeg, pepper flakes, pepper, and tamari. Stir well to distribute the spices. Sauté for 5 minutes, or until the tempeh mixture is dry.

On a floured board, roll out each ball of dough to a 10-inch round. Spread each crust with 3 tablespoons Puttanesca Sauce. Sprinkle the tempeh mixture over the crusts and bake until the toppings are hot, about 5 to 7 minutes. Garnish with the basil leaves. Slice and serve at once.

NUTRITIONAL INFORMATION PER SERVING TOPPING (SEE PAGE 92 FOR NUTRITIONAL INFORMATION FOR CRUST):

100 Calories (36% from fat), 5 g Protein, 11 g Carbohydrate, 4 g Fat, 0 mg Cholesterol, 275 mg Sodium, 2 g Fiber

(full pizza) 341 Calories (13% from fat), 12 g Protein, 62 g Carbohydrate, 5 g Fat, 0 mg Cholesterol, 591 mg Sodium, 5 g Fiber

HEIRLOOM TOMATO AND CORN PIZZAS WITH CHIPOTLE SPREAD

MAKES FOUR 10-INCH PIZZAS

3/4 cup Chipotle Paste (page 174)

4 tomatoes, thinly sliced

Kernels cut from 1 ear of fresh corn

2 teaspoons extra virgin olive oil (optional)

2 teaspoons minced fresh oregano

Sea salt and freshly ground pepper to taste

Millennium Pizza Dough (page 92)

On a floured surface, roll each ball of dough out to a 10-inch circle. Spread 3 tablespoons Chipotle Spread over each crust. Top with the tomato slices. Sprinkle on the corn and oil then the oregano, salt, and pepper. Bake or grill (see page 92). Slice and serve at once.

NUTRITIONAL INFORMATION PER SERVING TOPPING (SEE PAGE 92 FOR NUTRITIONAL INFORMATION FOR CRUST):

85 Calories (11% from fat), 2 g Protein, 17 g Carbohydrate, 1 g Fat, 0 mg Cholesterol, 225 mg Sodium, 2 g Fiber

(full pizza) 326 Calories (6% from fat), 9 g Protein, 68 g Carbohydrate, 2 g Fat, 0 mg Cholesterol, 541 mg Sodium, 5 g Fiber

OYSTER MUSHROOM, LEEK, AND FENNEL PIZZAS WITH LEMON AND LEMON THYME

MAKES FOUR 10-INCH PIZZAS

6 ounces oyster mushrooms

1/2 teaspoon minced lemon zest

2 tablespoons fresh lemon juice

2 teaspoons extra virgin olive oil

2 teaspoons minced fresh lemon thyme or regular thyme, plus more for garnish

1/2 teaspoon sea salt

Freshly ground pepper to taste

1 leek, white part only, washed and cut into 1/2-inch-thick slices

1 fennel bulb, cut into 1/2-inch-thick crescents

Red pepper flakes to taste

Millennium Pizza Dough (page 92)

3/4 cup Herb-Tofu Aioli (page 173)

1 teaspoon capers, drained

Juice of 1 lemon, for garnish

In a medium bowl, combine the mushrooms, lemon zest and juice, 1 teaspoon of the olive oil, the thyme, salt, and pepper. Let sit for 15 minutes.

In a large sauté pan or skillet, sauté the leek and fennel in the remaining 1 teaspoon olive oil over medium heat until just softened, about 1 minutes. Add the pepper flakes. Remove from heat.

On a floured surface, roll out each ball into a 10-inch circle. Spread each crust with 3 tablespoons of the aioli. Top with the leeks and fennel, then the marinated oyster mushrooms. Sprinkle with the capers. Bake until the mushrooms are soft and slightly browned, about 5 to 7 minutes. Garnish with more thyme and a squeeze of lemon juice. Slice and serve at once.

NUTRITIONAL INFORMATION PER SERVING TOPPING (SEE PAGE 92 FOR NUTRITIONAL INFORMATION FOR CRUST):

67 Calories (3% from fat), 1 g Protein, 9 g Carbohydrate, 3 g Fat, 0 mg Cholesterol, 385 mg Sodium, 3 g Fiber

(full pizza) 308 Calories (12% from fat), 8 g Protein, 60 g Carbohydrate, 4 g Fat, 0 mg Cholesterol, 701 mg Sodium, 6 g Fiber

SUN-DRIED TOMATO TAPENADE PIZZAS WITH WHITE BEAN AND GARLIC HUMUS

MAKES FOUR 10-INCH PIZZAS

The elements of these pizzas can also be served separately as flat breads with the humus and relish on the side.

WHITE BEAN AND GARLIC HUMUS

4 cloves garlic, minced

1 tablespoon olive oil

1½ teaspoons ground cumin

2 teaspoons minced fresh sage, or
    1 teaspoon dried sage

1 cup cooked white beans

1 teaspoon minced lemon zest

¼ cup fresh lemon juice

¼ cup water

1 teaspoon sea salt

¼ teaspoon black pepper

Millenium Pizza Dough (page 92)

Black pepper or cayenne pepper to taste

Sun-Dried Tapanade (page 91) or Tomato and
    Preserved Lemon Relish (page 121)

Fresh oregano and mint leaves and extra virgin
    olive oil, for garnish

1 lemon, cut into wedges

To make the humus: In a small sauté pan or skillet, sauté the garlic in the oil over medium heat until just starting to brown. Add the cumin and sage and sauté for 1 minute. Transfer to a medium bowl. Add the beans, zest and juice, water, salt, and pepper. Either mash by hand or purée in a blender until fairly smooth.

On a floured surface, roll out each ball into a 10-inch circle. Spread each crust with 3 tablespoons humus. Top with 2 tablespoons of tapenade or relish and bake until the toppings are heated through. Sprinkle with the oregano, mint, and olive oil. Slice and serve at once, with a wedge of lemon.

VARIATION:

For an oil-free version, substitute ¼ cup Millennium Braised Garlic (page 230) for the garlic and oil. Delete the sautéing procedure and toast the cumin (see page 234).

NUTRITIONAL INFORMATION PER SERVING TOPPING (SEE PAGE 92 FOR NUTRITIONAL INFORMATION FOR CRUST):

112 Calories (32% from fat), 4 g Protein, 15 g Carbohydrate, 4 g Fat, 0 mg Cholesterol, 587 mg Sodium, 3 g Fiber

(full pizza) 353 Calories (13% from fat), 11 g Protein, 66 g Carbohydrate, 5 g Fat, 0 mg Cholesterol, 903 mg Sodium, 6 g Fiber

SIDES AND COMPLEMENTS

Here are some of the dishes that complement our entrées. Don't pass up some of the bean and grain preparations, which make great entrées on their own.

SAFFRON BASMATI RICE PILAF

MAKES 6 SERVINGS

This pilaf finds many uses at Millennium. It is turned into salads, shaped into patties and sautéed for an appetizer, and served in our version of paella. Brown basmati rice is available at any natural foods store and some supermarkets.

1 yellow onion, finely diced
2 cloves garlic, minced
2 teaspoon olive oil
$1^1/2$ teaspoons ground cumin
1 teaspoon fennel seed
$1/4$ teaspoon ground pepper
1 teaspoon sea salt
2 cups brown basmati rice
$1/2$ teaspoon saffron steeped in $1/4$ cup warm water
$3^1/2$ cups water or light vegetable stock

In a medium, heavy saucepan, sauté the onion and garlic in the oil over medium heat until just softened. Add the cumin, fennel seed, pepper, and salt. Sauté for 1 minute. Add the rice and stir constantly for about 2 minutes, or until the rice smells fragrant. Add the saffron and water, bring to boil, and cover. Reduce the heat to medium-low and simmer for 20 to 25 minutes, or until the liquid is absorbed. Remove from heat and let sit for 10 minutes before serving.

NUTRITIONAL INFORMATION PER SERVING:
247 Calories (11% from fat), 5 g Protein, 50 g Carbohydrate, 3 g Fat, 0 mg Cholesterol, 429 mg Sodium, 3 g Fiber

MILLENNIUM MIXED-GRAIN PILAF

SERVES 6

We usually combine six grains in this hearty pilaf: basmati rice, wehani rice, and wild rice, along with barley, black barley, and wheat or rye berries. All of these grains cook in about the same amount of time, although some are softer or firmer than others, leading to a diversity of texture. Try this pilaf with your own selection of grains.

1 yellow onion, finely diced
1 carrot, peeled and finely diced
2 stalks celery, finely diced
$1/2$ cup vegetable stock or water
1 teaspoon dried sage
1 teaspoon dried thyme
$1/2$ teaspoon dried marjoram or savory (optional)
$1/4$ teaspoon ground pepper
1 teaspoon sea salt
$1/2$ cup brown basmati rice or long-grain brown rice
$1/2$ cup barley
$1/4$ cup wild rice
$1/4$ cup red rice or wehani rice
$1/4$ cup wheat or rye berries
$1/4$ cup black barley, buckwheat grouts, or grain of your choice
2 teaspoons Dijon mustard
2 teaspoons tamari soy sauce
4 cups water or light vegetable stock

In a medium, heavy saucepan, cook the onion, carrot, celery and stock over medium heat until the vegetables are just softened, about 5 minutes. Add the sage, thyme, marjoram, pepper, and salt. Add all the grains and stir constantly for about 2 minutes to toast them. Add the Dijon mustard, tamari, and water. Bring to a boil. Reduce heat to medium-low, cover, and simmer for 30 to 35 minutes, until the liquid is absorbed. Remove from heat and let sit for 10 minutes before serving.

NUTRITIONAL INFORMATION PER SERVING:

230 Calories (8% from fat), 6 g Protein, 47 g Carbohydrate, 2 g Fat, 0 mg Cholesterol, 539 mg Sodium, 6 g Fiber

BUTTERNUT SQUASH AND MIXED-GRAIN PILAF TORTE

SERVES 8

We top dried cranberry and walnut studded mixed grain pilaf with a butternut squash and tahini purée and bake until the purée is firm and then slice individual squares or wedges.

1 butternut or Kabocha squash, peeled, seeded, and cut into cubes

1 yellow onion, cut lengthwise into thin crescents

1/4 cup dry sherry, dry white wine, nonalcoholic red wine, or vegetable stock

1 teaspoon dried sage

1/2 teaspoon ground allspice

1/4 teaspoon ground nutmeg

1 teaspoon sea salt

2 tablespoons toasted sesame tahini

2 tablespoons cornstarch

2 tablespoons light miso (optional)

1/2 cup dried cranberries, soaked in stock or apple juice to plump

1/2 cup walnut, toasted and coarsely chopped (see page 234)

4 cups Millennium Mixed Grain Pilaf (page 104)

In a large pot of salted boiling water, cook the squash until tender, about 20 minutes. Drain well in a colander. In a medium sauté pan or skillet, cook the onion and sherry over medium heat until the onion softens, about 10 minutes. Add the sage, allspice, nutmeg, and salt. Mix well. Transfer the onion mixture to a blender or food processor. Add the cooked squash, tahini, cornstarch, and miso. Purée until smooth.

Drain the cranberries and toss with the walnuts and mixed-grain pilaf. Place in a lightly greased baking dish or 8-cup soufflé dish. Firmly pack in the grain mixture and pour the squash purée over it.

Cover with a lid or aluminum foil. Bake for 30 minutes. Remove the cover or foil and bake another 20 minutes, or until the top is lightly brown. Let cool for at least 15 minutes. Cut into serving portions and remove from the dish with a pie server.

VARIATION:

Use wild rice for half the grain in the pilaf and add chopped skinned toasted hazelnuts and a cubed apple.

NUTRITIONAL INFORMATION PER SERVING:

248 Calories (29% from fat), 6 g Protein, 38 g Carbohydrate, 8 g Fat, 0 mg Cholesterol, 545 mg Sodium, 7 g Fiber

MILLENNIUM BAKED BEANS

SERVES 6

We serve these beans on our macrobiotic plate and in our version of cassoulet, with chanterelle mushrooms and slices of seitan sausage. The master recipe usually includes a mirepoix of chopped carrot, onion, and celery, though in the fall and winter we may add other root vegetables, vegetable stock, Dijon mustard, and a little rice or maple syrup. Try a variety of beans of different sizes and textures, such as chestnut lima beans, cannellini, or calypso beans. Serve this as a main course as well as a side dish.

2 cups beans, cooked (see page 236)

1 yellow onion, cut into $\frac{1}{2}$-inch dice, or 2 leeks,
    white part only, cleaned and cut into $\frac{1}{2}$-inch dice

1 carrot, peeled and finely diced

2 stalks celery, finely diced

2 cups vegetable stock, or more as needed

1 tablespoon Dijon mustard

2 or 3 tablespoons brown rice syrup, or
    1 tablespoon maple syrup

$\frac{1}{2}$ teaspoon ground allspice

$\frac{1}{4}$ teaspoon ground cloves

$\frac{1}{4}$ teaspoon ground nutmeg

2 teaspoons minced fresh sage or
    $\frac{1}{2}$ teaspoon dried sage

2 teaspoons minced fresh thyme, or
    1 teaspoon dried thyme

$1\frac{1}{2}$ teaspoons sea salt, or 2 teaspoons miso

$\frac{1}{2}$ teaspoon ground pepper

2 bay leaves

1 small sprig fresh rosemary (optional)

Preheat the oven to 350°. Add the onion, carrot, and celery to the cooked beans and toss to evenly distribute the vegetables. Place the bean mixture in a small deep casserole or soufflé dish. In a medium bowl, combine the 2 cups stock, mustard, rice syrup, allspice, cloves, nutmeg, sage, thyme, salt, and pepper. Mix well, then pour over the beans. Place the bay leaves and rosemary sprig on top of the bean mixture. Add more stock if needed to just cover the beans. Cover with a lid or aluminum foil and bake for $1\frac{1}{2}$ hours, or until the liquid has reduced to a syrup. Remove the bay leaves and rosemary.

NUTRITIONAL INFORMATION PER SERVING:

129 Calories (7% from fat), 7 g Protein, 23 g Carbohydrate, 1 g Fat, 0 mg Cholesterol, 641 mg Sodium, 5 g Fiber

WINTER BAKED BEANS:

Substitute 2 cups cubed root vegetables for the carrot and celery. Add up to 1 cup sliced mushrooms of your choice.

NUTRITIONAL INFORMATION PER SERVING:

133 Calories (7% from fat), 8 g Protein, 23 g Carbohydrate, 1 g Fat, 0 mg Cholesterol, 640 mg Sodium, 5 g Fiber

SUMMER BAKED BEANS:

Use lima, cranberry, or fava beans. Use fresh oregano and/or marjoram or savory in place of the sage. Add 2 cups fresh corn kernels and 1 cup diced summer squash to the beans after the first hour of cooking. Toss the finished dish with minced fresh oregano, tarragon, or basil, a diced tomato, and a little extra virgin olive oil just before serving.

NUTRITIONAL INFORMATION PER SERVING:

158 Calories (11% from fat), 7 g Protein, 28 g Carbohydrate, 2 g Fat, 0 mg Cholesterol, 620 mg Sodium, 7 g Fiber

CHANTERELLE AND SMOKED ONION CASSOULET:

In place of the finely diced onion use 2 cubed lightly smoked yellow or red onions (see page 233), 1 cup or more of chanterelles, portobellos, shiitakes, or fresh porcini. Add 1 cup seitan sausage, cubed (page 108) or a packaged vegetarian sausage. Top with herbed bread crumbs (page 138) during the final 15 minutes of cooking. Serve as a main course with some sautéed greens and some good French bread.

NUTRITIONAL INFORMATION PER SERVING:

150 Calories (12% from fat), 10 g Protein, 23 g Carbohydrate, 2 g Fat, 0 mg Cholesterol, 720 mg Sodium, 5 g Fiber

SWEET AND SPICY BOSTON-STYLE BAKED BEANS:

Use pinto, calypso, anasazi, or black beans. Replace the onion with 2 smoked onions (see page 233). Add 1 tablespoon Chipotle Paste (page 174) or 1 canned chipotle chile, diced or puréed. Double the amount of Dijon mustard and use 3 or 4 tablespoons maple syrup as the sweetener. Add 1 tablespoon cider or balsamic vinegar, increase the allspice to 1 teaspoon, and add a pinch more cloves.

NUTRITIONAL INFORMATION PER SERVING:

141 Calories (6% from fat), 8 g Protein, 25 g Carbohydrate, 1 g Fat, 0 mg Cholesterol, 675 mg Sodium, 5 g Fiber

ADZUKI BEANS WITH SHIITAKES AND GINGER:

Use adzuki beans and add 1 cup sliced fresh shiitake mushrooms or $1/2$ cup reconstituted dried shiitakes. Add 3 or 4 tablespoons tamari soy sauce in place of the sea salt. Add up to 2 tablespoons minced fresh ginger. Delete the sage, rosemary, and bay.

NUTRITIONAL INFORMATION PER SERVING:

129 Calories (7% from fat), 7 g Protein, 23 g Carbohydrate, 1 g Fat, 0 mg Cholesterol, 725 mg Sodium, 5 g Fiber

MILLENNIUM FAT-FREE MASHED POTATOES

MAKES 6 SERVINGS

Our oil-free mashed potatoes are a real favorite. The addition of braised garlic gives them a creamy texture without the addition of fat.

4 russet potatoes, peeled
$1/4$ cup Millennium Braised Garlic (page 230)
1 teaspoon sea salt
Freshly ground pepper to taste

Bring a large pot of salted water to a boil. Cut the potatoes into 2-inch cubes and add to the boiling water. Cook the potatoes until tender, about 15 minutes. Pour the potatoes into a colander and let drain for 10 minutes to remove excess moisture. In a large bowl with a potato masher or fork, mash the potatoes with the garlic, salt, and pepper until smooth. Serve immediately.

NUTRITIONAL INFORMATION PER SERVING:

104 Calories (1% from fat), 2 g Protein, 24 g Carbohydrate, 0 g Fat, 0.1 mg Cholesterol, 395 mg Sodium, 2 g Fiber

SPICY FENNEL SEITAN SAUSAGE

SERVES 8: YIELDS 4 SAUSAGES

This and the Curry-Apple Seitan Sausage that follows are our versions of meat-free "sausages." These are the kind of thing that you see on the shelves of natural foods stores and (if you are like me) ignore. But if you think of these sausages, not as pretend meat, but as highly flavorful and texturally appealing additions to a dish, you might think differently. Try these in pasta sauces, on pizzas, or as additions to soups and stews, where they infuse their flavors throughout. There are two cooking methods given: boiling and braising. Boiling gives a firmer-textured sausage, while braising yields a softer texture.

2 cups gluten flour

2 to 4 cloves garlic, minced

1 teaspoon whole fennel seeds

1 1/2 teaspoon ground cumin

1 tablespoon mild chile powder or 2 teaspoons paprika

2/3 teaspoon ground nutmeg

1 1/2 teaspoon dried sage

1/4 teaspoon dried red chile flakes, plus more to taste

2 teaspoons sea salt

1/4 cup canola oil

4 tablespoons tamari

1 cup water

4 pieces single-layer cheesecloth, cut into
  6 x 4-inch pieces

4 cups vegetable stock or water

2 cloves garlic (optional)

2 bay leaves (optional)

Combine the flour, garlic, fennel seeds, cumin, chile powder, nutmeg, sage, chile flakes, and salt in a mixing bowl. In a separate bowl, combine the oil, 1 tablespoon tamari, and 1 cup water. Slowly add the oil mixture to the dry ingredients, kneading with your hands. Continue kneading until all the liquid is absorbed and the dough has the consistency of firm bread dough.

Cut the dough into 4 pieces. Roll out each piece so it is 4 inches long. Place one rolled out piece of dough at the bottom in the center of each piece of cheesecloth. Roll the cheesecloth around the dough. Cut off the excess cheesecloth at the ends of each roll, and tie the ends together with kitchen twine so that each sausage roll is sealed in cheesecloth.

To boil the sausage: In a large stock pot, combine the 4 cups vegetable stock, the remaining 3 tablespoons of the tamari, and the 2 cloves garlic and bay leaves. Make sure there is room enough for the sausages to lie in the pot without bending. Bring the liquid up to a boil and add the sausages. Reduce heat to a simmer and simmer, covered, for 1 hour, or until the sausages are firm and plump. Remove the sausages from the liquid and allow them to cool to room temperature before removing the cheesecloth and slicing the sausages. Store refrigerated with the remaining cooking liquid in an airtight container for up to 1 week.

To braise the sausage: Preheat the oven to 400°. Place the dough in an 8-inch baking dish or casserole. Add the 4 cups vegetable stock, the remaining 3 tablespoons of the tamari, and the 2 cloves garlic and bay leaves, if using. Cover the baking dish tightly with a lid or foil. Bake for 1 to 1 1/4 hours, or until most of the liquid has been absorbed and the sausage is firm and porous, with small air pockets. Remove from the oven and allow to cool to room temperature before slicing. Store refrigerated with the remaining cooking liquid in an airtight container for up to 1 week.

VARIATIONS:

For an oil-free version, substitute 3 ounces of silken tofu for the oil. The texture of the oil-free version will be a lot firmer than the standard recipe.

If you make the sausage in the traditional roll shape, try smoking it (see page 233). Lightly brush with oil before smoking to help the sausage retain moisture.

NUTRITIONAL INFORMATION PER SERVING:

(with oil) 208 Calories (35% from fat), 16 g Protein, 18 g Carbohydrate, 8 g Fat, 0 mg Cholesterol, 625 mg Sodium, 1 g Fiber

(without oil) 149 Calories (6% from fat), 16 g Protein, 19 g Carbohydrate, 1 g Fat, 0 mg Cholesterol, 625 mg Sodium, 1 g Fiber

ROOT VEGETABLE PURÉE

MAKES 4 SERVINGS

This recipe works with all root vegetables except potatoes and sweet potatoes. A favorite combination is parsnips and celery root. Serve with one of our seitan or tempeh dishes, or stuff into a baked pumpkin and serve as a side or main dish with one of our bean dishes.

4 cups cubed root vegetables

1 yellow onion, cut lengthwise into thin crescents

1/4 cup dry sherry, dry white wine, nonalcoholic white wine, or vegetable stock

1 teaspoon dried sage or tarragon

1/4 teaspoon ground nutmeg

1 teaspoon sea salt

3 tablespoons tahini or toasted almond butter

1 to 2 teaspoons light miso (optional)

Ground pepper to taste

In a large pot of salted boiling water, cook the root vegetables until they are tender, about 10 to 15 minutes. Drain well. In a medium sauté pan or skillet, sauté the onion and sherry over medium heat until the onion is soft. Add to the root vegetables. Add the remaining ingredients. Purée in a food processor, in batches if necessary, or mash with a potato masher or fork, until fairly smooth. Serve immediately, or reheat in a baking dish in the oven.

NUTRITIONAL INFORMATION PER SERVING:

183 Calories (34% from fat), 4 g Protein, 26 g Carbohydrate, 7 g Fat, 0 mg Cholesterol, 550 mg Sodium, 8 g Fiber

CURRY-APPLE
SEITAN SAUSAGE

SERVES 8; YIELDS 4 SAUSAGES

2 cups gluten flour

2 to 4 cloves garlic, minced

1 teaspoon whole fennel seeds

1^1/$_2$ teaspoon ground cumin

4 teaspoons mild curry powder

^{2}/$_3$ teaspoon ground nutmeg

1 teaspoon ground coriander

^{1}/$_4$ teaspoon cardamom

^{1}/$_4$ teaspoon dried red chile flakes

2 teaspoons sea salt

^{1}/$_4$ cup canola oil

4 tablespoons tamari

1 cup water

^{1}/$_2$ apple, peeled and grated or finely diced

4 pieces single-layer cheesecloth, cut into
    6 x 4-inch pieces

4 cups vegetable stock or water

2 cloves garlic (optional)

2 bay leaves (optional)

Combine the flour, garlic, fennel seeds, cumin, curry powder, nutmeg, coriander, cardamom, chile flakes, and salt in a mixing bowl. In a separate bowl, combine the oil, 1 tablespoon tamari, 1 cup water, and the apple. Slowly add the oil mixture to the dry ingredients, kneading with your hands. Continue kneading until all the liquid is absorbed and the dough has the consistency of firm bread dough.

Cut the dough into 4 pieces. Roll out each piece so it is 4 inches long. Place one rolled out piece of dough at the bottom in the center of each piece of cheesecloth. Roll the cheesecloth around the dough. Cut off the excess cheesecloth at the ends of each roll, and tie the ends together with kitchen twine to seal each sausage roll in cheesecloth.

To boil the sausage: In a large stock pot, combine the 4 cups vegetable stock, 3 tablespoons of the tamari, and the 2 cloves garlic and bay leaves, if using. Make sure there is room enough for the sausages to lie in the pot without bending. Bring the liquid up to a boil and add the sausages. Reduce heat to a simmer and simmer, covered, for 1 hour, or until the sausages are firm and plump. Remove the sausages from the liquid and allow them to cool to room temperature before removing the cheesecloth and slicing the sausages. Store refrigerated with the remaining cooking liquid in an airtight container for up to 1 week.

To braise the sausage: Preheat the oven to 400°. Place the dough in an 8-inch baking dish or casserole. Add the 4 cups vegetable stock, 3 tablespoons of the tamari, and the 2 cloves garlic and bay leaves, if using. Cover the baking dish tightly with a lid or foil. Bake for 1 to 1^1/$_4$ hours, or until most of the liquid has been absorbed and the sausage is firm and porous, with small air pockets. Remove from the oven and allow to cool to room temperature before slicing. Store refrigerated with the remaining cooking liquid in an airtight container for up to 1 week.

VARIATIONS:

For an oil-free version, substitute 3 ounces of silken tofu for the oil. The texture of the oil-free version will be firmer than the standard recipe.

If you make the sausage in the traditional roll shape, try smoking it (see page 233). Lightly brush with oil before smoking to help the sausage retain moisture.

Try making a sausage seasoned with 1 tablespoon of Thai curry paste and coarsely ground peanuts or pistachios: Add this to an Asian stir-fry.

NUTRITIONAL INFORMATION PER SERVING:

(with oil) 212 Calories (34% from fat), 16 g Protein, 19 g Carbohydrate, 8 g Fat, 0 mg Cholesterol, 627 mg Sodium, 1 g Fiber

(without oil) 149 Calories (6% from fat), 16 g Protein, 19 g Carbohydrate, 1 g Fat, 0 mg Cholesterol, 627 mg Sodium, 1 g Fiber

ENTRÉES

This chapter has a cross section of the entrées that are popular at Millennium, ranging from the very simple to the very complex. Some can be whipped up after work with little advance planning, while others entail a number of steps and subrecipes in order to present them in the true Millennium fashion. These will take longer, so be prepared to roll up your sleeves and spend some quality time in the kitchen. Also feel free not to do the dish in its entirety. Make a simple stir-fry with the Pumpkin Curry Sauce from the recipe for Pumpkins Stuffed with Sautéed Vegetables, for example.

We fuse a number of different elements from many different ethnic cuisines into our entrées. You'll find our versions of Thai curry, Indian tandoori marinade, Mexican chile sauce, as well as our take on German sauerbraten with spätzle and cabbage. Some of the dishes are seasonally oriented, and meant to utilize fresh foods in season; others can be prepared all year round.

MOROCCAN FILO CRESCENTS WITH CURRIED GOLDEN TOMATO SAUCE

MAKES 6 SERVINGS

The inspiration for this dish is Moroccan basilla. *We fill flaky filo dough with an aromatic vegetable sauté seasoned with cumin, rosemary, and mint. As with a traditional* basilla, *we sprinkle a mixture of ground almonds, cinnamon, and a little sugar between the layers. This is our summer version.*

FILLING

1 yellow onion, cut into 1/2-inch dice

4 cloves garlic, minced

2 red bell peppers, seeded, deribbed, and cut into 1/2-inch pieces

1 tablespoon olive oil (optional)

2 Japanese eggplants, halved lengthwise and cut into 1/2-inch-thick pieces

6 button, cremini, stemmed shiitake, or oyster mushrooms, thinly sliced

1 teaspoon ground cumin

2 teaspoons mild curry powder

2 teaspoons minced fresh rosemary

1 teaspoon minced fresh ginger

1/4 teaspoon cayenne pepper

1 cup tomato purée or mild tomato sauce

2 tablespoons tamari soy sauce

6 ounces firm tofu, sliced into 1/2-inch cubes

2 cups packed fresh spinach leaves, blanched until wilted, and drained

2 tablespoons fresh mint leaves, minced

Sea salt to taste

1/2 cup slivered almonds, toasted (see page 234)

2 tablespoons Sucanat

1 tablespoon ground cinnamon

1 package filo dough, thawed

1/4 cup canola or light vegetable oil

2 cups cooked Saffron Basmati Rice Pilaf (page 104) or Israeli couscous

Curried Golden Tomato Sauce (recipe follows)

1/4 cup Red Beet Reduction (page 174)

Fresh mint sprigs for garnish

To make the filling: In a large sauté pan or skillet, sauté the onion, garlic, and peppers in the oil over medium heat until the onion is soft, about 10 minutes. Add the eggplants and mushrooms, then the cumin, curry powder, rosemary, ginger, and cayenne. Stir well and sauté for 2 minutes. Stir in the tomato purée and tamari and simmer for 10 minutes, or until most of the liquid has evaporated. Remove from heat and stir in the tofu, spinach, and mint. Add salt. Let cool to room temperature.

Meanwhile, in a blender or food processor, grind the almonds, Sucanat, and cinnamon to a fine meal.

Preheat the oven to 400°. Line a baking sheet with parchment paper. Place 2 sheets of filo on a work surface. Keep the remaining filo covered with a damp cloth. Brush the filo with oil and sprinkle with a light dusting of the ground almond mixture. Repeat the process twice until 6 sheets of filo have been used. Cut filo stack in half to make 2 rough square stacks.

Place 1/3 cup pilaf 1 inch from nearest end of the filo strips. Top with 1 cup filling. Fold the farthest of the filo over the filling so the edges meet. Starting from the open side edges of the filo, fold the bottom edge over the top as tight as possible, work down the edges until the filo is completely sealed. The filo will take on a crescent shape. Place the filo on the prepared pan. Repeat with the second filo square, then repeat the entire stacking and filling process twice more, so that you have 6 crescents.

(recipe continues on page 116)

(continued from page 114)

Brush the tops of the crescents with the remaining oil and top with the remaining almond mixture. Bake in the center of the oven for 15 to 20 minutes, until the crescents are golden brown.

To serve, cover the center of each serving plate with $1/3$ cup of the curried golden tomato sauce. Place 1 filo crescent over the sauce and garnish with the beet reduction and mint sprigs.

VARIATION:

For a lower-fat version, substitute $1/4$ cup vegetable stock, dry white wine, or nonalcoholic white wine for the olive oil in both the filling and the tomato sauce.

For a fall presentation, serve the crescents over Pomegranate Sauce (page 146) with a drizzle of Saffron-Garlic Cream Sauce (page 91).

NUTRITIONAL INFORMATION PER SERVING:

545 Calories (21% from fat), 17 g Protein, 90 g Carbohydrate, 13 g Fat, 0 mg Cholesterol, 846 mg Sodium, 8 g Fiber

Curried Golden Tomato Sauce

MAKES 2$1/2$ CUPS

1 yellow onion, cut lengthwise into thin crescents
1 tablespoon olive oil (optional)
3 tablespoons dry sherry or nonalcoholic wine
1 tablespoon curry powder
1 teaspoon ground cumin
$1/4$ teaspoon ground cardamom
$1/4$ teaspoon cayenne pepper
6 ripe yellow tomatoes, cut into quarters
2 cups vegetable stock
1 teaspoon sea salt

In a heavy, medium saucepan, sauté the onions in the oil over medium heat until soft, about 10 minutes. Stir in the sherry, reduce heat, and simmer until almost evaporated. Stir in the curry powder, cumin, cardamom, and pepper. Add the tomatoes and stock. Cover and simmer for 20 minutes, or until the tomatoes are very tender. Transfer a blender and purée until smooth. Add the salt.

NUTRITIONAL INFORMATION PER $1/3$ CUP:

(with oil) 58 Calories (31% from fat), 1 g Protein, 8 g Carbohydrate, 2 g Fat, 0 mg Cholesterol, 328 mg Sodium, 1 g Fiber

(without oil) 36 Calories (0% from fat), 1 g Protein, 8 g Carbohydrate, 0 g Fat, 0 mg Cholesterol, 328 mg Sodium, 1 g Fiber

WILD MUSHROOM, WILD RICE, AND ROOT VEGETABLE ROULADES

MAKES 6 SERVINGS

This is a great fall or winter dish, and it can be made as elegant or as casual as you like. You can make both the filling and the Dijon Mustard–Lentil Sauce the day before, though the sauce actually comes together in under half an hour.

2 leeks, washed and cut into $1/2$-inch dice

4 cloves garlic, minced

$1/4$ cup dry sherry or vegetable stock

1 pound assorted cremini, shiitake, and chanterelle mushrooms, sliced thin

2 parsnips, cut into $1/2$-inch dice

1 turnip, cut into $1/2$-inch dice

1 small butternut squash, cut into $1/2$-inch dice

1 celery root bulb, peeled and cut into $1/2$-inch dice

1 teaspoon dried thyme

1 teaspoon dried marjoram (optional)

$1/2$ teaspoon ground nutmeg

1 teaspoon dried sage

2 teaspoons sea salt

1 cup vegetable stock

$1^{1}/2$ cups cooked wild rice

1 cup cubed seitan, tofu, or tempeh (optional)

$1/4$ cup dried cranberries (optional)

1 package filo dough, thawed

Canola oil for brushing filo

Dijon Mustard–Lentil Sauce (page 180)

Cooked French lentils, minced chives, or fresh tarragon for garnish

To make the filling: In a large saucepan, cook the leeks, garlic, and sherry over medium heat until the vegetables are softened, about 10 minutes. Add the mushrooms, parsnips, turnip, squash, celery root, thyme, marjoram, nutmeg, sage, salt, stock, and wild rice, as well as the seitan and cranberries, if desired. Cover and simmer until the root vegetables are just tender, about 15 minutes. Remove from heat, stir in the wild rice, and let cool.

To assemble: Preheat the oven to 350°. Remove 2 filo sheets, place them flat on a work surface. Place a damp towel over the remaining filo to keep it moist. Brush the 2 sheets with oil, the cover with 2 more sheets and brush with oil again. Repeat the process until 8 sheets have been used. Spread the filling on the bottom third of the filo stack in a bed about 2 inches deep and 2 inches thick. Starting at the bottom, roll the stack into a tight cylinder. Cut it into four portions, transfer them to a baking sheet, and bake for 20 minutes, or until crust is golden.

Place about $1/3$ cup of Dijon Mustard-Lentil Sauce in the center of a dinner plate. Slice a filo roulade in half diagonally so each piece of filo looks like a triangle. Place two filo triangles standing up in the center of the plate. Sprinkle with lentils, chives, or tarragon.

NUTRITIONAL INFORMATION PER SERVING:

433 Calories (10% from fat), 15 g Protein, 82 g Carbohydrate, 5 g Fat, 0 mg Cholesterol, 689 mg Sodium, 10 g Fiber

BAKED MADRAS-GLAZED TOFU WITH SAFFRON BASMATI PILAF, SAUTÉED VEGETABLES, AND PEACH-LIME CHUTNEY

MAKES 6 SERVINGS

After eating at a local Indian restaurant and being inspired by their tandoori dishes, we wondered if we could come up with something similar. I came up with a marinade that uses a bit of tofu, lime, paprika, and cardamom. Instead of chicken, we use tofu. Once you taste this, you'll be addicted to it. You can use it on grilled vegetables, sautéed vegetables, and as a base for a dressing for a grain salad.

CURRIED ONIONS

1 yellow onion, cut lengthwise into thin crescents

2 tablespoons canola oil or ¹/4 cup of vegetable stock or water

2 tablespoons mild curry powder

¹/4 teaspoon saffron threads

¹/4 cup fresh lemon juice

1 teaspoon sea salt

24 ounces extra-firm tofu

2 cups Tandoori Marinade (page 16)

1 teaspoon canola oil, or ¹/4 cup water or vegetable stock

4 cups chopped vegetables, cut into bite-size pieces, such as asparagus, carrots, bell peppers, zucchini, blanched broccoli and cauliflower florets, or blanched winter squash and root vegetables.

3 cups Saffron Basmati Rice Pilaf (page 104) or Millet-Almond Pilaf (page 121)

Peach-Lime Chutney (recipe follows)

Lime slices and fresh cilantro leaves, for garnish

To make the curried onions: Sauté the onions in a skillet over medium heat with the oil until softened, about 5 minutes. Add the curry powder and saffron threads, and continue to sauté another 2 minutes. Add the lemon juice and salt, remove from the heat, and reserve.

To prepare the tofu: Cut the tofu horizontally into 6 cutlets, each ¹/₂-inch thick. Pour half the marinade into a shallow glass or ceramic dish. Add the tofu to the marinade, making sure to coat the tofu thoroughly. Let set for at least 30 minutes at room temperature, or refrigerate for up to 4 hours if making ahead. Light a fire in a charcoal grill or preheat a gas grill. Brush the cooking rack of the grill with a bit of oil and grill the tofu for 2 to 3 minutes per side. To broil, place the tofu on a lightly oiled baking pan and broil for 5 to 7 minutes.

In a large sauté pan or skillet over high heat, heat the canola oil and sauté the vegetables and curried onions for 5 minutes, or until heated through and crisp-tender.

To serve: mound a ¹/₂ cup portion of pilaf in the center of each plate. Cut tofu into diagonal slices and place on top of the rice. Ring the rice with vegetables. Top the tofu with some marinade and 2 teaspoons chutney. Garnish with lime slices and cilantro leaves.

NUTRITIONAL INFORMATION PER SERVING:

(with oil) 376 Calories (38% from fat), 16 g Protein, 42 g Carbohydrate, 16 g Fat, 0 mg Cholesterol, 755 mg Sodium, 6 g Fiber

(without oil) 286 Calories (19% from fat), 16 g Protein, 42 g Carbohydrate, 6 g Fat, 0 mg Cholesterol, 755 mg Sodium, 6 g Fiber

Peach-Lime Chutney

MAKES 1 ¹/₂ CUPS

1 cup water

¹/₄ teaspoon sea salt

1 lime, with peel, cut into fine dice

1 tablespoons unrefined sugar, fructose, or Sucanat

¹/₄ cup rice vinegar or champagne vinegar

¹/₂ serrano chile, minced, or
   ¹/₄ teaspoon red pepper flakes

1 teaspoon coriander seeds, toasted (see page 234)

2 teaspoons minced fresh ginger

1 red bell pepper, seeded, deribbed, and finely diced

2 firm fresh peaches, or 4 apricots, peeled, pitted, and cut into ¹/₂-inch dice

¹/₄ teaspoon sea salt

In a medium saucepan, bring the water and salt to a boil. Add the lime, reduce heat, and simmer for 10 minutes. Drain the lime and set aside. In a large sauté pan or skillet, cook the sugar and vinegar over high heat until the sugar melts and the mixture becomes syrupy. Add the chile, coriander, and ginger, then the red pepper, lime, and peaches. Stir well and sauté for 5 minutes. Transfer to a bowl and cool.

VARIATIONS:

Substitute 1 cup dried peaches, apricots, or figs for the peach. Reconstitute by simmering in water or apple juice to cover until the fruit is soft. Drain, reserving about ¹/₂ cup liquid. Add to the chutney, with the reserved liquid, along with red pepper and lime. Simmer the chutney until all the liquid has evaporated.

NUTRITIONAL INFORMATION PER
2 TEASPOON SERVING:

8 Calories (0% from fat), 0.1 g Protein, 2 g Carbohydrate, 0 g Fat, 0 mg Cholesterol, 45 mg Sodium, 0.2 g Fiber

LENTIL STEW WITH MILLET-ALMOND PILAF AND MILLET CREPES

MAKES 6 SERVINGS

This dish was inspired by Dorinda Hafner's
A Taste of Africa *(Ten Speed Press) cookbook.*
Make a large batch of the Berber mix and let the
complex perfume of this seasoning envelop your
kitchen. Although the crepes are not authenti-
cally African, millet and corn flour are used in
the cuisine of certain regions of Africa.

LENTIL STEW

1 cup dried green or brown lentils

2 large yellow onions, cut into $1/2$-inch dice

4 teaspoons canola oil, or $1/4$ cup stock

1 tablespoon minced fresh ginger

1 tablespoon minced garlic

1 serrano chile, minced

2 tablespoons Berber Spice Mix (recipe follows)

2 red bell peppers, cut into $1/2$-inch dice

24 ounces canned tomatoes with juice

2 Japanese eggplants, cut into $1/2$-inch rounds

2 ripe plantains cut into $1/2$-inch dice

1 cup vegetable stock

1 teaspoon sea salt

Millet Crepes (recipe follows)

Millet-Almond Pilaf (recipe follows)

Tomato-Preserved Lemon Relish (recipe follows),
   optional

Cilantro leaves, for garnish

Bring 4 cups of water to a boil. Add lentils and simmer, covered, for 20 minutes, or until cooked al dente. Drain, and reserve.

In a large, heavy saucepan, sauté the onions in the oil until slightly softened, about 5 minutes. Add the ginger, garlic, chile, and Berber mix to the onions and sauté for 3 minutes, or until the mix-

ture smells fragrant. Add the peppers, tomatoes with juice, and eggplants. Reduce heat and simmer until the peppers just start to soften, about 5 to 7 minutes, then add the plantains, lentils, stock, and salt. Simmer, uncovered, for 20 to 30 minutes, or until the peppers and eggplant are very soft, adding more stock if necessary to keep the mixture from drying out. Taste and adjust the seasoning.

Place a crepe on the bottom of each serving plate. Mound 1 cup pilaf in the center of the crepe. Hollow out the center of the pilaf. Place 1 cup stew in the hollow. Top with tomato relish and garnish with cilantro. Serve extra crepes alongside.

NUTRITIONAL INFORMATION PER SERVING:

(with oil) 747 Calories (18% from fat), 26 g Protein, 127 g Carbohydrate, 15 g Fat, 0 mg Cholesterol, 1279 mg Sodium, 15 g Fiber

(without oil) 693 Calories (12% from fat), 26 g Protein, 127 g Carbohydrate, 9 g Fat, 0 mg Cholesterol, 1279 mg Sodium, 15 g Fiber

Berber Spice Mix

MAKES 2/3 CUP

1 teabag or 2 teaspoons mint tea

$1^{1}/2$ tablespoons cumin seeds

$1^{1}/2$ tablespoons coriander seeds

1 teaspoon cardamom seeds

$1^{1}/2$ teaspoon fenugreek seeds

1 teaspoon ground nutmeg

1 teaspoon ground cinnamon

1 teaspoon whole cloves

1 teaspoon allspice

$1^{1}/2$ tablespoon chile powder

1 teaspoon ground pepper

Remove the tea from the tea bag and combine with all remaining ingredients in a spice grinder or coffee mill. Grind until very fine. In a dry skillet, toast the mixture over medium heat, stirring constantly, about 5 minutes, or until the mixture slightly darkens in color.

Millet-Almond Pilaf

MAKES 6 CUPS

It is really worth spending the extra 5 minutes to toast the millet with the spices; this toughens the outer hull to help prevent overcooking.

1 cup finely diced yellow onion
1 clove garlic, minced
1 tablespoon canola oil, or ¼ cup vegetable stock
1 teaspoon ground cumin
½ teaspoon ground cinnamon
¼ teaspoon ground cardamom
¼ teaspoon ground turmeric
⅓ cup slivered almonds
1½ cups millet
3½ cups water
1 teaspoon sea salt

In a large sauté pan or skillet, sauté the onions and garlic in the oil until the onions are softened, about 8 minutes. Add the cumin, cinnamon, cardamom, turmeric, and almonds and sauté for 2 minutes, stirring constantly. Add the millet and stir constantly for 2 minutes to toast the millet. Add the water and salt. Bring to a boil, reduce heat, cover, and simmer for 20 minutes.

NUTRITIONAL INFORMATION PER 1 CUP SERVING:

(with oil) 384 Calories (28% from fat), 10 g Protein, 59 g Carbohydrate, 8 g Fat, 0 mg Cholesterol, 575 mg Sodium, 4 g Fiber

(without oil) 348 Calories (21% from fat), 10 g Protein, 59 g Carbohydrate, 8 g Fat, 0 mg Cholesterol, 575 mg Sodium, 4 g Fiber

Millet Crepes

MAKES 12 CREPES

1 cup millet
1 tablespoon egg replacement powder
3 cups water
2 cups corn flour
¼ teaspoon sea salt
2 tablespoons minced fresh cilantro

In a blender or spice grinder, grind the millet to a fine flour. In a large bowl, combine the egg replacement and water. Gradually whisk in the salt, cilantro, millet, and cornflour ½ cup at a time to make a smooth batter. Heat a 9-inch nonstick crepe pan over medium heat. Brush or spray with a thin layer of oil. Pour ⅓ cup batter into the pan. Cook for 2 to 3 minutes, until the bottom is brown. Flip crepe and cook for another minute. Transfer to a flat plate. Repeat to cook the remaining batter. Keep crepes warm in a 200° oven.

NUTRITIONAL INFORMATION PER SERVING:

121 Calories (7% from fat), 4 g Protein, 24 g Carbohydrate, 1 g Fat, 0 mg Cholesterol, 92 mg Sodium, 3 g Fiber

Tomato-Preserved Lemon Relish

MAKES 1½ CUPS

2 firm red tomatoes, sliced in small cubes
¼ to ⅓ cup preserved lemon, cut into small cubes (page 180)
1 teaspoon cumin seeds, toasted
2 tablespoon parsley or cilantro, minced

Toss all ingredients together. Store refrigerated for up to 2 days.

NUTRITIONAL INFORMATION PER SERVING:

5 Calories (0% from fat), 0.2 g Protein, 1 g Carbohydrate, 0 g Fat, 0 mg Cholesterol, 15 mg Sodium, 0 g Fiber

ROASTED CORN AND HEDGEHOG MUSHROOM TAMALES WITH MUSHROOM-CHILE CREAM SAUCE

SERVES 6

This dish is from one of our wild-mushroom tasting menus. Hedgehog mushrooms are available in specialty foods stores during the winter months, but any mushroom or any mix of varieties will work, from button mushrooms to morels.

ROASTED CORN AND MUSHROOM FILLING

Kernels cut from 3 ears fresh corn

1 red onion, finely diced

2 cloves garlic, minced

2 teaspoons light olive oil, vegetable stock, dry sherry, dry white wine, or nonalcoholic red or white wine

1/2 pound mushrooms, sliced 1/2-inch thick

1/2 teaspoon dried oregano

1 teaspoon ground cumin

1/2 teaspoon sea salt plus more to taste

1/4 teaspoon cayenne pepper

1/4 cup dry sherry, dry white wine, or nonalcoholic white wine

1 cup cooked pinto or black beans (see page 236)

2 tablespoons minced fresh cilantro

TAMALE BATTER

3 cups masa harina

1/2 teaspoon sea salt

Ground black pepper to taste

1/2 teaspoon dried oregano

1/2 teaspoon baking powder

2 cups water or soy milk

1 teaspoon light vinegar

2 teaspoons light olive oil (optional)

6 dried corn husks or 4 x 5-inch parchment paper rectangles

Canola oil for brushing

Mushroom-Chile Cream Sauce (recipe follows)

Tomato Relish for garnish (page 177) optional

Roasted Tomatillo Sauce for garnish (page 176) optional

To make the filling: Preheat the oven to 450°. Put the corn kernels in an 8-inch baking pan and bake, turning once or twice, until they start to brown, 8 to 10 minutes. Set aside.

In a large sauté pan or skillet, sauté the onions and garlic in the oil over medium heat until the onions are translucent, about 3 minutes. Add the mushrooms, oregano, cumin, salt, and cayenne and sauté until the mushrooms soften, 5 to 8 minutes. Stir in the sherry. Remove from heat and mix in the beans, cilantro, and roasted corn. Let cool to room temperature.

To make the tamale batter: In a large bowl, combine the masa harina, salt, pepper, oregano, and baking powder together. In a liquid measuring cup, combine the water, vinegar, and oil. Stir the liquid into the masa mixture, using a spoon or your hands. The resulting batter should be thick enough to roll into a ball, yet soft enough to spread.

Place the tamale wrapper flat and lightly brush or spray with oil. Spread a 1/4-inch-thick layer masa batter over the tamale wrapper. Place 1/2 cup filling in the center of the wrapper. If using corn husks, tie the ends with string or strips of corn husk, making sure both sides of the masa are sealed with each other. If using parchment paper, either leave the ends open or crimp them together.

Place the tamales in a steamer and steam for 20 minutes. Let sit for 10 to 15 minutes before serving.

To serve: Remove the tamales from their wrappers and serve each on a plate over $^1/_3$ cup of the Mushroom Chile Cream Sauce. Serve with Tomato Relish or Roasted Tomatillo Salsa if desired.

NUTRITIONAL INFORMATION PER SERVING:

(with oil) 383 Calories (16% from fat), 11 g Protein, 69 g Carbohydrate, 7 g Fat, 0 mg Cholesterol, 787 mg Sodium, 11 g Fiber

(without oil) 356 Calories (10% from fat), 11 g Protein, 69 g Carbohydrate, 4 g Fat, 0 mg Cholesterol, 787 mg Sodium, 11 g Fiber

Mushroom-Chile Cream Sauce

MAKES 3 CUPS

4 cups Mushroom Stock (page 228)

1 ounce dried porcini

1 ancho chile

1 dried or canned chipotle chile, or 2 teaspoons Chipotle Paste (page 174)

1 cup water

1 red or yellow onion, cut into $^1/_2$-inch dice

3 cloves garlic, minced

2 teaspoons light olive oil or canola oil, vegetable stock, dry sherry, dry red wine, or nonalcoholic red wine

$^1/_3$ pound button, cremini, or portobello mushrooms, thinly sliced

$^1/_2$ teaspoon dried thyme

1 teaspoons ground cumin

$^1/_4$ teaspoon ground nutmeg

1 teaspoon sea salt

$^1/_4$ cup dry sherry (optional)

1 teaspoon tamari soy sauce

1 cup Cashew Cream (page 85)

In a small saucepan, bring the mushroom stock to a boil and add the porcini. Reduce heat to a simmer and cook to reduce by one half. Strain through cheesecloth to remove the porcini and any grit. Reserve the stock and mince the porcini. In a dry skillet, toast the chile over high heat until they darken. Remove from heat, let cool, and remove the seeds. In a small saucepan, bring the water to a boil and cook the chiles until soft, about 15 minutes. In a blender, purée the chiles and water until smooth.

In a medium saucepan, sauté the onions and garlic with the oil over medium heat for 5 minutes. Add the mushrooms and continue to sauté until they soften and release their liquid. Add the thyme, cumin, nutmeg, and salt, followed by the chile puree and the reserved stock. Remove from the heat and stir in the Cashew Cream. Add the sherry, if desired, and the tamari, and adjust the salt to taste.

NUTRITIONAL INFORMATION PER $^1/_3$ CUP SERVING:

29 Calories (31% from fat), 1 g Protein, 4 g Carbohydrate, 1 g Fat, 0 mg Cholesterol, 312 mg Sodium, 1 g Fiber

GRILLED SEITAN, BEAN, AND CHILE TAMALES WITH MANCHAMANTELES SAUCE

MAKES 6 SERVINGS

Another tamale from another special dinner. This dish comes from our chile-tasting dinner. It pairs a savory, smoked tamale filling with a sweet and spicy sauce. Manchamanteles, which means "tablecloth stainer," is a traditional purée of fruit, chiles, and nuts. Our version is loosely based on a recipe from Mark Millers Coyote Cafe Cookbook *(Ten Speed Press).*

SEITAN, BEAN, AND CHILE FILLING

1 yellow onion, cut into 1/2-inch dice

4 cloves garlic, minced

2 large bell peppers, seeded, deribbed, and cut into 1/2-inch dice

1 Anaheim, pasilla, or Hungarian chile, finely diced (optional)

1 tablespoon olive oil, or 1/4 cup dry sherry or nonalcoholic red wine, or vegetable stock

1 teaspoon ground cumin

2 teaspoons minced fresh oregano

1 serrano chile, minced (optional)

Kernels cut from 2 ears fresh corn

2 cups cooked pinto or anasazi beans (see page 236)

1/4 cup diced green olives, or 1 tablespoon capers, drained

8 ounces grilled seitan, cubed

1/4 cup Manchamanteles Sauce (recipe follows), Moroccan Marinade (page 13), or barbecue sauce

2 tablespoons minced fresh cilantro leaves

Sea salt to taste

TAMALE BATTER

3 cups masa harina

1/2 teaspoon sea salt

Ground black pepper to taste

1/2 teaspoon dried oregano

1/2 teaspoon baking powder

2 cups water or soy milk

1 teaspoon light vinegar

2 teaspoons light olive oil (optional)

6 dried corn husks or 4 x 5-inch parchment paper rectangles

Canola oil for brushing

Roasted Tomatillo Sauce for garnish (page 176) optional

To make the filling: In a large, heavy saucepan, sauté the onion, garlic, peppers and chile in the oil over high heat until the vegetables soften. Reduce heat to medium-low and add the cumin, oregano, and serrano chile. Stir in the corn, beans, olives, and seitan. Add the sauce and remove from heat. Stir in the cilantro and salt. Let cool to room temperature.

To make the tamale batter: In a large bowl, combine the masa harina, salt, pepper, oregano, and baking powder together. In a liquid measuring cup, combine the water, vinegar, and oil. Stir the liquid into the masa mixture, using a spoon or your hands. The resulting batter should be thick enough to roll into a ball, yet soft enough to spread.

On a steamer tray large enough to hold all the tamales, place a lightly oiled tamale wrapper. Spread tamale batter over the wrapper approximately 1/4 inch thick. Place 1/2 cup of the filling in the center of the wrapper. Fold the wrapper over the filling, making sure both sides of the masa are sealed with each other. If you are using bakers parchment, either leave the ends open, or crimp the ends together. If you are using triangular masa wrappers fold the top third of the triangle over the filling before folding over the sides. If you are using corn husks, fold over and tie the ends together with bakers twine or pieces of softened corn husk. Place the tamales in a steamer and steam for 20 minutes. Allow the tamales to sit for 10 to 15 minutes before serving: this allows the masa to firm up, which makes it easier to remove the wrappers.

Remove the tamales from the wrappers and serve each over 1/3 cup of warm Manchamanteles Sauce. Serve with Roasted Tomatillo Salsa, if desired.

NUTRITIONAL INFORMATION PER SERVING:

(with oil) 379 Calories (17% from fat), 23 g Protein, 56 g Carbohydrate, 7 g Fat, 0 mg Cholesterol, 780 mg Sodium, 13 g Fiber

(without oil) 343 Calories (8% from fat), 23 g Protein, 56 g Carbohydrate, 3 g Fat, 0 mg Cholesterol, 780 mg Sodium, 13 g Fiber

Manchamanteles Sauce

MAKES 3 CUPS

1 dried ancho chile
1 dried guajillo chile
2 cloves garlic
1/2 yellow onion, cut lengthwise into thin crescents
1/4 cup vegetable stock or water
1/2 teaspoon dried oregano
1 teaspoon ground cinnamon
1/4 teaspoon ground allspice
1/4 teaspoon ground cloves
1 teaspoon ground coriander
1/2 serrano chile, seeded and minced
1 cup tomato purée or tomato sauce
2 cups vegetable stock or water
1/2 ripe banana, cut into 1/2-inch dice
1/2 cup 1/2-inch diced pineapple
1/2 ripe mango, cubed

1 tablespoon sesame seeds, toasted (see page 234) optional
1 tablespoon cashews or hazelnuts, toasted (see page 234) optional
Sea salt to taste
Extra vegetable stock, as needed, or water

Preheat a broiler. Put the ancho and guajillo chiles under the broiler and roast, turning the chiles every 10 seconds until the skin darkens slightly and the chiles puff up. Remove from the broiler and cool before handling. When cool, remove the stems and seeds.

Place the garlic cloves in a pan under the broiler. Broil until the upper half of the cloves blacken. Remove from the broiler and reserve.

In a saucepan over medium heat, braise the onion in the stock until soft and lightly caramelized, about 10 minutes. Add the roasted chiles and garlic and all the remaining ingredients except the salt. Bring to a boil and reduce heat to a simmer. Simmer, covered, for 30 minutes. Remove sauce from the heat and purée in batches until smooth, adding extra stock if sauce is too thick. Add salt to taste, and use or refrigerate in an airtight container for up to 1 week.

NUTRITIONAL INFORMATION PER 1/3 CUP SERVING:

57 Calories (16% from fat), 1 g Protein, 11 g Carbohydrate, 1 g Fat, 0 mg Cholesterol, 354 mg Sodium, 3 g Fiber

TAMALE TORTE WITH BLACK BEAN CHILE AND RED CHILE SAUCE

MAKES 8 SERVINGS

Instead of being made into individual tamales, corn masa and black bean chili are layered in a casserole and baked together. The sauce is quite easy and a good beginning recipe for people who have not cooked with whole dried chiles.

BLACK BEAN CHILI

2 red onions, cut into 1/2-inch dice

4 cloves garlic, minced

1/2 cup vegetable stock

1 tablespoon ground cumin

1 tablespoon mild chile powder

1 teaspoon dried oregano

2 bay leaves

4 cups cooked black beans

1 cup tomato purée or mild tomato sauce

1 tablespoon molasses (optional)

1 cup vegetable stock

1 teaspoon sea salt

RED CHILE SAUCE

2 ancho chiles

2 guajillo or ancho chiles

8 cloves garlic

24 ounces canned puréed tomatoes

2 cups water

2 tablespoons Sucanat or unrefined sugar

1 tablespoon ground cumin powder

2 teaspoons dried oregano

1 teaspoon sea salt

MASA BATTER

4 cups masa harina

1 teaspoon baking powder

1/2 teaspoon sea salt

4 cups (32 ounces) soy milk

Kernels cut from 2 ears fresh corn

Cilantro-Tofu Cream (recipe follows)

To make the chile: In a large skillet with a cover, sauté the onions and garlic in the stock over medium-high heat until the liquid evaporates. Add the cumin, chile powder, oregano, and bay leaves. Stir well to toast the spices for 1 minute before adding the beans, tomato purée, and stock. Cover and simmer for 10 minutes, then remove the cover and simmer for 5 minutes. Add salt and set aside.

To make the sauce: In a dry medium saucepan, toast the chiles over high heat, turning them, until they darken, about 3 to 5 minutes. Remove from the pan and let cool to the touch. Remove the stem and seeds of the chiles. Toast the garlic cloves in the same manner until half of each clove is blackened. Remove from the pan and set aside.

Combine the chiles, garlic, puréed tomatoes, water, Sucanat, cumin, oregano, and salt. Bring to a boil, then reduce heat, cover, and simmer for 30 minutes, stirring every 10 minutes to prevent scorching. Remove from the heat and let cool. In a blender, blend the sauce in batches until fairly smooth. Set aside.

To make the batter: In a large bowl, combine the masa, baking powder, and salt. Gradually whisk in the soy milk. Fold in the corn kernels.

Preheat the oven to 350°. Lightly oil an 11 x 9 inch baking dish. Spread half the masa batter on the bottom. Top with the black beans, followed by the remaining masa batter. Cover with aluminum foil and bake for 40 minutes. Remove the foil and bake for 10 minutes, until crisp. Let cool for 10 to 15 minutes before serving. Slice into 8 portions. Serve each portion with 4 ounces chili sauce and a dollop of Cilantro-Tofu Cream.

NUTRITIONAL INFORMATION PER SERVING:

518 Calories (10% from fat), 20 g Protein, 97 g Carbohydrate, 6 g Fat, 0 mg Cholesterol, 907 mg Sodium, 19 g Fiber

Cilantro-Tofu Cream

MAKES 1 1/2 CUPS

1 bunch cilantro, stemmed
12.3 ounces low-fat silken tofu
1/3 cups fresh lime juice
1/2 cup water

In a blender, combine all the ingredients and blend until smooth. Store in an airtight container in the refrigerator for up to 4 days.

NUTRITIONAL INFORMATION PER 2 TABLESPOON SERVING:

16 Calories (0% from fat), 2 g Protein, 2 g Carbohydrate, 0 g Fat, 0 mg Cholesterol, 22 mg Sodium, 1 g Fiber

INDONESIAN RICE TAMALES WITH CARROT-LEMONGRASS SAUCE

SERVES 6

This is a flavor tour de force and oil free! It's worth searching out banana leaves, which are available frozen in most Asian and Latino markets. The sauce has subtle aromatic flavors of lemongrass and coriander, and the salsa with kumquats is not to be missed.

RICE

1 tablespoons sesame seeds

2 cups jasmine rice or brown basmati rice

1 teaspoon minced lime zest

2 tablespoons fresh lime juice

1^1/$_2$ teaspoons sea salt

4 cups water

FILLING

1 yellow onion, cut into ^{1}/$_2$-inch dice

4 cloves garlic, minced

2 red bell peppers, seeded, deribbed, and cut into thin strips

2 carrots, peeled and cut into ^{1}/$_2$-inch matchsticks

^{3}/$_4$ cup vegetable stock or water

3 Japanese eggplants, halved lengthwise and cut into ^{1}/$_2$-inch pieces

4 ounces shiitake mushrooms, stemmed and thinly sliced

2 teaspoons fermented black beans, rinsed and minced

2 tablespoons minced fresh ginger

^{1}/$_4$ teaspoon red pepper flakes

3 tablespoons ketchup

2 tablespoons Sucanat or unrefined sugar

2 tablespoons tamari soy sauce

4 ounces firm tofu, cut into ^{1}/$_2$-inch dice

^{1}/$_2$ cup fresh or canned water chestnuts, peeled and thinly sliced

^{1}/$_4$ cup finely shredded fresh basil leaves

1 package frozen banana leaves, thawed

Carrot Lemon Grass Sauce (recipe follows)

Carmelized Pineapple Salsa (recipe follows)

1 ounce bean sprouts, for garnish

Blanched snow peas for garnish

To prepare the rice: Preheat a dry large saucepan over medium heat. Add the sesame seeds and jasmine rice and toast, stirring constantly, for 1 minute, or until the rice smells fragrant. Add the zest, juice, salt, and water. Cover and simmer for 30 minutes, or until all the liquid is evaporated and the rice is soft. Remove from heat and let stand for 10 minutes. Transfer the rice to a baking sheet pan and let cool to room temperature.

To make the filling: In a large sauté pan or skillet, sauté the onion, garlic, red peppers, and carrot in ^{1}/$_2$ cup of the vegetable stock until the onion starts to soften, about 7 minutes. Add the eggplant, mushrooms, black beans, ginger, pepper flakes, ketchup, Sucanat, tamari, and the remaining ^{1}/$_4$ cup stock. Cook until the eggplants are soft and most of the liquid has evaporated, about 15 minutes. Remove from heat and add the tofu, water chestnuts, and basil. Let cool to room temperature.

Preheat the oven to 400°. Unroll a banana leaf. Using a sharp knife or a pair of shears, cut the banana leaf into six 6 x 5-inch-long segments. Lay a segment on a work surface. Moistening your hands with water, pat about 1 cup of the rice in a ^{1}/$_2$-inch-thick layer for the entire 5 inches of the width. Spread a heaping ^{1}/$_2$ cup of the filling over the entire length of the bottom of the rice, leaving a ^{1}/$_2$-inch border along the length of the bottom. Carefully roll up the banana leaf into a tight cylinder. Place seam-side down in a baking dish.

Repeat to fill and roll the remaining banana leaf segments. Place ¼ inch water in the bottom of the baking dish. Cover with aluminum foil and bake for 20 minutes. Remove from baking dish and let sit at room temperature for 5 to 10 minutes before serving.

Ladle ½ cup carrot sauce on the bottom of each serving plate. Place a wrapped banana leaf tamale on the sauce, seam-side-up, and halfway unroll the banana leaf, exposing the rice. Top with 2 tablespoons pineapple salsa and a few sprouts. Serve with a fan of blanched snow peas.

NUTRITIONAL INFORMATION PER SERVING:

367 Calories (7% from fat), 11 g Protein, 74 g Carbohydrate, 3 g Fat, 0 mg Cholesterol, 1,020 mg Sodium, 5 g Fiber

Carrot-Lemongrass Sauce

MAKES 4 CUPS

1 yellow onion, cut lengthwise into thin crescents

¼ cup dry sherry or dry white wine or nonalcoholic white wine

½ teaspoon sea salt

2 teaspoons Sucanat

2 carrots, peeled and thinly sliced

¼ teaspoon ground turmeric

1 teaspoon ground coriander

1 tablespoon minced fresh ginger

2 stalks lemongrass, bottom half crushed with a cleaver or rolling pin

¼ cup fresh lime juice

4 cups vegetable stock

2 tablespoons light miso

Sea salt and cayenne or white pepper to taste

In a medium saucepan, cook the onion with the sherry, salt, and Sucanat until the liquid evaporates and the onions are soft and lightly caramelized, about 15 minutes. Add the carrots, turmeric, coriander, ginger, lemongrass, lime juice, and stock. Cover and simmer for 40 minutes. The carrots should be very soft. Remove the lemongrass. Transfer to a blender, add the miso and blend until thoroughly puréed. Add salt and cayenne.

NUTRITIONAL INFORMATION PER ½ CUP SERVING:

53 Calories (17% from fat), 1 g Protein, 10 g Carbohydrate, 1 g Fat, 0 mg Cholesterol, 337 mg Sodium, 1 g Fiber

Caramelized Pineapple Salsa

MAKES 2 CUPS

½ small ripe pineapple, peeled, cored, and cut into ½-inch-thick slices

1 teaspoon minced lime zest

2 tablespoons fresh lime juice

4 to 6 kumquats, thinly sliced (optional)

1 serrano chile, minced

4 scallions, white part only, thinly sliced on the diagonal

1 ripe tomato, cut into ¼-inch cubes

1 teaspoon sea salt

3 tablespoons finely shredded fresh mint leaves

Preheat the broiler. Broil the pineapple until the flesh closest to the heat source starts to brown. Remove from heat and let cool to room temperature. Cut the pineapple into small cubes, place in a medium bowl, and toss with the remaining ingredients.

NUTRITIONAL INFORMATION PER 2 TABLESPOON SERVING:

13 Calories (0% from fat), 0.2 g Protein, 3 g Carbohydrate, 0 g Fat, 0 mg Cholesterol, 135 mg Sodium, 0.4 g Fiber

ROSA BIANCA EGGPLANT TORTE WITH SMOKED ONION RATATOUILLE AND FLAGEOLET-SAGE SAUCE

MAKES 6 SERVINGS

This dish elevates humble vegetables and beans into an elegant entrée. The smoked onions, flageolet beans, sage, and cumin evoke the rustic cuisine of the South of France and the Mediterranean. In the late summer, we use Rosa Bianca eggplant, which are large, white- and lavender-skinned eggplants with very little acid in their flesh. If you cannot find Rosa Biancas, use globe or purple Italian eggplants—just rub the slices with salt and leave them to drain in a colander, then rise and pat them dry.

FLAGEOLET-SAGE SAUCE

1 yellow onion, cut into $1/2$-inch cubes

1 carrot, peeled and cut into $1/2$-inch cubes

2 stalks celery, cut into $1/2$-inch pieces

1 tablespoon minced garlic

3 tablespoons extra virgin olive oil or $1/4$ cup vegetable stock, dry sherry, or nonalcoholic red wine

1 teaspoon minced rosemary

2 teaspoons minced fresh sage

2 bay leaves

$1/4$ teaspoon ground cloves

$1/3$ teaspoon ground allspice

$1/2$ teaspoon ground pepper

3 cups cooked flageolets or white beans

1 cup dry white wine or nonalcoholic white wine

4 cups vegetable stock

1 tablespoon Dijon mustard

1 teaspoon sea salt

SMOKED ONION RATATOUILLE

2 red onions, smoked and cut into 1-inch cubes (see page 233)

1 tablespoon minced garlic

2 bell peppers (red, gold, or green), pimientos, or gypsy peppers, seeded, deribbed, and cut into 1-inch squares

2 tablespoons extra virgin olive oil or $1/4$ cup vegetable stock, dry sherry, or nonalcoholic red wine

$1/2$ teaspoon sea salt

1 teaspoon minced fresh rosemary

1 teaspoon dried oregano

$1/2$ teaspoon ground pepper

1 large Rosa Bianca or purple Italian eggplant, cut into 1-inch cubes

2 zucchini or summer squash, cut into 1-inch cubes

1 cup corn kernels

2 red or gold tomatoes, cut into $1/2$-inch dice

2 teaspoons minced fresh mint, or 1 tablespoon minced fresh basil

Sea salt to taste

HERB-CRUSTED EGGPLANT

$1^1/2$ cups unbleached all-purpose flour

$^1/3$ cup polenta

1 teaspoon dried thyme

1 teaspoon dried basil

1 teaspoon dried oregano

1 teaspoon paprika

$^1/2$ teaspoon ground pepper

1 cup soy milk

2 tablespoons Dijon mustard

2 Rosa Bianca or purple Italian eggplants,
    cut into twelve $^1/2$-inch-thick rounds

$^1/4$ cup canola oil (optional)

$^1/2$ cup Romesco Sauce (page 173), optional

Chopped Niçoise olives and
    chopped fresh parsley for garnish

To make the sauce: In a large saucepan, sauté the onion, carrot, celery, and garlic in the oil over medium heat until the onion softens and lightly browns, about 10 minutes. Add the herbs and spices, stir well, and sauté for 5 minutes. Add the beans, wine, stock, mustard, and salt. Reduce heat, cover, and simmer for 20 minutes. Remove from heat. Taste and adjust the seasoning.

To make the ratatouille: In a large skillet, sauté the onions, garlic, and peppers in the oil over high heat until the onions soften and lightly brown, about 5 minutes. Add the seasonings, reduce heat to medium, and sauté 5 minutes. Add the eggplant and zucchini, stirring well to incorporate the seasonings. Cover and cook, stirring the first few minutes, for 10 to 15 minutes, or until the eggplant and zucchini are just soft. Remove from heat and stir in the corn, tomatoes, and fresh herbs. Add salt and set aside.

To make the eggplant: In a shallow bowl, combine the flour, polenta, herbs, and spices. Stir to mix well. In another shallow bowl, whisk the soy milk and mustard together. Dredge the eggplant slices in the flour mixture to coat well, then place in the soy milk mixture to coat well. Dredge in the flour mixture again to coat well.

In a large nonstick sauté pan or skillet, heat the oil over medium-high heat until a drop of the flour mixture fries immediately. Cook the eggplant rounds in batches on both sides until golden brown, about 2 to 3 minutes per side. Drain on paper towels and keep warm in a low oven.

For an oil-free version, preheat the oven to 400°. Line a baking sheet with parchment paper. After the eggplant is coated with the flour mixture the second time, place back in the soy milk mixture and coat well. Place on the prepared pan. Bake for 15 to 20 minutes, or until the crust is hard and slightly brown while the center is soft.

On each serving plate, pour $^1/2$ cup flageolet sauce. Place $^1/2$ cup ratatouille in the center. Top with an eggplant round. Place more ratatouille on top of the eggplant and follow with another round of eggplant. Drizzle the top with a little Romesco sauce. Place a few chopped Niçoise olives on top of the eggplant and sprinkle with chopped parsley.

NUTRITIONAL INFORMATION PER SERVING:

(with oil) 564 Calories (26% from fat), 16 g Protein, 87 g Carbohydrate, 16 g Fat, 0 mg Cholesterol, 807 mg Sodium, 15 g Fiber

(without oil) 448 Calories (8% from fat), 16 g Protein, 87 g Carbohydrate, 4 g Fat, 0 mg Cholesterol, 807 mg Sodium, 15 g Fiber

THAI GREEN CURRY EGGPLANT STACK

MAKES 6 SERVINGS

In summer we serve vegetables sautéed in green curry and sandwiched between layers of crunchy herb-crusted baked eggplant.

GREEN CURRY SAUCE

1 cup Curry Paste (recipe follows)

14 ounces canned low-fat coconut milk

1 cup rice milk or soy milk

1 cup green summer squash cubes, cooked until soft and drained

1/2 bunch Thai or Italian basil leaves, stemmed

1/2 bunch fresh cilantro leaves, stemmed

Sea salt to taste

Herb Crusted Eggplant (page 131)

BARLEY SALAD

3 cups cooked barley

2 scallions, white part only, thinly sliced

1 tomato, finely diced

1 small cucumber, peel on, seeded and finely diced

1/4 cup fresh lime juice

1 teaspoon sea salt

2 tablespoons chopped fresh mint

2 teaspoons sesame seeds, toasted (see page 234), optional

SAUTÉED VEGETABLES

1 1/2 pounds seasonal vegetables, cut into bite-sized pieces (broccoli, cauliflower, carrots, zucchini, sliced shiitake and whole oyster mushrooms, green beans, long beans, bok choy and other greens, cubed tomato, peppers, and Japanese eggplant)

1/4 cup bean sprouts

4 shallots, sliced thin

2 teaspoons canola oil (optional)

1 tablespoon finely shredded fresh mint leaves

1 tablespoon finely shredded fresh basil leaves

1 red onion, peeled and sliced thin

To make the curry sauce: In a medium saucepan, combine the curry paste, coconut milk, and rice milk and bring to a boil. Reduce heat and simmer for 20 minutes. Strain the sauce. Transfer to a blender and add the squash, basil, and cilantro. Blend until smooth. Add salt. Set aside.

To make the salad: In a medium bowl, combine all the ingredients and mix well.

To make the sautéed vegetables: In a large sauté pan or skillet, sauté the vegetables and shallots in the oil over very high heat, about 5 minutes. Or cook them in a dry nonstick pan just until they start to soften. Add the curry sauce, bean sprouts, mint, basil, and onion and cook for another 2 to 3 minutes.

To assemble: Put 1/2 cup barley salad in the bottom of shallow soup or pasta bowl. Place 1 eggplant round on top of the salad, place 1 cup sautéed vegetables on the eggplant, and top with a second eggplant round. Pour 1/2 cup curry sauce around the plate. Top the eggplant with some sprouts and some basil and mint.

NOTE:

For a lower-fat dish, replace the coconut milk with 14 ounces or rice milk, with 1 teaspoon of coconut extract.

NUTRITIONAL INFORMATION PER SERVING:

(with oil) 551 Calories (25% from fat), 12 g Protein, 92 g Carbohydrate, 15g Fat, 0 mg Cholesterol, 1,020 mg Sodium, 15 g Fiber

(without oil) 488 Calories (15% from fat), 12 g Protein, 92 g Carbohydrate, 8 g Fat, 0 mg Cholesterol, 1,020 mg Sodium, 15 g Fiber

(recipe continues on next page)

Curry Paste

MAKES 2 CUPS

4 shallots, coarsely chopped

6 cloves garlic, coarsely chopped

2 tablespoons minced peeled garlic

1 tablespoon minced galangal (optional)

$1/2$ bunch cilantro, coarsely chopped, including stems and roots

3 stalks lemongrass, bottom half coarsely chopped

2 serrano or Thai chiles

1 teaspoon coriander seeds, toasted and ground (see page 234)

1 teaspoon cumin seeds, toasted and ground (see page 234)

$1/2$ teaspoon ground pepper

2 teaspoons minced lime zest

$1/4$ cup fresh lime juice

2 teaspoons sea salt

1 tablespoon light miso

2 tablespoons brown rice syrup (optional)

In a food processor or blender, blend all the ingredients until ground to a coarse paste. If using a blender, you will need to up $1/3$ cup or more of water to pull the mix together. Store in an airtight container in the refrigerator for up to 2 weeks.

NUTRITIONAL INFORMATION PER
$1/2$ CUP SERVING:

59 Calories (8% from fat), 2 g Protein, 10 g Carbohydrate, 0.5 g Fat, 0 mg Cholesterol, 1,226 mg Sodium, 1 g Fiber

PUMPKINS STUFFED WITH SAUTÉED VEGETABLES IN PUMPKIN CURRY SAUCE

MAKES 6 SERVINGS

We've been strongly influenced by the southeast Asian cuisine represented in the Bay Area, especially Thai cuisine. This variation on a Thai coconut curry is served in the fall when baby pumpkins and winter squash are plentiful. To make this dish simpler, forgo the whole pumpkin and serve it in a soup bowl with plenty of sauce.

PUMPKIN CURRY SAUCE

1 cup Curry Paste (this page)

14 ounces canned low-fat coconut milk or 14 ounces rice milk with 1 teaspoon coconut extract

1 cup rice milk or soy milk

2 cups pumpkin or butternut squash cubes, cooked until soft and drained

Sea salt to taste

Six 8-inch-diameter pumpkins, such as Baby Bears, or acorn or buttercup winter squash

1 teaspoon sea salt

$1/2$ teaspoon ground pepper

1½ pounds seasonal vegetables, cut into bite-sized pieces (broccoli, cauliflower, carrots, zucchini, slices of shiitake and whole oyster mushrooms, green beans, long beans, Chinese bok choy, blanched cubes of winter squash or root vegetables)

6 shallots, peeled and thinly sliced

2 teaspoons canola oil (optional)

3 to 4 cups cooked barley or jasmine rice

Asian Pear Chutney (recipe follows)

1 tablespoons finely shredded fresh mint leaves

2 tablespoons finely shredded fresh basil leaves

1 tablespoon finely shredded fresh cilantro leaves

To make the curry sauce: In a large saucepan, bring the paste, coconut milk, and rice milk to a boil. Reduce heat and simmer for 20 minutes. Strain. In a blender, combine the sauce and pumpkin and blend until smooth. Add salt and set aside.

Preheat oven to 400°. Cut the top 2 inches off the pumpkin. Scoop out the seeds and pith. Salt and pepper the cavity. Using two 8-inch baking pans, place the pumpkins, upside down. Place the pumpkin tops in the pans. Pour in ½-inch water. Cover the pans with aluminum foil. Bake for 30 to 40 minutes, until just slightly soft when squeezed. Remove from the oven and let cool.

In a large sauté pan or skillet, sauté the vegetables and shallots in the oil over very high heat, just until they start to soften, about 5 minutes. Or cook them in a dry nonstick pan. Add the curry sauce and cook for another 2 minutes.

Divide the vegetable mixture among the baked pumpkins. Set each pumpkin on a bed of barley. Top each serving with 2 teaspoons chutney and sprinkle with mint, basil, and cilantro.

NUTRITIONAL INFORMATION PER SERVING:

253 Calories (18% from fat), 5 g Protein, 47 g Carbohydrate, 5 g Fat, 0 mg Cholesterol, 824 mg Sodium, 6 g Fiber

Asian Pear Chutney

MAKES 2 CUPS

2 tablespoons fructose or Sucanat

¼ cup rice vinegar or champagne vinegar

¼ teaspoon red pepper flakes

½ teaspoon cumin seeds, toasted (see page 234)

1 red bell pepper, seeded, deribbed, and finely diced

2 Asian pears, apples, or pears, peeled, cored, and cut into ½-inch-dice

½ teaspoon sea salt

In a large sauté pan or skillet, heat the sugar and vinegar over high heat until the sugar melts and the mixture becomes syrupy. Add the pepper flakes and cumin seeds, followed by the remaining ingredients. Stir well and cook for 10 minutes if using Asian pears, and 5 to 7 minutes if using apples or pears. Transfer to a bowl and let cool. Store in an airtight container in the refrigerator for up to 4 days.

NUTRITIONAL INFORMATION PER 2 TEASPOON SERVING:

8 Calories (0% from fat), 0 g Protein, 2 g Carbohydrate, 0 g Fat, 0 mg Cholesterol, 22 mg Sodium, 0.2 g Fiber

POLENTA TORTE WITH PUTTANESCA SAUCE

MAKES 8 SERVINGS

Created by former Milly's chef Steve Mclaine, this torte has layers of duxelles and a tofu-basil filling sandwiched between layers of firm polenta.

POLENTA LAYER
8 cups water
1 teaspoon sea salt
2 cups polenta
1 teaspoon dried oregano
1/2 teaspoon minced rosemary

DUXELLES
1 red onion, finely diced
2 cloves garlic, minced
1/2 cup dry red wine or nonalcoholic red wine
1 pound button or cremini mushrooms, minced by pulsing in a blender or food processor
1 1/2 teaspoons dried sage
1 teaspoon dried thyme
2 teaspoons tamari soy sauce or 1 teaspoon sea salt
1/2 teaspoon ground pepper

TOFU-BASIL FILLING
1 bunch spinach, washed and stemmed
1 clove garlic, minced
1 bunch basil, stemmed
2 tablespoons light miso
1 1/2 pounds firm tofu, finely crumbled
2 teaspoons champagne vinegar or rice vinegar
1/3 teaspoon ground nutmeg (optional)

Puttanesca Sauce (recipe follows)
Basil Cashew Cream (page 90)

To make the polenta: In a large, heavy pot, bring the water to a boil and add the salt. Gradually whisk in the polenta. Reduce heat to low, add the oregano and rosemary, and whisk for another 5 minutes. Cook the polenta for another 10 minutes, or until it pulls away from the sides of the pan. Divide the polenta between two 8-inch baking dishes. Let cool for 1 hour.

To make the duxelles: In a large sauté pan or skillet, combine all the ingredients and cook over medium heat for about 30 minutes, or until soft and dry. Stir often during the last few minutes of cooking time to prevent scorching. Set aside.

To make the filling: In a large pot of salted boiling water, blanch the spinach leaves for 2 minutes, or until thoroughly wilted. Rinse under cold water, drain, and squeeze out all excess water. In a medium bowl, combine the spinach, garlic, basil, miso, tofu, vinegar, and nutmeg. Blend all the ingredients together. Transfer half of the mixture to a blender and purée until smooth. Add back to the remaining mixture and mix well.

To assemble and bake: preheat the oven to 400°. Spread the duxelles on one of the polenta layers. Carefully lift the other layer of polenta out of the baking pan and place on top of the duxelles. Spread the tofu mixture on top of the second layer of polenta. Cover with aluminum foil and bake for 20 minutes. Remove the foil and bake for 10 minutes. Cut into 8 squares and serve each with 1/2 cup Puttanesca Sauce. Garnish with Basil Cashew Cream.

NUTRITIONAL INFORMATION PER SERVING:
321 Calories (25% from fat), 20 g Protein, 40 g Carbohydrate, 9 g Fat, 0 mg Cholesterol, 792 mg Sodium, 4 g Fiber

Puttanesca Sauce

MAKES 8 CUPS

4 cloves garlic, minced

4 peperoncini (pickled Italian peppers), finely diced

2 tablespoons capers, drained

1 teaspoon dried oregano

2 teaspoons dried basil

1/2 cup dry red wine or nonalcoholic red wine

32 ounces canned diced tomatoes

Sea salt to taste

2 teaspoons Sucanat or unrefined sugar, if needed

In a large saucepan, combine the garlic, peperoncini, capers, oregano, basil, and wine. Bring to a boil and cook to reduce the liquid by half. Add the tomatoes. Cover, reduce heat, and simmer for 30 minutes. Add salt and Sucanat.

NUTRITIONAL INFORMATION PER 1/2 CUP SERVING:

27 Calories (0% from fat), 0.7 g Protein, 6 g Carbohydrate, 0 g Fat, 0 mg Cholesterol, 206 mg Sodium, 0.4 g Fiber

MILLENNIUM MOUSSAKA

MAKES 8 SERVINGS

A lower-fat version of this popular dish, this uses baked eggplant.

2 Italian eggplants, cut into ¼-inch-thick crosswise slices

2 red onions, finely diced

1 tablespoon minced garlic

1 pound cremini mushrooms, thinly sliced

1 cup dry red wine or nonalcoholic red wine

2 pounds Marinated Tempeh (page 231) or packaged marinated tempeh, crumbled

1 tablespoon minced fresh rosemary

2 teaspoons ground cinnamon

½ teaspoon ground allspice

2 teaspoons dried oregano

1 teaspoon sea salt

1 teaspoon ground pepper

1½ cups tomato purée or sauce

SAVORY CUSTARD

16 ounces low-fat silken tofu

1 cup Millennium Braised Garlic (page 230)

3 tablespoons light miso

2 tablespoons nutritional yeast (optional)

1 tablespoon egg replacement powder (optional)

1 teaspoon ground nutmeg

½ teaspoon sea salt

3 tablespoons soy milk

HERBED BREAD CRUMBS

1 cup toasted bread cubes

1 teaspoon fennel seeds, toasted (see page 234)

1 teaspoon dried thyme

1 teaspoon dried oregano

⅓ teaspoon ground nutmeg

4 cups Puttanesca Sauce (page 137)

Preheat the oven to 350°. Line a baking sheet with parchment paper. Soak the eggplant in warm salted water for 10 minutes. Drain, then place on the prepared pan and bake for 10 minutes, or until it just starts to soften. Set aside and let cool.

To make the sauce: Combine the onions, garlic, mushrooms, and wine in a large saucepan. Cook for 10 minutes over medium heat. Add the tempeh, seasonings, and tomato purée and simmer, covered, for 20 minutes, or until thick. Let cool.

To make the custard: Blend all custard ingredients in a food processor leaving some texture. Or mash together. Set aside.

To make the bread crumbs: In a blender or food processor combine all the ingredients for the bread crumbs and pulse until ground.

To assemble and bake: Preheat the oven to 350°. Spread a thin layer of puttanesca sauce on the bottom of a 12-inch baking dish. Add a layer of one-third of the eggplant, followed by half of the tempeh filling. Add a second layer of eggplant, and moisten with a little sauce. Top with the remaining eggplant and and tempeh filling. Top with the custard.

Bake, uncovered, for 30 minutes. Top with the bread crumbs and bake for 10 to 15 minutes more, or until lightly browned. Let sit a few minutes before serving. Serve over heated Puttanesca Sauce.

NUTRITIONAL INFORMATION PER SERVING:

351 Calories (18% from fat), 25 g Protein, 47 g Carbohydrate, 7 g Fat, 0 mg Cholesterol, 807 mg Sodium, 7 g Fiber

MILLENNIUM VEGETABLE PAELLA

MAKES 6 SERVINGS

Instead of seafood and sausage, we hint at those flavors in this vegetarian dish with smoked tofu, oyster mushrooms, and arame sea vegetable. We start with a saffron pilaf, and add sautéed vegetables. Finally, we serve it over braised kale and top it with our chile aioli.

2 yellow onions, cut into $1/2$-inch dice

4 cloves garlic, minced

2 red bell peppers, seeded, deribbed, and cut into $1/2$-inch dice

3 tablespoons light olive oil, dry sherry, or nonalcoholic red wine

$1^1/2$ teaspoons dried oregano

$1/3$ teaspoon red pepper flakes

$1/2$ teaspoon minced orange zest

$1/3$ teaspoon whole cumin seeds (optional)

2 cups fresh or canned peeled Roma tomatoes with juice

6 ounces smoked tofu, cut into $1/2$-inch dice (page 235), or seitan sausage, cubed (page 108)

2 zucchini, halved lengthwise and cut into $1/2$-inch crescents

1 ounce dried arame, soaked in warm water for 10 minutes

2 teaspoons capers, drained

$1/4$ cup pitted black olives, thinly sliced (optional)

8 ounces oyster mushrooms or mushroom of choice

4 cups Saffron Basmati Rice Pilaf (page 104)

2 tablespoons chopped fresh parsley

1 teaspoon sea salt

2 bunches kale

6 tablespoons Chile Tofu Aioli (page 173)

Chopped fresh parsley for garnish

1 lemon or orange, thinly sliced for garnish

In a large sauté pan or skillet, sauté the onions, garlic, and peppers in the olive oil over high heat until the onions soften, about 5 minutes. Add the oregano, pepper flakes, zest, and cumin. Stir and sauté for 1 minute. Add the tomatoes, smoked tofu, zucchini, arame, capers, and black olives. Reduce heat to medium-low and simmer for 5 minutes. Add the mushrooms and sauté another minute or two. Stir in the rice pilaf, parsley, and salt. Heat through. Taste and adjust the seasonings. Set aside and keep warm.

Steam or blanch the kale until it is softened, about 8 minutes. Drain and set aside to cool.

For each serving, line the rim of the plate with some kale and place one-sixth of the paella in the center of the plate. Top with a small dollop of the chile aioli. Garnish with chopped parsley and a lemon or orange slice.

NUTRITIONAL INFORMATION PER SERVING:

331 Calories (30% from fat), 10 g Protein, 48 g Carbohydrate, 11 g Fat, 0 mg Cholesterol, 976 mg Sodium, 7 g Fiber

PUMPKINS STUFFED WITH SAGE POLENTA AND SEITAN BOURGUIGNON

MAKES 6 SERVINGS

This fun and elegant entrée is perfect for a special fall or winter dinner. An earthy combination of flavors, textures, and aromas are served in baby pumpkins.

PUMPKINS

Six 8-inch-diameter pumpkins, such as
    Baby Bears or acorn or buttercup squash

$1/2$ teaspoon sea salt

$1/2$ teaspoon black pepper

SAGE POLENTA

5 cups water or light vegetable stock

$1^1/2$ cups polenta

1 teaspoon minced garlic

2 teaspoons minced fresh sage, or
    $1/2$ teaspoon dried sage

$1/2$ teaspoon ground pepper

1 tablespoon nutritional yeast

1 teaspoon sea salt

SEITAN BOURGUIGNON

$1^1/2$ cups pearl onions

1 tablespoon minced garlic

2 teaspoons olive oil or $1/4$ cup vegetable stock, or
    dry red wine, or nonalcoholic red wine

$1/2$ pound portobello mushrooms,
    cut into 1-inch cubes

2 teaspoons minced fresh thyme

2 teaspoons minced fresh rosemary

1 teaspoon minced fresh sage

1 teaspoon dried tarragon

2 bay leaves

2 cups dry red wine (good-quality Burgundy,
    Rhône or Zinfandel) or nonalcoholic red wine

2 cups Dark Vegetable Stock or Mushroom Stock
    (page 228)

2 tablespoons tomato paste, or $1/4$ cup reconstituted
    sun-dried tomatoes

1 tablespoon Dijon mustard

1 turnip, peeled and cut into 1-inch cubes

2 parsnips, peeled, sliced lengthwise, and
    cut into $1/2$-inch pieces

2 carrots, peeled, sliced lengthwise, and
    cut into $1/2$-inch pieces

1 celery root, peeled and cut into $1/2$-inch dice

1 cup winter squash, peeled, seeded, and
    cut into 1-inch cubes

6 to 8 dried chestnuts, blanched to reconstitute
    and halved

8 ounces prepared seitan, cut into 1-inch cubes

$1^1/2$ teaspoons ground pepper

4 teaspoons tamari soy sauce

2 tablespoons cornstarch or arrowroot,
    dissolved in $1/4$ cup cold water

Sea salt to taste

6 fresh rosemary sprigs, for garnish

Chopped fresh parsley, for garnish

To prepare the pumpkins: Preheat the oven to 400°. Cut the top 2 inches off the pumpkins. Scoop out the seeds and pith. Salt and pepper the cavity. In two 8-inch baking pans, place the pumpkins upside down, and put the pumpkins lids in the pans. Pour in 1/2 inch water. Cover the pans with aluminum foil and bake for 30 to 40 minutes, or until just slightly soft when squeezed. Let cool.

To make the polenta: In a large saucepan, bring the water to a boil. Gradually whisk in the polenta and whisk constantly for 5 minutes. Reduce heat to a simmer and add the remaining ingredients. Continue cooking, whisking every 5 minutes, until the polenta starts to pull away from the sides of the pan, about 15 minutes. Set aside and keep warm.

To make the seitan bourguignon: In a large saucepan, sauté the onions and garlic in the oil over medium heat until they lightly brown, about 5 to 7 minutes. Add the mushrooms and seasonings and sauté for 2 minutes. Add all the remaining ingredients except the cornstarch mixture and salt. Cover and simmer until the root vegetables are just tender, about 30 minutes. Stir in the cornstarch mixture and cook for about 5 minutes. Remove from heat. Adjust the salt.

Heat the pumpkins in a 350° oven for 10 minutes. Fill each with 1 cup polenta, then top with 1 heaping cup seitan bourguignon. Insert a rosemary sprig in the top of each pumpkin. Sprinkle with parsley and serve.

NUTRITIONAL INFORMATION PER SERVING:

425 Calories (11% from fat), 20 g Protein, 75 g Carbohydrate, 5 g Fat, 0 mg Cholesterol, 1024 mg Sodium, 11 g Fiber

WILD RICE–STUFFED CABBAGE WITH PARSNIP-PERNOD SAUCE

MAKES 6 SERVINGS

This entrée takes stuffed cabbage to a new level of elegance not usually associated with that dish. We serve this in the late fall when we get our hands on fresh porcini and other boletus mushroom varieties, but it also works with other mushrooms.

FILLING

2 leeks, white part only, washed and cut into 1/3-inch pieces

2 cloves garlic, minced

2 carrots, peeled and finely diced

1 large celery root, peeled and finely diced

1/4 cup dry sherry or nonalcoholic red wine

1 pound wild mushrooms, porcini, shiitakes, chanterelles

1 teaspoon minced fresh thyme

1 tablespoon minced fresh tarragon

1 teaspoon dried sage

1/2 cup vegetable stock

2 tablespoons tamari soy sauce

1/2 teaspoon ground pepper

2 cups cooked wild rice

6 ounces smoked tofu, finely diced (optional)

1 large head Savoy cabbage

1/2 cup vegetable stock

Parsnip-Pernod Sauce (recipe follows)
Minced fresh chives for garnish

(recipe continues on next page)

To make the filling: In a large saucepan, cook the leeks, garlic, carrots, celery root, and sherry over medium heat for 10 minutes. Add the mushrooms, thyme, tarragon, and sage, followed by the stock. Simmer until most of the stock evaporates, about 15 minutes. Add the tamari, pepper, rice, and tofu. Mix together and remove from heat. Cool to room temperature.

To prepare the cabbage: Separate the leaves from the head to yield 24 large leaves. Blanch the leaves in salted boiling water for 4 to 6 minutes. Drain and let cool.

To assemble and cook: Preheat the oven to 350°. On a work surface, lay 2 cabbage leaves side by side and overlapping by 1/2 inch. Place 1/2 cup filling in the center. Fold the sides of the leaves in, then roll into a cylinder. Add the stock to a 12-inch baking dish. Add the cabbage rolls and bake for 15 to 20 minutes, or until the cabbage rolls are heated through and slightly dry.

Serve 2 rolls per person on 1/2 cup of sauce.

NUTRITIONAL INFORMATION PER SERVING:

283 Calories (10% from fat), 11 g Protein, 53 g Carbohydrate, 3 g Fat, 0 mg Cholesterol, 705 mg Sodium, 10 g Fiber

Parsnip-Pernod Sauce

MAKES 6 CUPS

1 yellow onion, cut lengthwise into 1/2-inch crescents
1 clove garlic, minced
2 parsnips, peeled and cut into 1/3-inch thick slices
1/3 cup vegetable stock
1 teaspoon minced fresh thyme
1 teaspoon minced fresh tarragon
1/2 teaspoon ground nutmeg
1 teaspoon sea salt
1/2 teaspoon ground pepper
3 cups rice milk or soy milk
2 tablespoons light miso
1/3 cup Pernod liqueur

In a large saucepan, combine the onion, garlic, parsnips, and stock. Cover and cook over low heat for 20 minutes. Add the thyme, tarragon, nutmeg, salt, pepper, rice milk, and miso and simmer until the parsnips are very soft and the liquid reduces by a third, about 10 minutes. Transfer the mixture to a blender in batches and purée until smooth. Return to low heat. Add the Pernod and simmer for 10 minutes. Taste and adjust the seasonings. Serve warm.

NUTRITIONAL INFORMATION PER 1/2 CUP SERVING:

77 Calories (12% from fat), 1 g Protein, 16 g Carbohydrate, 1 g Fat, 0 mg Cholesterol, 316 mg Sodium, 2 g Fiber

GRILLED SEITAN WITH STAR ANISE, PEAR, AND PORT SAUCE AND CORN AND MUSHROOM RAGOUT

SERVES 6

This is a popular dish. The flavors of the sauce and the ragout combine the Asian flavors of star anise and ginger with the more familiar western flavor of thyme. The sauce is a rich, savory-sweet wine reduction that pairs beautifully with grilled or breaded seitan or tempeh. I prefer to prepare the sauce and the ragout in advance, then grill the seitan, brushing the sauce over the seitan as it grills. Serve the seitan over the corn and mushroom ragout, or with our mixed grain pilaf or one of our grain salads and some grilled vegetables.

RAGOUT

2 leeks, sliced thin

1 bulb fennel, sliced in $1/2$-inch cubes

2 tablespoons extra-virgin olive oil or
    $1/4$ cup sherry or vegetable stock

3 tablespoons sherry

$1/4$ pound fresh shiitake mushrooms

$1/4$ pound oyster mushrooms

$1/2$ teaspoon sea salt

1 tablespoon fresh thyme

2 cups fresh corn kernels cut from ears (about 4 ears)

1 teaspoon tamari soy sauce

1 tablespoon grated ginger

SAUCE

1 leek, white part only, sliced

2 comice or Bosc pears, sliced thin

1 cup marsala wine

1 cup red wine or nonalcoholic red wine

$1/2$ cup Ponzu Sauce (page 87)

1 cup vegetable stock plus more if needed

4 whole star anise

$1/2$ teaspoon dried thyme

$1/4$ teaspoon dried red chile flakes

$1/4$ teaspoon ground black pepper

2 teaspoons Sucanat

2 teaspoons balsamic vinegar

$1/2$ teaspoon green peppercorns

2 teaspoons corn starch

$1/4$ cup cold water

6 4-ounce portions seitan medallions or
    marinated tempeh

Mixed Grain Pilaf (page 104) optional

To make the ragout: In a large sauté pan over high heat, sauté the leeks and fennel in the oil or stock until the leeks soften, about 10 minutes. Remove from the pan and reserve. Deglaze the pan with the sherry, then add the mushrooms and salt. Sauté until the mushrooms soften, then add the thyme, corn, tamari, ginger, and the reserved leeks and fennel. Stir to combine thoroughly, remove pan from the heat, and set aside.

To make the sauce: In a saucepan, braise the leeks and 2 of the pears in the marsala wine over medium heat until the leeks just start to soften, about 10 minutes. Add the red wine, ponzu sauce, stock, star anise, thyme, chile flakes, black pepper, Sucanat, and vinegar. Bring to a boil, then reduce to a simmer. Simmer, uncovered, for 20 minutes, until the mixture is reduced by about one-third. Stir in the green peppercorns.

Mix the cornstarch with the water until the starch is dissolved. Slowly whisk half the starch mixture into the sauce. Increase heat and allow sauce to come back to a low boil and thicken slightly before adding the rest of the starch slurry. Remove from the heat and let cool slightly before using.

Brush the seitan with sauce and grill over a medium flame for 2 minutes each side, or broil for 2 minutes each side, brushing again after flipping it over. Serve each portion of seitan over $1/2$ cup of the corn and mushroom ragout, topped with the sauce. Serve with mixed grain pilaf on the side if you like, and garnish with the remaining sliced pear.

VARIATION:

If you like, substitute 2 tablespoons tamari, 1 tablespoon lemon juice, $1/3$ cup vegetable stock, and 1 teaspoon Sucanat for the Ponzu Sauce.

NUTRITIONAL INFORMATION PER SERVING:
446 Calories (12% from fat), 37 g Protein, 61 g Carbohydrate, 6 g Fat, 0 mg Cholesterol, 908 mg Sodium, 10 g Fiber

SEITAN, WILD MUSHROOM, AND CORN-STUFFED PEPPERS WITH POBLANO CHILE SAUCE AND QUINOA PILAF

MAKES 6 SERVINGS

We serve this in late summer and early fall, when peppers and corn are plentiful and the first of the wild mushrooms start to show up. Surprisingly, the flavors of the mushrooms stand up to smoky grilled seitan and the spicy sauce.

SEITAN, WILD MUSHROOM, AND CORN FILLING

6 ounces Millennium Seitan Medallions (page 231) or substitute packaged seitan

1/2 cup Moroccan Marinade (page 13) or your favorite barbecue sauce

1 tablespoon canola oil (optional)

1 yellow onion, cut into 1/2-inch dice

1 tablespoon minced garlic

1 fennel bulb, cut into 1/2-inch dice

2 tablespoons extra virgin olive oil, or 1/4 cup dry sherry, nonalcoholic wine, or vegetable stock

1 teaspoon ground cumin

2 teaspoons minced fresh oregano

1/4 teaspoon red pepper flakes

8 ounces mixed wild mushrooms or portobellos, cut into bite sized pieces

Kernels cut from 4 ears fresh corn

2 tablespoons finely shredded fresh mint

Sea salt to taste

12 gypsy, pimiento, or Anaheim chiles

Poblano Chile Sauce (recipe follows)

1/2 cup Romesco Sauce (page 173), optional

Quinoa Pilaf (page 53)

1 cup Mango Salsa (page 178), or salsa of choice

To make the filling: Preheat the broiler. Toss the seitan with 1/2 cup of the marinade and the canola oil. Broil for 5 minutes, or until browned, brushing with the marinade several times. Let cool to room temperature. Cut into 1/2-inch dice.

In a large sauté pan or skillet, sauté the onion, garlic, and fennel in the olive oil or stock over high heat until the onion softens, about 5 minutes. Add the cumin, oregano, and pepper flakes, followed by the mushrooms. Stir well and sauté until the mushrooms just soften, about 5 minutes. Add the corn, seitan, and remaining 1/4 cup marinade. Sauté for 5 minutes, or until the mixture is fairly dry. Remove from heat. Stir in the mint and salt.

Broil the chiles until they just start to soften, but do not char the skin. Let cool to room temperature. Slit the peppers lengthwise, remove the seeds, and stuff each with 2/3 cup seitan filling. Broil the stuffed peppers for 5 to 7 minutes, or until the filling is warmed through. Spread 1/3 cup Poblano Chile Sauce on the bottom of each dinner plate.

Pour 2 tablespoons Romesco sauce on top of the green sauce. Drag a knife through to make a pattern. Place 1/2 cup pilaf at the end of the plate and arrange 2 stuffed chiles over the pilaf and sauce. Serve with the Mango Salsa of your choice.

NUTRITIONAL INFORMATION PER SERVING:

388 Calories (19% from fat), 18 g Protein, 6 g Carbohydrate, 8 g Fat, 0 mg Cholesterol, 510 mg Sodium, 15 g Fiber

Poblano Chile Sauce

MAKES 2 1/2 CUPS

4 poblano chiles or Anaheim chiles, roasted and peeled (see page 235)

1/3 cup fresh lime juice

1 clove garlic, minced

2 tablespoons Millennium Braised Garlic (page 230)

1/3 teaspoon red pepper flakes

1/2 bunch cilantro, stemmed and coarsely chopped

1 teaspoon minced fresh oregano

1 teaspoon sea salt

1 cup water

In a blender, combine all the ingredients and blend to a coarse sauce. Set aside.

NUTRITIONAL INFORMATION PER SERVING:

28 Calories (0% from fat), 0 g Protein, 7 g Carbohydrate, 0 g Fat, 0 mg Cholesterol, 469 mg Sodium, 3 g Fiber

TEMPEH OR SEITAN PICCATA

MAKES 6 SERVINGS

This is our take on the classic piccata—whether you use seitan or tempeh, you'll be pleased with the result. As in the traditional version of this dish, the pungent lemons and capers add a balance and contrast You can use our marinated seitan or tempeh (see page 231 or 232), or buy commercial marinated tempeh or seitan from a natural foods store or supermarket. Serve this with any of our pilafs, or with mashed potatoes.

HERB CRUST

$1^1/2$ cups all-purpose unbleached flour

$1/3$ cup polenta

1 teaspoon dried thyme

1 teaspoon dried basil

1 teaspoon dried oregano

1 teaspoon paprika

$1/2$ teaspoon ground pepper

1 cup soy milk

2 teaspoons Dijon mustard

6 servings ($1^1/2$ pounds) marinated tempeh, each 4-ounce portion cut into triangles, or use the same amount of seitan medallions

$1/4$ cup canola oil

PICCATA SAUCE

2 teaspoons minced garlic

6 paper-thin lemon slices

$1/2$ cup fresh lemon juice

2 cups dry white wine (you can use non-alcoholic wine)

1 tablespoon nutritional yeast

1 tablespoon capers, drained

$1/2$ teaspoon ground pepper

$1/2$ teaspoon sea salt

1 tablespoon cornstarch or arrowroot, dissolved in 3 tablespoons cold water

Thin lemon slices and minced fresh parsley or chives for garnish

In a shallow bowl, combine all the ingredients for the herb crust. In another shallow bowl, combine the soy milk and mustard. Dredge the tempeh with the crust mixture, dip in the soy milk mixture, then dredge again in the crust mixture. In a large nonstick sauté pan or skillet, sauté the tempeh in batches on each side in the oil over medium-high heat until lightly brown, about 2 to 3 minutes per side. Or, cook the seitan in batches in a dry nonstick pan. Keep warm in a low oven.

To make the sauce: Wipe out the pan and place it over medium heat. Add the garlic and toast until lightly browned. Add the lemon slices, the remaining sauce ingredients. Boil until the volume is reduced by almost half. Stir in the cornstarch mixture and cook until thickened. Serve the hot sauce over the tempeh. Garnish with more lemon slices and parsley.

NUTRITIONAL INFORMATION PER SERVING:

324 Calories (11% from fat), 34 g Protein, 38 g Carbohydrate, 4 g Fat, 0 mg Cholesterol, 781 mg Sodium, 3 g Fiber

GRILLED JERKED SEITAN WITH COCONUT MASHED YAMS

SERVES 6

The key elements of our jerk marinade are the sweet, spicy, and unmistakable flavors of allspice and clove. The addition of our onion marmalade to the marinade adds volume and sweetness. If you decide to make the marinade without oil, watch the seitan carefully as you grill it, as it will dry out fast. The coconut mashed yams have the flavor of toasted thyme. They are truly yummy.

MARINADE

$1/2$ cup Red Onion Marmalade (page 24) or caramelized onions

2 cloves garlic, chopped

$3/4$ cup fresh lime juice

$1/4$ cup canola oil or light olive oil (optional)

$3/4$ to 1 cup water

1 teaspoon Sucanat or brown sugar

2 tablespoons tamari soy sauce

1 serrano chile, seeded and chopped (leave seeds in if you want it hotter)

1 teaspoon minced fresh ginger

1 teaspoon dried thyme

$1^1/4$ teaspoons ground allspice

$1/2$ teaspoon ground black pepper

$1/4$ teaspoon ground cloves

1 cup cilantro leaves

6 servings seitan medallions (page 231)

Coconut Mashed Yams (recipe follows)

1 cup Mango Salsa or other salsa of choice for garnish

Braised collard greens or kale

To make the marinade: In a blender, blend all the ingredients to a fairly smooth, thin purée. Reserve or refrigerate for up to a week (it will separate if stored: just shake it to recombine).

To prepare the seitan: Pour half the marinade in a shallow pan and add the seitan, making sure that the seitan is coated thoroughly. Allow to marinate for $1/2$ hour to 1 hour at room temperature (if you must keep it longer, put it in the refrigerator. To grill the seitan, brush a bit of oil over a very hot grill just before you put the seitan on. Grill for 2 minutes each side. Brush with marinade after turning. To broil, place the seitan on a lightly oiled baking pan and broil until the top starts to brown. Do not turn it: This will keep it from drying out.

To serve: Heat through the remaining marinade. Place the seitan over a portion of the mashed yams and serve with the heated marinade, salsa, and greens.

NUTRITIONAL INFORMATION PER SERVING:

517 Calories (16% from fat), 34 g Protein, 75 g Carbohydrate, 9 g Fat, 0 mg Cholesterol, 483 mg Sodium, 9 g Fiber

Coconut Mashed Yams

3 large garnet yams, peeled
1 teaspoon canola oil
3 or 4 cloves garlic, minced
1 teaspoon dried thyme
1/4 teaspoon nutmeg
1 teaspoon sea salt
1/2 cup coconut milk or rice milk
   with coconut extract

Slice the yams into 2-inch cubes and store them in cold water until ready to cook. Bring 3 quarts of water to a boil, add the yams, and boil, covered, for 15 minutes or until the yam cubes are soft and easily crushed with a fork. Drain the yams in a strainer or colander, leaving them there for 5 minutes.

In a small sauté pan over medium heat, heat the oil and add the garlic and thyme. Sauté for 1 minute, or until the garlic is golden. Remove to a large mixing bowl.

Add the drained yams, nutmeg, sea salt, and 1/4 cup of the coconut milk. Mash with potato masher or large whisk until the mixture is smooth. If the mash is overly stiff or lumpy, add the remaining 1/4 cup of coconut milk. Set aside while you prepare the seitan, or store for up to 2 days refrigerated, covered, and airtight.

NUTRITIONAL INFORMATION PER SERVING:

213 Calories (21% from fat), 3 g Protein, 39 g Carbohydrate, 5 g Fat, 0 mg Cholesterol, 369 mg Sodium, 5 g Fiber

CURRY-CRUSTED TEMPEH WITH POMEGRANATE SAUCE

MAKES 6 SERVINGS

With its Turkish-Middle Eastern roots and pungent sweet and sour flavors, this sauce is a perfect match for our curry-herb crusted tempeh served over saffron basmati pilaf. Also try it with seitan or tofu. Look for pomegranate juice in natural foods stores and Middle Eastern markets.

POMEGRANATE SAUCE

8 to 10 shallots, or 1 medium red onion, sliced thin
2 cloves garlic, minced
1/2 cup dry red wine or nonalcoholic red wine
1/2 teaspoon dried thyme
1 1/2 teaspoons curry powder
1/3 teaspoon ground cinnamon
1/4 teaspoon red pepper flakes
2/3 cup orange juice
1 1/2 cups pomegranate juice
2/3 cup vegetable stock
1 tablespoon tamari soy sauce
1/2 teaspoon sea salt

CURRY CRUST

1 1/2 cups unbleached white flour
1/2 cup polenta
1 teaspoon dried thyme
1 tablespoon mild curry powder
1 teaspoon ground coriander
1/2 teaspoon whole cumin seeds
1 teaspoon paprika
1/2 teaspoon black pepper

1 cup soy milk
2 tablespoons Dijon mustard
6 4-ounce portions tempeh or seitan
4 tablespoons Canola oil

Saffron Basmati Rice Pilaf (page 104)

To make the sauce: In a medium saucepan, combine shallots, garlic, and red wine. Cook over medium heat until the wine evaporates and the shallots are soft and lightly carmelized, about 15 minutes. Add the thyme, curry powder, cinnamon, and pepper flakes and cook for 2 minutes. Add the orange juice, pomegranate juice, stock, and tamari. Reduce heat and simmer for 20 to 30 minutes, or until reduced by one third. Transfer to a blender and purée until smooth. Return to heat and cook to reduce a little more if needed to thicken the sauce. Add the salt. Set aside.

To make the crust: Combine the ingredients in a medium bowl. In a separate bowl, whisk together the soy milk and Dijon mustard. Coat the tempeh with the crust mixture, then dip into the soy milk mixture, then dredge again in the crust mixture. In a sauté pan over medium-high heat, sauté the tempeh in batches in a minimum of oil until each side is browned, about 2 minutes per side. Keep warm in a low oven or covered.

To serve: Pool 6 tablespoons of the pomegranate sauce on each plate, and place the tempeh on the sauce. Serve with Saffron-Basmati Rice Pilaf.

VARIATION:

For a lower fat version, place the tempeh on a parchment-lined baking sheet and bake in a 400° oven for 10 minutes. The crust should be lightly brown.

NUTRITIONAL INFORMATION PER SERVING:

(with oil) 572 Calories (31% from fat), 29 g Protein, 69 g Carbohydrate, 20 g Fat, 0 mg Cholesterol, 488 mg Sodium, 4 g Fiber

(without oil) 491 Calories (20% from fat), 29 g Protein, 69 g Carbohydrate, 11 g Fat, 0 mg Cholesterol, 488 mg Sodium, 4 g Fiber

ALLSPICE-ROASTED BUTTERNUT SQUASH

MAKES 6 SERVINGS

This simple yet flavorful preparation is a great accompaniment for many fall entrees.

1 small to medium butternut squash
2 teaspoons canola oil
1/2 teaspoon ground allspice
1/4 teaspoon ground cinnamon
1/4 teaspoon black pepper
1/4 teaspoon salt

Preheat a 350° oven. Cut the squash in half lengthwise and remove the seeds, then slice into 1/3 inch crescents. Toss with remaining ingredients and place on a baking sheet. Roast in the oven for 20 minutes or until the squash is cooked through, but still firm. Serve hot or at room temperature.

NUTRITIONAL INFORMATION PER SERVING OF SQUASH:

25 Calories (36% from fat), 0 g Protein, 4 g Carbohydrate, 1 g Fat, 0 mg Cholesterol, 100 mg Sodium, 1 g Fiber

TEMPEH WITH ORANGE-GINGER SAUCE

MAKES 6 SERVINGS

The simple citrus and ginger sauce is a perfect complement for the rich flavor of the tempeh and the crunch of its polenta crust. Also try the sauce with sautéed seitan. Also, try making this sauce with blood oranges or ruby grapefruit segments.

1½ pounds tempeh or seitan, cut into 12 triangles
¼ cup canola oil (optional)

HERB CRUST

1½ cups unbleached all-purpose flour
½ cup polenta
1 teaspoon dried thyme
1 teaspoon dried basil
1 teaspoon dried oregano
1 teaspoon paprika
½ teaspoon ground pepper

1 cup soy milk
2 tablespoons Dijon mustard

Orange Ginger Sauce (recipe follows)
Orange segments and chopped basil
   and/or cilantro for garnish

In a shallow bowl, mix all the herb crust ingredients together. In another shallow bowl, whisk the soy milk and mustard together. Dredge the tempeh or seitan with the crust mixture, dip into the soy milk mixture, then dredge again in the crust mixture. In a large sauté pan or skillet, cook the tempeh in batches on each side in the oil over medium-high heat until lightly browned. Keep warm in a low oven. Serve each serving of tempeh on ⅓ cup orange sauce. Garnish with orange segments and basil and/or cilantro.

VARIATION:

For an oil-free version, place the coated tempeh on a parchment-lined baking sheet and bake in a preheated 400° oven for 10 minutes. Turn the tempeh and bake for 5 minutes, or until lightly brown.

NUTRITIONAL INFORMATION PER SERVING:

(with oil) 564 Calories (32% from fat), 29 g Protein, 67 g Carbohydrate, 20 g Fat, 0 mg Cholesterol, 650 mg Sodium, 6 g Fiber

(without oil) 483 Calories (20% from fat), 20 g Protein, 67 g Carbohydrate, 11 g Fat, 0 mg Cholesterol, 650 mg Sodium, 6 g Fiber

Orange-Ginger Sauce

MAKES 2 ½ CUPS

1 red onion, cut lengthwise into thin crescents
2 cloves garlic, minced
3 cups fresh orange juice
¼ cup tamari soy sauce or Ponzu Sauce (page 87)
¼ teaspoon red pepper flakes, plus more to taste
1 tablespoon capers, drained (optional)
2 tablespoons minced fresh ginger
2 teaspoons cornstarch or arrowroot dissolved in
   3 tablespoons water
1 orange, peeled, cut into quarters lengthwise
   and thinly sliced (slices should look like
   small triangles)

In a medium saucepan, combine the onion, garlic, orange juice, tamari, pepper flakes, and capers. Simmer for 15 minutes. Add the ginger, then whisk in the cornstarch mixture and cook for 5 more minutes to thicken. Remove from the heat and stir in the orange segments.

NUTRITIONAL INFORMATION PER ⅓ CUP SERVING:

70 Calories (3% from fat), 2 g Protein, 16 g Carbohydrate, 0.2 g Fat, 0 mg Cholesterol, 509 mg Sodium, 1 g Fiber

TEMPEH SAUERBRAUTEN STYLE WITH BRAISED RED CABBAGE AND APPLES AND SPÄTZLE

MAKES 6 SERVINGS

For the past few Octobers, we've held a special Octoberfest dinner, serving German-influenced vegan cuisine with different kinds of beer, including our own house-brewed pumpkin beer. This sauce is our variation of the classic sauerbraten marinade. We serve it over sautéed tempeh with spätzle, and braised red cabbage.

SAUERBRAUTEN SAUCE

2 red onions, cut lengthwise into thin crescents
1/4 cup dry red wine or nonalcoholic red wine
2 teaspoons Sucanat
1/2 teaspoon sea salt
1 teaspoon ground allspice
1/3 teaspoon ground cloves
1/2 teaspoon ground nutmeg
4 juniper berries
2 bay leaves
3 cups dry red wine or nonalcoholic red wine
1 cup apple juice
2 cups vegetable stock
1/2 cup champagne vinegar or cider vinegar
1/4 cup golden raisins
4 ounces gingersnap cookies, finely ground
1 teaspoon minced fresh ginger
1/2 teaspoons ground pepper
1 teaspoon sea salt

1 preparation Herb-Crusted Tempeh (page 150)
Braised Red Cabbage and Apples (recipe follows)
Spätzle (recipe follows)
Allspice Roasted Butternut Squash (page 149)

To make the sauce: In a large, heavy saucepan, cook the onions with the 1/4 cup red wine, Sucanat, and salt over medium heat, stirring often, until the onions are soft and reddish brown, about 15 minutes. Add the allspice, cloves, nutmeg, juniper berries, and bay leaves. Stir well. Add the 3 cups red wine, apple juice, stock, vinegar, and the raisins.

Simmer for 30 minutes, or until the mixture is reduced by half. Whisk in the ground gingersnaps and continue whisking until the sauce starts to thicken. Add the ginger, pepper, and salt and cook for 10 minutes, or until the sauce is thick enough to coat the back of a spoon. Prepare the Herb-Crusted Tempeh, as described on page 152.

To serve, mound equal portions of the cabbage in the center of each of 6 plates. Lean the tempeh up against the cabbage and ladle 1/2 cup of the sauce around each serving of tempeh. Place a portion of spätzle next to each mound of cabbage. Serve with Allspice Roasted Butternut Squash.

NUTRITIONAL INFORMATION PER SERVING:

555 Calories (18% from fat), 26 g Protein, 88 g Carbohydrate, 11 g Fat, 0 mg Cholesterol, 651 mg Sodium, 13 g Fiber

Braised Red Cabbage and Apples

MAKES 6 SERVINGS

1 red onion, cut lengthwise into thin crescents
1 small head red cabbage, halved lengthwise, cored, and cut into thin crescents
1 cup apple juice
1 tablespoon wine vinegar (optional)
1 teaspoon sea salt
1/4 teaspoon caraway seeds
1/2 teaspoon fennel seeds
1 apple, cored and thinly sliced

(reicpe continues on next page)

(continued from previous page)

In a large saucepan, combine the onion, cabbage, apple juice, vinegar, salt, caraway, and fennel seeds. Cover and cook, stirring often, over medium heat for 15 minutes. Reduce heat, add the apple and cook another 15 minutes, or until soft and lightly browned. Serve hot or at room temperature.

NUTRITIONAL INFORMATION PER SERVING:

72 Calories (2% from fat), 2 g Protein, 16 g Carbohydrate, 0.2 g Fat, 0 mg Cholesterol, 365 mg Sodium, 3 g Fiber

Spätzle

MAKES 6 SERVINGS

This is about as simple as dumplings get: flour, water, a little leavening, and salt. Traditionally, eggs are added as a binder, but this recipe works well without them. The secret is to really whisk the batter to develop the gluten in the flour. There are two ways to make these dumplings. One method is to force the batter through the holes of a colander to yield thin, noodle-like dumplings. The other method is to cut the batter off the edge of a small cutting board into boiling water, to yield plumper dumplings (this method takes a little practice to perfect, so be warned— you might end up with one giant dumpling if the dough slips off the cutting surface into the pot). Serve these plain with plenty of sauce, or sauté them in olive oil with garlic and parsley for an addictive side dish or snack.

2 cups high-gluten unbleached white flour

1 teaspoon egg replacer

$^1/_2$ teaspoon sea salt plus more for the water

$^2/_3$ cup warm water

2 teaspoons vegetable oil

In a mixing bowl, combine the flour, egg replacer, and $^1/_2$ teaspoon of salt. Whisk in the warm water in a slow stream. Continue whisking for a few minutes to develop the gluten. The batter should be thick and stretchy. Bring 2 quarts of water to a boil and add a pinch of salt and the oil.

To make dumplings using the colander method: Holding a colander over the boiling water, push a quarter of the batter through the holes of the colander, cutting the strings of batter after they are 2 inches long. Boil for 5 to 7 minutes, until the dumplings float and their centers are cooked through. Remove to a baking sheet with a strainer or slotted spoon. Repeat until all the batter is used up.

To make dumplings using the cutting board method: Wet a small hand-held cutting board with the boiling water. Spoon on about a quarter of the batter. Using a pastry spatula or butter knife, shape the dough down the length of the board in a shape about $1^1/_2$ to 2 inches wide. Keeping the spatula wet by dipping it into the cooking water, cut off $^1/_2$-inch-thick sections of dough and push them into the cooking water. Boil for 5 to 7 minutes, until dumplings float and their centers are cooked through. Remove to a baking sheet with a strainer or slotted spoon. Repeat until all the batter is used up.

Serve the dumplings immediately: Use as a side dish, float in a soup, or sauté with olive oil, garlic, and parsley. To store the dumplings, lightly oil them to prevent their sticking together, and refrigerate in an airtight container for up to days.

NUTRITIONAL INFORMATION PER SERVING:

136 Calories (13% from fat), 1 g Protein, 33 g Carbohydrate, 2 g Fat, 0 mg Cholesterol, 180 mg Sodium, 1 g Fiber

SPRING ONION, MOREL, FRESH PEA, AND LEMON THYME RISOTTO

MAKES 6 SERVINGS

This risotto captures the essence of spring in our area. We add a little cashew cream and finish off with fresh carrot juice to intensify the spring flavors and give the dish a striking orange hue. If by chance you come upon some fresh porcini in your search for morels, don't pass them up!

4 spring onions or 8 shallots

2 cloves garlic, minced

2 tablespoons olive oil (optional)

1/4 cup dry sherry, nonalcoholic wine, or vegetable stock

8 ounces morel mushrooms, halved lengthwise

2 teaspoons minced fresh lemon thyme

1 teaspoon dried sage

2 cups Arborio rice

6 cups light vegetable stock or Mushroom Stock, simmering (page 22)

1 bunch baby carrots, cleaned, peeled, and sliced in half

1 pound English peas, shucked (2 cups)

1 cup fresh carrot juice

1 cup Cashew Cream (page 85)

1/3 teaspoon ground nutmeg

2 teaspoons sea salt

1 teaspoon ground pepper

ROASTED ONIONS AND MORELS

2 bunches spring onions, trimmed of roots and all but 1 inch of greens

12 morels

1/4 cup dry red wine, sherry, or non-alcoholic red wine

1 teaspoon olive oil (optional)

1/2 teaspoon sea salt

1/3 teaspoon ground pepper

Chopped fresh parsley and 8 sprigs of thyme or lemon thyme for garnish

To make the risotto: In a large, heavy saucepan, cook the onions, garlic, oil, and sherry over medium heat until the onions are soft and lightly caramelized, about 10 minutes. Reduce heat to medium and add the mushrooms and seasonings. Stir in the rice, mixing well to incorporate the ingredients. Add 2 cups stock and cook, stirring constantly, until the stock is absorbed. Add the carrots and peas followed by 2 cups stock. Repeat until the rice is al dente. Stir in the carrot juice, cashew cream, nutmeg, salt, and pepper. Simmer for 5 more minutes. Remove from heat and serve.

Meanwhile, to make the roasted vegetables: Preheat the oven to 400°. Toss the onions and mushrooms with the wine, oil, salt, and pepper. Place on a baking sheet and bake for 10 to 15 minutes, or until soft and fairly dry. Set aside and keep warm.

Serve the risotto topped with the roasted onions and mushrooms, sprinkled with parsley, and garnished with a thyme sprig.

VARIATION:

For an oil-free vesion, delete the olive oil and substitute corn purée for the cashew cream.

NUTRITIONAL INFORMATION PER SERVING:

(with oil) 488 Calories (22% from fat), 11 g Protein, 84 g Carbohydrate, 12 g Fat, 0 mg Cholesterol, 814 mg Sodium, 8 g Fiber

(without oil) 420 Calories (9% from fat), 9 g Protein, 87 g Carbohydrate, 4 g Fat, 0 mg Cholesterol, 805 mg Sodium, 9 g Fiber

BARLEY RISOTTO WITH CORN AND ROASTED VEGETABLES

MAKES 6 SERVINGS

The starches of the barley, enhanced with a little corn and roasted garlic purée, give the dish a creamy appeal, while the barley adds a firm, chewy texture not found in traditional risotto. The corn-basil-garlic purée added at the end gives the dish a vibrant flavor and summer-green color. The bed of baby arugula adds jolt of fresh summer flavor.

ROASTED VEGETABLES

2 leeks, white part only, cleaned and cut into 1/2-inch thick slices

1 purple Italian or Rosa Bianca eggplant, cut into 1/2-inch dice, soaked in salted water for 10 minutes, and drained

2 zucchini or summer squash, cut into 1/2-inch dice

1 red bell pepper, seeded, deribbed, and cut into 1/2-inch dice

1 yellow bell pepper, seeded, deribbed, and cut into 1/2-inch dice

8 large green olives, pitted and coarsely chopped

2 teaspoons minced garlic

1 teaspoon dried thyme

1 teaspoon dried oregano

1 tablespoon olive oil (optional)

1/4 cup dry white wine, nonalcoholic white wine, or vegetable stock

1/2 teaspoon ground pepper

CORN, BASIL, AND BRAISED GARLIC PURÉE

1 cup corn kernels (about 2 ears fresh corn)

1 bunch basil, stemmed

1/4 cup Millennium Braised Garlic (page 230)

1 cup soy milk or rice milk

BARLEY RISOTTO

1 yellow onion, finely diced

1 teaspoon minced garlic

1 stalk celery, finely diced

1 carrot, peeled and finely diced

1/2 teaspoon sea salt

1/4 cup dry sherry, nonalcoholic white wine, or vegetable stock

2 cups barley, rinsed

6 cups light vegetable stock or Tomato-Corn Stock (page 228), simmering

2 teaspoons minced fresh thyme

1 cup corn kernels

1 teaspoon sea salt

1 bunch baby arugula, stemmed

1 teaspoon minced lemon zest, plus extra for garnish

Finely diced tomatoes for garnish

To make the roasted vegetables: Preheat the oven to 450°. In a large bowl, toss all the ingredients together. Pour into an 8-inch baking dish and bake for 20 minutes, stirring, or until the eggplant and zucchini are soft and lightly browned.

To make the purée: In a blender, combine all the ingredients and purée until smooth.

To make the risotto: In a large, heavy saucepan, cook the onion, garlic, celery, carrot, salt, and sherry over high heat until the liquid evaporates, about 10 minutes. Reduce heat to medium, add the barley, and sauté until the barley is dry. Add 2 cups stock. When most of the stock is absorbed, add 2 cups stock. Repeat until barley is al dente. Add the roasted vegetables and thyme and toss with the barley. Remove from heat and fold in the corn purée, corn kernels, lemon zest, and salt.

Serve over a bed of baby arugula, topped with lemon zest and tomatoes.

NUTRITIONAL INFORMATION PER SERVING:

(with oil) 437 Calories (10% from fat), 10 g Protein, 88 g Carbohydrate, 5 g Fat, 0 mg Cholesterol, 814 mg Sodium, 11 g Fiber

(without oil) 419 Calories (6% from fat), 10 g Protein, 88 g Carbohydrate, 3 g Fat, 0 mg Cholesterol, 814 mg Sodium, 11 g Fiber

SAFFRON AND BUTTERNUT SQUASH RISOTTO

MAKES 6 SERVINGS

Chanterelle mushrooms and winter squash are a classic fall combination. Saffron and cumin flavor this risotto and give the dish a Mediterranean touch. At the restaurant we serve this with braised greens and a wedge of our cumin and rosemary chickpea flat bread.

2 yellow onions, finely diced

2 cloves garlic, minced

$1/4$ cup dry sherry, nonalcoholic wine, or
    vegetable stock

8 ounces chanterelle mushrooms, halved

4 cups finely diced butternut squash
    1 teaspoon dried thyme

2 teaspoons ground cumin

$1/3$ teaspoon saffron threads

1 cup light vegetable stock

2 cups Arborio rice

6 cups light vegetable stock or Mushroom Stock,
    simmering (page 228)

2 tomatoes, finely diced (optional)

2 teaspoons minced fresh winter savory, oregano,
    or marjoram

2 cups cooked chickpeas, chestnut limas, or
    pinto beans

1 cup corn kernels, puréed with 1 cup soy milk
    or rice milk

2 teaspoons sea salt

1 teaspoon ground pepper

In a large sauté pan or skillet, cook the onions, garlic, and sherry over high heat until the liquid evaporates. Reduce heat to medium and add the mushrooms, squash, thyme, cumin, saffron, and 1 cup vegetable stock. Simmer until most of the stock is evaporated and the squash just begins to soften. Stir in the rice, mixing well to incorporate the ingredients. Add 2 cups stock and cook, stirring frequently, until most of it is absorbed. Continue to add stock, 2 cups at a time, until all of it is absorbed or the rice is al dente. Add the tomatoes, savory, chickpeas, and corn purée. Cook for 5 more minutes, or until the risotto is thick and creamy. Add the salt and pepper. Remove from heat and serve.

NUTRITIONAL INFORMATION PER SERVING:

455 Calories (6% from fat), 13 g Protein, 94 g Carbohydrate, 3 g Fat, 0 mg Cholesterol, 813 mg Sodium, 9 g Fiber

BRUNCH AND LUNCH

We offer up a cross-section of our brunch and lunch fare. Some are simple, some are complex, and many are our renditions and adaptations of classic favorites. Don't wait 'til Sunday to try out these recipes! Some may well end up being part of your everyday repertoire.

BRUNCH

LUNCH

BRUNCH

SMOKED TEMPEH AND POTATO SAUSAGES

MAKES 8 SERVINGS

Some of our carnivorous friends claim these sausages are better than the real thing. They're perfect complements to our French toast.

8 ounces marinated, smoked tempeh, finely crumbled

1 russet or 2 yellow Finn potatoes, peeled, finely diced into $1/4$-inch cubes, boiled until soft, and drained

2 to 3 scallions, finely chopped

$1/4$ cup unbleached flour or 2 tablespoons cornstarch

1 teaspoon dried sage

$1/2$ teaspoon dried thyme

$1/4$ teaspoon ground nutmeg

$1/2$ teaspoon ground pepper

2 teaspoons tamari soy sauce

Sea salt to taste

2 tablespoons canola oil (optional)

In a large bowl, combine all the ingredients except the oil and mix well with your hands. Form the mixture into eight $1/2$-inch-thick patties. In a large sauté pan or skillet, cook in the oil over medium heat on both sides until browned. Or, cook in a dry nonstick pan. Serve warm.

NUTRITIONAL INFORMATION PER SERVING:

(with oil) 126 Calories (43% from fat), 6 g Protein, 12 g Carbohydrate, 6 g Fat, 0 mg Cholesterol, 138 mg Sodium, 1 g Fiber

(without oil) 90 Calories (20% from fat), 6 g Protein, 12 g Carbohydrate, 2 g Fat, 0 mg Cholesterol, 138 mg Sodium, 1 g Fiber

THE BENEDICT

MAKES 4 SERVINGS

Our version of eggs Benedict uses smoked tofu, sautéed spinach, and grilled onion and tomato served on focaccia, and smothered with our citrus béarnaise sauce. It will make converts of those who grew up with the traditional version.

GRILLED ONIONS AND TOMATOES

$1/4$ cup fresh orange juice

1 clove garlic, minced

$1/2$ teaspoon sea salt

1 large red onion, cut into $1/3$-inch slices

2 tomatoes, halved crosswise

2 teaspoons olive oil

SAUTÉED SPINACH

1 clove garlic, minced

2 teaspoons olive oil

4 cups packed spinach leaves

Sea salt

12 ounces smoked tofu, cut lengthwise into 4 slices

1 teaspoon canola oil

4 slices focaccia or English muffin halves, toasted

Citrus Béarnaise-Style Sauce (recipe follows)

Chopped fresh parsley or chives for garnish

Sea salt to taste

To make the grilled vegetables: Preheat the broiler. In a shallow bowl, combine the orange juice, garlic, and salt, onion, tomatoes, and oil. Let set for 10 minutes. Broil the onions and tomato halves until the onions are slightly soft and browned, about 10 minutes. Set aside.

To make the spinach: In a medium sauté pan or skillet, sauté the garlic in the oil over medium heat until lightly browned. Remove from heat and add the spinach. Toss the spinach until just wilted. Add salt to taste and set aside.

Brush the tofu slices with the oil. Broil for 2 minutes, or until the top is lightly browned and blistered. Or, if you prefer, grill the tofu for 1 or 2 minutes on each side.

For each serving, place a focaccia slice in the center of a plate. Top with a slice of tofu, a portion of wilted spinach, slices of grilled onion, and a grilled tomato half. Ladle over $^1/_3$ cup sauce and garnish with the chopped herbs. Serve immediately.

NUTRITIONAL INFORMATION PER SERVING:

213 Calories (21% from fat), 14 g Protein, 28 g Carbohydrate, 5 g Fat, 0 mg Cholesterol, 592 mg Sodium, 5 g Fiber

Citrus Béarnaise-Style Sauce

MAKES 1 $^1/_3$ CUPS

4 shallots, minced

$^2/_3$ cup dry white wine or nonalcoholic white wine

2 tablespoons champagne vinegar

2 teaspoons minced fresh thyme

$^1/_2$ teaspoon dried sage

1 tablespoon minced fresh tarragon

$^1/_2$ teaspoon ground pepper

$^1/_4$ teaspoon saffron threads

$^1/_2$ teaspoon minced lemon zest

$^1/_2$ teaspoon minced orange zest

$^1/_4$ cup fresh lemon juice

$^1/_4$ cup fresh orange juice

2 teaspoons nutritional yeast

$^1/_2$ cup Cashew Cream (page 85), or low-fat silken tofu blended with $^1/_2$ cup soy milk)

$^1/_2$ cup rice milk or soy milk

Sea salt to taste

In a medium nonreactive saucepan, bring the shallots, wine, and vinegar to a boil over medium heat. Cook to reduce by half, then add the thyme, sage, tarragon, pepper, saffron, zests, and juices. Cook to reduce by half again. Remove from heat and stir in the yeast, cashew cream, and rice milk, Add the salt. Serve warm, or store in an airtight container in the refrigerator for up to 4 days. Reheat to serve.

NUTRITIONAL INFORMATION PER SERVING:

100 Calories (36% from fat), 3 g Protein, 13 g Carbohydrate, 4 g Fat, 0 mg Cholesterol, 83 mg Sodium, 1 g Fiber

DATE-WALNUT SPREAD

MAKES 1 $^1/_4$ CUPS

Try this simple spread on morning pastries or just plain old toast.

1 cup dates, pitted

1 cup walnuts, toasted (page 234)

1 tablespoon light miso

10 ounces silken tofu

1 tablespoon maple syrup

$^1/_2$ teaspoon ground nutmeg

$^1/_2$ teaspoon sea salt

Soak the dates in warm water until soft, about 15 minutes. Drain. In a blender or food processor, combine the dates and all of the remaining ingredients and blend until smoothly puréed. Store in an airtight container in the refrigerator for up to 4 days.

NUTRITIONAL INFORMATION PER TABLESPOON:

67 Calories (40% from fat), 2 g Protein, 8 g Carbohydrate, 3 g Fat, 0 mg Cholesterol, 78 mg Sodium, 0.9 g Fiber

FLAXSEED-APPLE-BATTERED FRENCH TOAST WITH WARM APPLE COMPOTE

MAKES 4 SERVINGS

The flaxseeds in the batter give this French toast an eggy quality that's missing in a lot of vegan recipes. Don't skip the compote; it's a perfect complement and easy to make, too.

FLAXSEED-APPLE BATTER

1 tablespoon flaxseeds

$^1/_2$ cup applesauce

2 cups soy milk

$^1/_2$ teaspoon ground nutmeg

1 teaspoon ground cinnamon

$^1/_4$ teaspoon sea salt

8 thick slices whole-grain bread, stale or air-dried overnight

$^1/_4$ cup oil (optional)

Warm Apple Compote (recipe follows)

To make the batter: Combine all of the ingredients in a blender and purée until smooth. Place in a large shallow bowl.

Dip 2 slices of bread at a time into the batter to coat evenly. In a large sauté pan or skillet, cook the bread in the oil over medium heat on both sides until lightly brown. Or, cook the bread in a dry nonstick pan. Repeat with the remaining bread. Serve 2 slices per serving with $^1/_2$ cup of the apple compote.

NUTRITIONAL INFORMATION PER SERVING:

(with oil) 343 Calories (50% from fat), 10 g Protein, 33 g Carbohydrate, 19 g Fat, 0 mg Cholesterol, 398 mg Sodium, 7 g Fiber

(without oil) 217 Calories (21% from fat), 10 g Protein, 33 g Carbohydrate, 5 g Fat, 0 mg Cholesterol, 398 mg Sodium, 7 g Fiber

Warm Apple Compote

MAKES 2 CUPS

3 apples, peeled, cored, and cut into $^1/_2$-inch-thick slices

1 cup apple juice

2 tablespoons maple syrup or Sucanat

1 teaspoon minced orange zest

$^1/_4$ teaspoon ground cloves

$^1/_4$ teaspoon ground allspice

$^1/_2$ teaspoon ground cinnamon

2 teaspoons minced fresh ginger

$^1/_4$ teaspoon ground pepper

$^1/_4$ teaspoon sea salt

In a large nonreactive saucepan, combine all the ingredients and bring to a boil. Reduce to a simmer and cook until the liquid reduces to a light syrup, about 15 minutes. Serve warm. Store in an airtight container in the refrigerator for up to 4 days.

NUTRITIONAL INFORMATION PER SERVING:

116 Calories (0% from fat), 0 g Protein, 29 g Carbohydrate, 0 g Fat, 0 mg Cholesterol, 137 mg Sodium, 2 g Fiber

Polenta, Tofu, and Vegetable Quiche

MAKES 6 SERVINGS

A popular and relatively easy brunch entrée, this quiche is really a hearty layered torte.

POLENTA

4 cups water

1/2 teaspoon sea salt

1 cup polenta

1/2 teaspoon dried oregano

1/4 teaspoon minced fresh rosemary

TOFU-VEGETABLE FILLING

1 clove garlic, minced

1 bunch basil, stemmed

2 tablespoons light miso

1 1/2 pounds firm tofu, finely crumbled

2 teaspoons champagne vinegar or rice vinegar

2 teaspoons nutritional yeast

1/3 teaspoon ground nutmeg

2 leeks, white part only, washed well and
    cut into 1/2-inch-thick slices

1 clove garlic, minced

2 teaspoons olive oil, or 3 tablespoons vegetable stock

8 ounces cremini or button mushrooms, thinly sliced

1 zucchini, thinly sliced

1 teaspoon sea salt

1/4 teaspoon ground pepper

1 tomato, thinly sliced

Chopped fresh herbs such as oregano, parsley, basil,
    tarragon, and rosemary

1/2 cup fresh bread crumbs (optional)

Citrus Bernaise-Style Sauce (page 161)

To make the polenta: In a medium heavy pot, bring the water to a boil and add the salt. Gradually whisk in the polenta. Reduce heat to low, add the oregano and rosemary, and whisk for 5 minutes. Cook the polenta for another 10 minutes, or until it pulls away from the sides of the pot. Pour the polenta into an 8-inch square baking dish and smooth the top. Let cool for 1 hour.

To make the filling: Preheat the oven to 400°. In a large bowl, combine the garlic, basil, miso, tofu, vinegar, yeast, and nutmeg. Transfer half the mixture to a blender or food processor and blend until smooth. Return the purée to the bowl and set aside.

In a large sauté pan or skillet, sauté the leeks and garlic in the olive oil over medium heat until the leeks are just wilted, about 5 minutes. Add the mushrooms and zucchini and sauté until the vegetables are soft and the liquid has evaporated. Add the salt and pepper and remove from heat. Add the tofu mixture and stir well. Spread this mixture on the polenta in the baking dish.

Cover with aluminum foil and bake for 20 minutes. Remove the foil and top with the tomato slices, herbs, and bread crumbs. Bake, uncovered, for 20 minutes, or until the top is lightly browned and the filling is firm. Let cool for 15 minutes to set up the filling before serving. Slice into even portions and serve each with some sauce.

NUTRITIONAL INFORMATION PER SERVING:

333 Calories (35% from fat), 23 g Protein, 31 g Carbohydrate, 13 g Fat, 0 mg Cholesterol, 785 mg Sodium, 5 g Fiber

MILLENNIUM OAT AND WALNUT PANCAKES WITH BLUEBERRY-ORANGE SAUCE

MAKES 4 SERVINGS

Our multigrain pancakes have both texture and a delightful, nutty flavor, thanks to the walnuts. Make these a weekend staple with our quick blueberry-orange sauce.

1 cup unbleached all-purpose flour

1/2 cup whole-wheat flour

1/2 cup corn flour

1/3 cup walnuts, toasted (see page 234) and crushed in a plastic bag with a rolling pin

1/4 cup rolled oats

2 teaspoons Sucanat or unrefined sugar (optional)

1/4 teaspoon ground allspice

1/2 teaspoon ground cinnamon

1/4 teaspoon sea salt

1 teaspoon baking powder

3 cups soy milk or rice milk

1 teaspoon champagne vinegar or rice vinegar

Blueberry-Orange Sauce (recipe follows)

In a large bowl, mix the flours, walnuts, oats, Sucanat, allspice, cinnamon, salt, and baking powder together well. In a medium bowl, mix the soy milk and vinegar together. Add the liquid ingredients to the dry ingredients and whisk until well incorporated. The resulting batter should be a little thicker than heavy cream.

Pour 1/2 cup batter per pancake onto a lightly oiled nonstick sauté pan or skillet and cook until lightly browned on each side. Serve with blueberry-orange sauce.

NUTRITIONAL INFORMATION PER SERVING (WITHOUT SAUCE):

379 Calories (26% from fat), 14 g Protein, 56 g Carbohydrate, 11 g Fat, 0 mg Cholesterol, 304 mg Sodium, 8 g Fiber

Blueberry-Orange Sauce

MAKES 2 CUPS

2 cups fresh or frozen blueberries

1/2 cup apple juice

1/2 cup fresh orange juice

1 teaspoon minced orange zest

1 tablespoon Sucanat or unrefined sugar

1 teaspoon minced fresh ginger

Place all the ingredients in a nonreactive saucepan. Cook over medium heat, stirring occasionally, for 15 minutes, or until the blueberries are soft and the remaining liquid is syrupy. Serve warm.

NUTRITIONAL INFORMATION PER 1/4 CUP SERVING:

40 Calories (0% from fat), 0 g Protein, 10 g Carbohydrate, 0 g Fat, 0 mg Cholesterol, 3 mg Sodium, 1 g Fiber

LUNCH

MOROCCAN CREPES

MAKES 6 SERVINGS

In this popular lunch entrée, sautéed vegetables sauced with our Moroccan marinade and rolled in a chickpea-flour crepe, are served with a dollop of raita and our Saffron-Basmati Rice Pilaf.

CHICKPEA CREPES

$2/3$ cup chickpea flour

$1/3$ cup unbleached all-purpose flour

$1/2$ teaspoon baking powder

$1/2$ teaspoon sea salt

$1/4$ teaspoon ground pepper

$1/2$ teaspoon cumin seeds, toasted (see page 234)

$1/4$ teaspoon ground turmeric (optional)

2 tablespoons chopped fresh cilantro (optional)

$1/2$ cups soy milk or rice milk, plus extra to thin

2 tablespoons canola oil

FILLING

1 red onion, cut lengthwise into thin crescents

2 cloves garlic, minced

2 teaspoons olive oil or vegetable stock

$1/2$ pounds seasonal vegetables cut into bite-sized pieces (carrots, peppers, broccoli and cauliflower florets, fresh peas and corn, blanched cubed winter squash and root vegetables)

1 cup cooked chickpeas or another firm bean (optional)

$2/3$ cup Moroccan Marinade (page 13)

$1/2$ cup Tofu, Mint, and Cilantro Raita (page 176)

To make the crepes: In a medium bowl, combine all the dry ingredients and add the $1^1/2$ cups soy milk. Whisk until the batter is smooth and the consistency of heavy cream. Add more soy milk if batter thickens on standing.

Heat a 9-inch nonstick crepe pan or shallow sauté pan over medium-high heat. Wipe or spray with a thin layer of oil. Pour $1/3$ cup of the batter into the pan, turning the pan as you pour to evenly coat it with batter. When the edges of the crepe are light brown and crisp, carefully flip the crepe and cook the other side until firm. Transfer to a plate and keep warm, covered. Repeat with the remaining batter to make 6 crepes.

To make the filling: In a large sauté pan or skillet, sauté the onion and garlic in the oil over medium-high heat until lightly browned, about 5 to 7 minutes. Add the seasonal vegetables and chickpeas and sauté until they just start to soften, about 5 minutes. Add the Moroccan Marinade and sauté until the vegetables are just tender, another 2 to 3 minutes.

Place 1 cup vegetables on the bottom half of each crepe and fold the top of the crepe over the vegetables. Serve with a dollop of tofu raita.

NUTRITIONAL INFORMATION PER FILLED CREPE:

293 Calories (15% from fat), 11 g Protein, 51 g Carbohydrate, 5 g Fat, 0 mg Cholesterol, 819 mg Sodium, 9 g Fiber

NUTRITIONAL INFORMATION PER CREPE:

118 Calories (46% from fat), 4 g Protein, 12 g Carbohydrate, 6 g Fat, 0 mg Cholesterol, 257 mg Sodium, 1 g Fiber

SEITAN GYRO

MAKES 4 SERVINGS

Serve this sandwich to nonvegetarians and see how amazed they are that it's vegetarian. Seitan grilled with Moroccan marinade and wrapped in warm flat bread with grilled onions and tofu raita is so good and so satisfying.

1 recipe Millennium Pizza Dough (page 92)

8 Marinated Seitan Medallions (page 231)

1 large red onion, cut into 1/3-inch slices

1/2 cup Moroccan Marinade (page 13)

2 teaspoons olive oil (optional)

2 cups Tofu, Mint, and Cilantro Raita (page 176)

1 cup Millennium Tomato Relish (page 177)
    or salsa of choice

Leaves from 1 head romaine lettuce, shredded

On a lightly floured board, roll out each ball of dough to a 10-inch circle. Wrap in aluminum foil and keep warm in a low oven.

Preheat the broiler. Place the seitan and onion in a shallow bowl, add the marinade and oil, and turn the seitan and onion to coat evenly. Let sit for 10 minutes. Broil the seitan and onions until the onions soften and the seitan is browned and heated through, about 5 minutes. Cut the seitan into strips and coarsely chop the onion. Bake or grill the dough in a 350° oven for 7 to 10 minutes (see pizza procedures, page 93).

Place each flatbread on a work surface and spread with 2 tablespoons raita, then 1 tablespoon tomato relish. Top with the shredded romaine, seitan strips, and broiled onion, Roll the flat bread around the filling and cut in half on a diagonal. Serve the remaining raita and tomato relish alongside.

NUTRITIONAL INFORMATION PER SERVING:

391 Calories (7% from fat), 22 g Protein, 69 g Carbohydrate, 3 g Fat, 0 mg Cholesterol, 723 mg Sodium, 5 g Fiber

SMOKED PORTOBELLO SANDWICHES

MAKES 4 SERVINGS

A favorite since day one of the restaurant, this recipe takes all the components of our grilled smoked portobello mushroom appetizer and stuffs it between house-made focaccia for substantial sandwiches. Add a couple of slices of fresh tomato and some crisp romaine and you're set.

1/2 cup Moroccan Marinade (page 13)

2 teaspoons extra-virgin olive oil (optional)

4 smoked portobello mushrooms (page 233)

1/2 cup Herb-Tofu Aioli (page 173)

4 x 4-inch slices focaccia or 8 lengthwise
    French baguette slices, toasted

1/4 cup Red Onion Marmalade (page 24)

16 thin tomato slices

8 romaine lettuce leaves

To grill the mushrooms, combine the marinade with the oil (if using) in a shallow bowl. Add the mushrooms, grill for 2 to 3 minutes per side, or broil for 4 to 5 minutes, until heated through.

For each sandwich, spread 2 tablespoons aioli on each of 2 slices of focaccia. Cut the mushroom in thin diagonal slices and fan out over 1 slice of focaccia. Top with 1 tablespoon red onion marmalade, then 2 slices tomato and a romaine leaf.

NUTRITIONAL INFORMATION PER SERVING:

174 Calories (10% from fat), 8 g Protein, 31 g Carbohydrate, 2 g Fat, 0 mg Cholesterol, 420 mg Sodium, 3 g Fiber

EMILIANO'S POTATO BURRITO WITH ANASAZI BEAN CHILI

MAKES 4 SERVINGS

This was originally a staff lunch that our dishwasher Emiliano would request. It was so well liked we had to put it on the menu. It's simple— just sautéed yellow Finn potatoes and onions with Anasazi bean chili and mango salsa rolled in a large whole-wheat tortilla.

YELLOW FINN POTATO SAUTÉ

1 yellow onion, cut into $1/2$-inch dice

1 clove garlic, minced

1 tablespoon olive oil

1 red bell pepper, seeded, deribbed, and cut into $1/2$-inch dice

4 yellow Finn potatoes, cut into $1/2$-inch dice

$1/2$ cup water

Sea salt and freshly ground pepper to taste

4 large whole-wheat tortillas, warmed in the oven

$1/4$ cup Garlic-Herb Aioli (page 173) or 4 tablespoons

2 cups Anasazi Bean Chili (recipe follows)

1 cup Mango Salsa (page 178)

$1/2$ cup chopped cilantro

1 cup shredded romaine lettuce

To make the potato sauté: In a large saucepan, sauté the onions and garlic in the olive oil over medium heat until the onions are softened, about 10 minutes. Add the red pepper and potatoes, then the water. Cover and cook until the potatoes are just soft and lightly browned, about 5 minutes. Remove the cover and cook until the potato mixture is dry, about another 5 minutes. Remove from heat. Add salt and pepper.

Wrap the tortillas in foil and warm them in a 350° oven for 5 minutes. For each burrito, spread 1 tablespoon aioli over a tortilla. Spread $1/2$ cup potato sauté over the tortilla, then $1/2$ cup Anasazi Bean Chili. Top with 2 tablespoons salsa and some chopped cilantro and romaine lettuce. Roll in the sides of the tortilla, then roll it into a cylinder. Cut in half and serve with the remaining Mango Salsa.

NUTRITIONAL INFORMATION PER SERVING:

512 Calories (14% from fat), 15 g Protein, 95 g Carbohydrate, 8 g Fat, 0 mg Cholesterol, 980 mg Sodium, 13 g Fiber

Anasazi Bean Chili

MAKES 2 CUPS

2 tablespoons mild ancho chile powder

2 tablespoons ground cumin

1 yellow onion, cut into $1/2$-inch dice

2 cloves garlic, minced

$1/4$ cup vegetable stock or water

1 jalapeno chile, minced

1 teaspoon dried oregano, preferably Mexican

2 bay leaves (optional)

1 cup tomato purée

1 cup vegetable stock or water

2 cups cooked anasazi or pinto beans

Sea salt to taste

Toast the chile and cumin in a dry skillet over high heat for about 30 seconds, until the spices darken slightly and start to smoke. Remove from the pan and set aside. In a medium, heavy saucepan, sauté the onions and garlic in vegetable stock over medium heat until softened, about 5 to 7 minutes. Add the jalapeno, toasted spices, oregano, and bay leaves. Sauté for 2 minutes. Add the tomato purée, stock, and beans. Cover and simmer for 20 minutes. Add salt. Serve warm.

NUTRITIONAL INFORMATION PER $1/2$ CUP SERVING:

192 Calories (5% from fat), 10 g Protein, 38 g Carbohydrate, 1 g Fat, 0 mg Cholesterol, 273 mg Sodium, 11 g Fiber

ROASTED EGGPLANT AND TOMATO SANDWICHES WITH ARUGULA PESTO

MAKES 4 SERVINGS

A great summer sandwich with the sharp zing of arugula pesto.

2 Italian globe eggplants cut into 1/2-inch slices
Salt for sprinkling
2 teaspoons olive oil
1 teaspoon balsamic vinegar
1 teaspoon Sucanat or unrefined sugar
1/4 teaspoon sea salt
1/4 teaspoon dried oregano

4 tablespoons Arugula Pesto (page 83)
Four 4 x 8-inch slices focaccia, cut in half
    horizontally, or country bread slides, toasted
4 tablespoons Garlic-Herb Aioli (page 173)
Thin tomato slices
Thin red onion slices
4 romaine lettuce leaves

Preheat the oven to 400°. Line a baking sheet with parchment paper. Sprinkle salt on the eggplant and let sit in a colander for 5 minutes. Rinse. In a shallow dish, toss the eggplant slices with the remaining ingredients. Let sit for 10 minutes. Place the eggplant slices on the prepared pan and bake for 15 to 20 minutes, or until soft. Remove from the oven.

For each sandwich, place 1 tablespoon pesto on the cut half of a focaccia slice. Place 1 tablespoon aioli on the top half. Place 1 eggplant slice on the bottom half and top with tomato, onion, and lettuce.

NUTRITIONAL INFORMATION PER SERVING:

245 Calories (33% from fat), 8 g Protein, 33 g Carbohydrate, 9 g Fat, 0 mg Cholesterol, 507 mg Sodium, 4 g Fiber

SALSAS, CHUTNEYS, AND RELISHES

Here are the condiments and garnishes that finish a dish. Some help to tie all the elements of a dish together while others add a new contrasting element, whether flavor or texture, to the finished recipe.

MILLENNIUM TOFU SPREAD

MAKES ABOUT 2¹/₂ CUPS

When you sit down for a meal at Millennium, this spread and some bread are one of the first things to greet you. Tofu spread seems to have developed its own cult following, and why not? With its mixture of caramelized onions and garlic, herbs, and miso, it's a lot more flavorful than butter. It can even be served as a dip or pâté at a party. This recipe is easily doubled.

1 yellow onion, cut lengthwise into thin crescents

3 cloves garlic, peeled but left whole

1 teaspoon sea salt

¹/₄ cup dry white wine, nonalcoholic white wine, sherry, or vegetable stock

¹/₂ teaspoon dried thyme

¹/₂ teaspoon dried sage

¹/₂ teaspoon minced fresh rosemary

¹/₂ teaspoon dried basil

¹/₂ teaspoon dried oregano

³/₄ teaspoon ground pepper

¹/₄ teaspoon ground nutmeg

¹/₂ cup light vegetable stock or water

12 ounces firm tofu, drained

¹/₄ cup light miso

In a large sauté pan or skillet, cook the onions, garlic, salt, and wine over medium heat until the onions just start to soften, about 5 minutes. Add the thyme, sage, rosemary, basil, oregano, pepper, nutmeg, and vegetable stock. Cover and cook until the liquid evaporates and the onion and garlic are very soft and light brown, about 20 minutes. Remove from heat and let cool to room temperature.

Crumble the tofu into a medium bowl. Add the miso and the onion mixture and blend well. In a food processor, process this mixture, in batches if necessary, until smooth. Serve at room temperature or chilled.

NUTRITIONAL INFORMATION PER TABLESPOON:

33 Calories (27% from fat), 2 g Protein, 4 g Carbohydrate, 1 g Fat, 0 mg Cholesterol, 294 mg Sodium, 0.3 g Fiber

GARLIC-HERB AIOLI

MAKES 2 CUPS

12.3 ounces silken tofu

1/4 cup Millennium Braised Garlic (page 230)

2 tablespoons light miso

1/2 cup fresh lemon juice

1 teaspoon minced lemon zest

1 tablespoon capers, drained

1/2 teaspoon dried oregano

2 tablespoons coarsely chopped parsley

1/2 teaspoon dried dill (optional)

1 tablespoon fresh tarragon or
    1 teaspoon dried tarragon (optional)

2 teaspoons nutritional yeast (optional)

1/4 teaspoon cayenne pepper (optional)

1/2 teaspoon ground pepper

1/2 teaspoon sea salt

2 tablespoons water

In a blender or food processor, combine all the ingredients, adding more water as necessary to thin to the consistency of mayonnaise. Store in an airtight container in the refrigerator for up to 1 week.

NUTRITIONAL INFORMATION PER
2 TABLESPOON SERVING AIOLI:

  35 Calories (43% from fat), 3 g Protein, 2 g Carbohydrate, 1.7 g Fat, 0 mg Cholesterol, 179 mg Sodium, 0.3 g Fiber

VARIATIONS:

SAFFRON TOFU AIOLI: Add 1/4 to 1/2 teaspoon saffron threads soaked in 2 tablespoons of water.

DIJON TOFU SPREAD: Add 2 to 3 tablespoons Dijon mustard.

ROASTED RED PEPPER TOFU AIOLI: Add 2 peeled roasted red peppers or pimientos.

DILL AND GREEN PEPPERCORN
TOFU AIOLI: Add 2 tablespoons minced fresh dill, 2 teaspoons green peppercorns, and 2 chopped scallions.

CHILE TOFU AIOLI: Add 2 teaspoons toasted ancho chile powder, 1/2 teaspoon ground cumin, 2 cloves garlic, and cayenne to taste.

ROMESCO SAUCE

MAKES 1 1/2 CUPS

Our version of this Spanish sauce can be used as a dipping sauce, a flavorful complement to our savory tortes, and as a dressing for pasta, grain, or bean salads.

1/2 cup slivered almonds, toasted (see page 234)

1 clove garlic, minced

2 tablespoons Millennium Braised Garlic
    (page230), optional

1 red bell pepper or pimiento, roasted and peeled
    (page 235)

2 tablespoons champagne vinegar or other
    light vinegar

1/2 teaspoon ground cumin

1/2 teaspoon ground caraway seed

2 teaspoons sea salt

1 cup water

In a blender, purée all the ingredients together until thoroughly smooth. Store in an airtight container in the refrigerator for 1 week.

NUTRITIONAL INFORMATION PER
TABLESPOON:

  21 Calories (68% from fat), 0.6 g Protein, 1 g Carbohydrate, 1.6 g Fat, 0 mg Cholesterol, 210 mg Sodium, 0.4 g Fiber

CHIPOTLE PASTE

MAKES 1 CUP

While you can usually buy canned chipotle chiles in red sauce in Latino markets and some supermarkets, you can easily make your own—without refined sugar and preservatives, and adjusted to your tastes with different kinds of chiles. Dried chipotles are available in Latino markets as well as specialty food stores. Try little dab of this whenever you want to add heat along with a subtle, smoky nuance.

4 dried chipotle chiles, stemmed
$1/2$ cup mild tomato sauce or tomato purée
$1/2$ cup water
1 tablespoon champagne vinegar or another light vinegar
$1^1/2$ tablespoons Sucanat or sugar

In a medium saucepan, combine all the ingredients and bring to a boil. Cover and simmer for 30 minutes. Remove the cover and simmer for 5 minutes. Remove from heat and let cool to room temperature. In a blender, purée the mixture until smooth. Store in an airtight container in the refrigerator for up to 2 weeks.

NUTRITIONAL INFORMATION PER TABLESPOON:

13 Calories (0% from fat), 0.3 g Protein, 3 g Carbohydrate, 0 g Fat, 0 mg Cholesterol, 20 mg Sodium, 0.2 g Fiber

RED BEET REDUCTION

MAKES $1/2$ CUP

This brilliant red syrup is an outstanding enhancement to many dishes where presentation is important.

1 red beet, peeled and sliced thin
2 cups vegetable stock or water
2 tablespoons balsamic vinegar
$1/2$ teaspoon sea salt
$1/4$ teaspoon caraway seeds
$1/4$ teaspoon coriander seeds
$1/4$ teaspoon fennel seeds
$1/4$ teaspoon red pepper flakes or ground pepper (optional)
$1/2$ teaspoon cornstarch, dissolved in 2 tablespoons water

In a medium nonreactive saucepan, combine all the ingredients except the cornstarch mixture and bring to a boil. Cover and simmer until the beets are soft, about 20 minutes. Strain the mixture through a fine-meshed sieve. Discard the solids and return the strained liquid to medium low heat. Simmer until reduced to about $1/2$ cup. Gradually whisk in the cornstarch solution. Simmer for 1 minute and remove from heat. Use warm or at room temperature. Store in an airtight container in the refrigerator for up to 1 week.

NUTRITIONAL INFORMATION PER TEASPOON:

4 Calories (6% from fat), 0 g Protein, 1 g Carbohydrate, 0 g Fat, 0 mg Cholesterol, 52 mg Sodium, 0 g Fiber

CASHEW SOUR CREAM

MAKES 1 CUP

Use this cream to add a little more body and richness to a dish, especially a soup or stew. A little, usually a few teaspoons, goes a long way. The variations can be endless, from the addition of chile, cumin, and roasted garlic for Mediterranean dishes, to sesame seeds and wasabi for miso soup.

1/2 cup raw cashews
2 teaspoons light miso
1/4 cup fresh lemon juice
1/4 teaspoon ground nutmeg
1 cup water
Sea salt to taste

In a blender, combine the cashews, miso, lemon juice, nutmeg, and 1/2 cup of the water. Blend to make a thick, coarse purée. With the machine running, gradually add the remaining water and blend until smooth and the consistency of whipped cream. Add salt to taste. Add more water to make a thinner cream for soup garnishes. Store in an airtight container in the refrigerator for up to 4 days.

VARIATIONS:

TARRAGON-LEMON CASHEW SOUR CREAM: Add an additional 1/4 cup fresh lemon juice and 1/2 bunch fresh tarragon, stemmed.

CILANTRO-MINT CASHEW SOUR CREAM: Add 1/2 bunch stemmed cilantro and 1/2 bunch stemmed mint and up to 1/2 cup water.

BASIL-GARLIC CASHEW SOUR CREAM: Delete the lemon juice and add 1/2 bunch stemmed basil and 1 clove garlic.

SAFFRON-GARLIC CASHEW SOUR CREAM: Steep 1/4 teaspoon saffron threads in 3 tablespoons warm water. Add to main recipe ingredients along with 1 clove garlic.

CHILE CASHEW SOUR CREAM: Add 2 teaspoons toasted mild chile powder or paprika, 1 teaspoon toasted ground cumin, and 2 tablespoons Millenium Braised Garlic (page 230) along with additional water to thin.

CHIPOTLE CASHEW SOUR CREAM: Add 1 to 2 tablespoons of our Chipotle Paste (page 174).

HORSERADISH CASHEW SOUR CREAM: Add 2 teaspoons prepared white horseradish.

SESAME AND WASABI CASHEW SOUR CREAM: Delete 2 tablespoons cashews and replace with 2 tablespoons toasted sesame seeds. Add up to 2 teaspoons wasabi paste and 1 teaspoon grated fresh ginger, if desired, plus additional water to thin.

LOW-FAT SOUR CREAM: Replace the cashews with 1/2 cup (6 ounces) low-fat silken tofu.

NUTRITIONAL INFORMATION PER 2-TEASPOON SERVING (ALL VARIATIONS EXCEPT LOW-FAT):

19 Calories (66% from fat), 0.5 g Protein, 1.2 g Carbohydrate, 1.4 g Fat, 0 mg Cholesterol, 36 mg Sodium, 0.3 g Fiber

NUTRITIONAL INFORMATION PER 2-TEASPOON SERVING (LOW-FAT VERSION):

6 Calories (15% from fat), 0.5 g Protein, 1 g Carbohydrate, 0.1 g Fat, 0 mg Cholesterol, 24 mg Sodium, 0 g Fiber

TOFU, MINT, AND CILANTRO RAITA

MAKES 1 CUP

This is our version of the Indian yogurt-based condiment. We use it as a garnish on some of our entrées. Try it stirred into curries and soups.

6 ounces silken tofu

1/3 cup fresh lime juice

1 tablespoon light miso

1/2 bunch mint, stemmed

1/2 bunch cilantro, stemmed

Sea salt to taste

1/2 apple, peel on, cored and finely diced

1/2 English cucumber, finely diced (optional)

In a blender or food processor, combine the tofu, lime juice, miso, mint, and cilantro. Blend until smooth. Add salt. Fold in the apple and cucumber. Refrigerate in an airtight container for up to 4 days.

NUTRITIONAL INFORMATION PER TABLESPOON:

14 Calories (26% from fat), 0.7 g Protein, 2 g Carbohydrate, 0.4 g Fat, 0 mg Cholesterol, 46 mg Sodium, 0.5 g Fiber

ROASTED PEPPER HARISSA

MAKES 1 CUP

2 red bell peppers or pimientos, roasted and peeled (see page 235)

1 serrano or jalapeno chile, roasted and peeled (see page 235)

1/3 cup water

1 small clove garlic, minced

1/4 cup fresh lime juice

1/2 teaspoon caraway seeds, toasted and ground (see page 234)

1/2 teaspoon cumin seeds, toasted and ground (see page 234)

1/2 teaspoons sea salt

In a blender, combine all the ingredients and blend until smooth. Store in an airtight container for up to 1 week.

NUTRITIONAL INFORMATION PER TEASPOON:

4 Calories (0% from fat), 0 g Protein, 1 g Carbohydrate, 0 g Fat, 0 mg Cholesterol, 26 mg Sodium, 0.1 g Fiber

ROASTED TOMATILLO SALSA

MAKES 1 CUP

6 ounces tomatillos, husked

1/2 yellow onion

2 cloves garlic

2 serrano chiles

Juice of 2 limes

1 teaspoon dried oregano, preferably Mexican

1/2 bunch cilantro, stemmed

1 teaspoon sea salt

Preheat the broiler. Place the tomatillos, onion, garlic, and chiles on a baking pan. Place in the broiler and roast, turning them frequently, until about half of each vegetable is blackened. Remove from the broiler and let cool to the touch. If you like, remove some of the charred skin.

Transfer the vegetables to a blender or food processor with the remaining ingredients and pulse until uniformly diced. Refrigerate in an airtight container for up to 1 week.

NUTRITIONAL INFORMATION PER
2-TABLESPOON SERVING:

10 Calories (9% from fat), 0.2 g Protein, 2 g Carbohydrate, 0.1 g Fat, 0 mg Cholesterol, 158 mg Sodium, 0.2 g Fiber

CARROT-HABANERO SALSA

MAKES 1 1/2 CUPS

This salsa was created for a special chile dinner at the restaurant. It's very easy and very hot.

1 habanero or Scotch bonnet chile, seeded if you
    want to lessen the burn
1/2 red onion, chopped
2 carrots, peeled, and chopped
1/2 cup fresh lime juice
2 teaspoons Sucanat or fructose
2 tablespoons minced fresh oregano
2 tablespoons minced fresh mint leaves
1/4 cup minced fresh cilantro
1 teaspoon sea salt

In a food processor, combine all the ingredients and process until the carrots are finely minced. Store in an airtight container in the refrigerator for up to 4 days.

NUTRITIONAL INFORMATION PER
2-TABLESPOON SERVING:

14 Calories (0% from fat), 0.2 g Protein, 3 g Carbohydrate, 0 g Fat, 0 mg Cholesterol, 184 mg Sodium, 0.4 g Fiber

MILLENNIUM TOMATO RELISH

MAKES 1 1/2 CUPS

Our tomato relish is part Mexican salsa and part Italian salsa cruda. We add diced apple for a sweet crunch and capers for a pungent zip, giving the relish complex flavors and textures.

1/2 red onion, finely diced
3 tomatoes, finely diced
4 tomatillos, husked and finely diced
1 apple, peeled, cored, and finely diced
1 teaspoon minced lemon zest
1/3 cup fresh lemon juice
1 tablespoon capers, drained
1 jalapeno chile, minced
1 bell pepper, roasted, peeled, and minced
    (see page 235)
1 teaspoon dried oregano
2 tablespoons minced fresh basil
2 tablespoons minced fresh parsley
2 teaspoons sea salt

In a medium bowl, toss all the ingredients together. Mix well and serve. Store in the refrigerator for up to 4 days.

NUTRITIONAL INFORMATION PER
2-TABLESPOON SERVING:

24 Calories (8% from fat), 0.6 g Protein, 5 g Carbohydrate, 0.2 g Fat, 0 mg Cholesterol, 448 mg Sodium, 1 g Fiber

Mango Salsa

MAKES 1 CUP

This is indispensable with our Plantain Torte (page 28).

1 ripe yet firm mango, peeled, cut from pit, and
  finely diced
1 tomato, finely diced
1/2 red onion, finely chopped
1/3 cup fresh lime juice
1 serrano chile, minced
1/2 teaspoon dried oregano
2 tablespoons minced fresh cilantro
1 teaspoon sea salt

In a small bowl, toss all of the ingredients together. Store in an airtight container in the refrigerator for up to 2 days.

NUTRITIONAL INFORMATION PER
2-TABLESPOON SERVING:

27 Calories (3% from fat), 0.4 g Protein, 6 g Carbohydrate, 0.1 g Fat, 0 mg Cholesterol, 269 mg Sodium, 1 g Fiber

VARIATIONS:

Add 1/2 cup diced peeled jicama or 1/2 cup fresh corn kernels. Also try it with 1/2 roasted banana in place of the tomato.

Quick Fig Relish

MAKES 1 CUP

Very simple, yet very exotic. Serve this with our Moroccan Filo Crescents, or with our Tempeh with Pomegranate Sauce.

6 fresh Mission figs, cut into quarters
1/4 teaspoon fennel seed, toasted
1/2 teaspoon crack black pepper
1/2 teaspoon sea salt
3 tablespoons balsamic vinegar

In a small bowl, combine all the ingredients. Let sit for 10 minutes. Serve the same day it is made.

NUTRITIONAL INFORMATION PER 1/4 CUP:

58 Calories (0% from fat), 0.4 g Protein, 14 g Carbohydrate, 0 g Fat, 0 mg Cholesterol, 268 mg Sodium, 3 g Fiber

Cranberry-Mandarin Relish

MAKES 2 CUPS

This is our Thanksgiving cranberry sauce. Try it with potato or butternut squash pancakes.

4 mandarin oranges
3 cups (one 12-ounce bag) cranberries
2 cups apple juice
1/4 cup Sucanat or unrefined sugar
1 teaspoon ground allspice
1/4 teaspoon ground nutmeg
1 tablespoon minced fresh ginger
1/4 teaspoon red pepper flakes
1 teaspoon grated mandarin orange zest
1/4 teaspoon sea salt

Peel the oranges by hand or with a knife, and separate the segments. In a heavy, medium saucepan, combine the cranberries, apple juice, and Sucanat. Bring to a boil and simmer until the cranberries soften and the liquid becomes syrupy, about 20 minutes. Add the allspice, nutmeg, ginger, pepper flakes, oranges, orange zest, and salt and remove from the heat. Let cool or serve chilled. Store in an airtight container in the refrigerator for up to 1 week.

NUTRITIONAL INFORMATION PER ¹/4 CUP:

98 Calories (3% from fat), 0.7 g Protein, 23 g Carbohydrate, 0.3 g Fat, 0 mg Cholesterol, 87 mg Sodium, 2 g Fiber

PUMPKIN-HABANERO SAUCE

MAKES 2 CUPS

This ultra-spicy and flavorful condiment is not for the faint of heart. We let it sit out and naturally ferment for a week before boiling it and using or storing it. Try it in the early fall when the first of the pumpkins and last of the chiles are around. Freeze a batch so you can spice up your life in the dead of winter.

1 cup pumpkin purée (see page 230)
2 habanero or Scotch bonnet chiles, seeded if you want to reduce the heat
1 apple, peeled, cored, and chopped
¹/2 teaspoon ground allspice
¹/4 teaspoon cloves
1 tablespoon sea salt
1 cup water

In a blender, purée all of the ingredients until smooth. Place in an airtight container and cover.

Let sit at room temperature for 1 week to 10 days to sour and ferment. In a small pan, boil the sauce for 5 minutes. Let cool before serving. Store in an airtight container in the refrigerator for up to 2 weeks.

NUTRITIONAL INFORMATION PER TEASPOON:

4 Calories (0% from fat), 0 g Protein, 1 g Carbohydrate, 0 g Fat, 0 mg Cholesterol, 79 mg Sodium, 0 g Fiber

SWEET AND SPICY PUMPKIN SPREAD

MAKES 1 CUP

We serve this in the fall as a part of our antipasto platter. Spread it on bread—it's delicious. It makes a great addition to any holiday table.

1 cup pumpkin purée (see page 230)
¹/2 cup Caramelized Onions (page 229)
8 ounces firm tofu
2 tablespoons light miso
1 tablespoon maple syrup
¹/2 teaspoon ground allspice
¹/4 teaspoon ground cloves
¹/2 teaspoon nutmeg
1 teaspoon curry powder
¹/4 teaspoon cayenne pepper
Sea salt to taste

In a blender or food processor, combine all of the ingredients except the salt and purée until smooth. Stir in the salt. Store in an airtight container in the refrigerator for up to 2 days.

NUTRITIONAL INFORMATION PER TABLESPOON:

29 Calories (31% from fat), 2 g Protein, 3 g Carbohydrate, 1 g Fat, 0 mg Cholesterol, 115 mg Sodium, 0.4 g Fiber

Dijon Mustard-Lentil Sauce

Makes 3 cups

With this sauce, I prefer using a red ale with a strong bitter hop flavor; stouts and heavy Belgian beers also work well. Any good beer of your choice will do—except maybe fruit beer.

2 tablespoons cornstarch
1 large yellow onion, cut into 1/3-inch dice
1 tablespoon olive oil (optional)
1/4 cup sherry or white wine
1/2 bunch fresh thyme leaves, or 2 teaspoons dried
1 twelve-ounce bottle of beer or non-alcoholic beer
1 cup apple juice
2/3 cup dijon mustard
3 cups light vegetable stock
1 cup cooked French lentils
1/4 bunch fresh tarragon, leaves only
1/2 teaspoon ground black pepper
    (or half black pepper, half green pepper)
2 teaspoons salt

Dissolve the corn starch in 1/4 cup cold water and set aside. In a saucepan over medium heat, cook the onion, oil, and sherry until the onions are lightly caramelized, about 15 minutes. Add the thyme leaves and stir into the onions. Add the beer, apple juice, mustard, and stock. Simmer until reduced by one third, about 20 minutes. Add the lentils, tarragon, pepper, and salt, and whisk in the cornstarch until the sauce is thick enough to coat the back of a spoon. Simmer 5 more minutes, remove from heat, and use or set aside. Will keep up to a week in the refrigerator.

Nutritional information per tablespoon:

(with oil) 25 Calories (36% from fat), 1 g Protein, 3 g Carbohydrate, 1 g Fat, 0 mg Cholesterol, 188 mg Sodium, 0.3 g Fiber

(without oil) 16 Calories (0% from fat), 1 g Protein, 3 g Carbohydrate, 0 g Fat, 0 mg Cholesterol, 188 mg Sodium, 0.3 g Fiber

Preserved Lemons

Makes 24 wedges

This Middle Eastern staple is also a staple in our kitchen. Preserved lemons add a pungent bite to relishes and salsas as well as to stews and sautés. It takes only 5 days to ferment the lemons.

4 lemons, each cut into 6 wedges
1/2 cup fresh lemon juice
1 tablespoon sea salt

Place the lemon wedges in a clean 1 quart heavy glass or ceramic container with a large opening. Add the lemon juice and salt and mix well with the lemons. Add warm water to cover the lemons. Cover the surface of the mixture with plastic wrap and top with a saucer to weigh down the lemons and keep them submerged.

Let sit at room temperature for 5 days. After 5 days the lemons will be ready for use, though 3 to 4 more days will make softer, less pungent lemons.

To store, refrigerate the preserved lemons in their brine for up to 2 weeks. To use, rinse the lemon wedges of excess brine and salt.

Nutritional information per wedge:

8 Calories (0% from fat), 0 g Protein, 2 g Carbohydrate, 0 g Fat, 0 mg Cholesterol, 125 mg Sodium, 0.1 g Fiber

SAFFRON-LOTUS ROOT PICKLES

MAKES 10 TO 12 PICKLES

For this quick pickle, we add a little turmeric to the brine to produce day-old golden lotus root pickles. We use these to garnish many of our Asian-inspired dishes. If you use the saffron as well, they will complement Indian or Middle Eastern dishes.

1 lotus root, cut into 10 to 12 $^{1}/_{4}$-inch-thick slices
1 cup rice or white wine vinegar
1 cup water
1 tablespoon sea salt
2 whole cloves garlic
$^{1}/_{4}$ teaspoon saffron threads (optional)
1 teaspoon turmeric
2 whole cloves
$^{1}/_{2}$ teaspoon fennel seeds

In a medium saucepan, combine all the ingredients. Bring to a boil and boil for 15 minutes. Chill and serve, or store with the brine in an airtight container in the refrigerator for up to 2 weeks.

NUTRITIONAL INFORMATION PER SLICE PICKLE:

8 Calories (0% from fat), 0.1 g Protein, 2 g Carbohydrate, 0 g Fat, 0 mg Cholesterol, 62 mg Sodium, 0 g Fiber

Curry and Fennel Marinated Beets

MAKES 6 SERVINGS

This flavorful pickled beet is a great addition to salads or a condiment for a main dish.

18 small beets, any variety
1/3 cup champagne vinegar
1 cup apple juice
1/4 teaspoon red pepper flakes
1 teaspoon curry powder
1 teaspoon fennel seed
2 whole cloves
1/2 teaspoon sea salt

Remove the tops of the beets and peel. Cut the beets in half. In a large saucepan, combine the beets and all the remaining ingredients. Cover and simmer until the beets are cooked through but still firm, about 20 minutes.

Using a slotted spoon, transfer the beets to a 1-quart glass jar. Cook the pan liquid over medium heat until reduced to a syrup. Pour over the beets and let cool to room temperature before serving. To store, cover and refrigerate for up to 2 weeks.

NUTRITIONAL INFORMATION PER BEET:

12 Calories (0% from fat), 0.2 g Protein, 3 g Carbohydrate, 0 g Fat, 0 mg Cholesterol, 77 mg Sodium, 0.5 g Fiber

Arame Sea Vegetable Salad

MAKES 1 1/2 CUPS

This is a condiment we always have around for our Macrobiotic Plate. It makes a great salad paired with thinly sliced cucumber and a little red onion over some crunchy lettuce or shredded cabbage. We also use it as a garnish on some of our Asian-inspired plates.

1/2 cup loosely packed dried arame
1 small carrot, shredded or julienned
1 cup shredded red cabbage
2 teaspoons minced fresh dill
2 teaspoons Ginger Juice (see page 230)
2 tablespoons tamari soy sauce plus more to taste
3 tablespoons unseasoned rice vinegar
1 tablespoon toasted sesame seeds (see page 234)

Reconstitute the arame by steeping it in boiling water for 15 minutes. Drain and set aside to cool.

Combine the arame with all other ingredients and allow to marinate for 30 minutes before using. Will keep refrigerated in an airtight container for up to 1 week.

NUTRITIONAL INFORMATION PER 1/4 CUP:

29 Calories (31% from fat), 1 g Protein, 4 g Carbohydrate, 1 g Fat, 0 mg Cholesterol, 19 mg Sodium, 1 g Fiber

DESSERTS

When I start talking about the sort of pastry work I do, I always feel like I have to defend it—but I'd much rather celebrate. After all, dessert is an important part of the meal, a sensual, exciting pleasure, no matter what ingredients you use. At Millennium, we use all of the ingredients that you are familiar with, as well as a few exotic ones. We just don't use dairy or eggs. We do use chocolate in all of its forms, from cocoa powder to dark, rich varieties (contrary to popular belief, most dark chocolate is dairy free). We use sweeteners ranging from barley malt to maple syrup to Sucanat. On the more exotic side, you'll find cakes using Japanese-style silken tofu, and cookies featuring egg-replacement powder. True, even with all of these riches, some people still wonder about the missing eggs and dairy. I say, there's nothing missing. Open your mind and your mouth and allow yourself to savor a sinfully dark chocolate cake or the full tangy force of a Meyer lemon sorbet. The secret to making a truly luscious, decadent dessert without eggs, dairy, or much fat is to concentrate on flavor. Use the freshest, best ingredients available, and you'll never feel like anything is missing.

So, where do my ideas come from? To some extent, I do this for myself: I want to be able to have a vegan biscotti with my coffee! In addition, there's the challenge of bringing together the traditions of classic pastry work with my own sometimes strange inspirations, creating a whole new kind of cooking. Finally, there's the gratification of looking out of the kitchen and seeing people enjoying these desserts. I hope that you will enjoy creating and eating these dishes as much as I've enjoyed making them for everyone who's stopped by Millennium in the past two years.

—Sascha Weiss, Pastry Chef

184

SORBETS

DESSERT SAUCES

Lemon–Caramel and Hazelnut Napoleon
with Kiwifruit and Mango Sauce

LEMON-CARAMEL AND HAZELNUT NAPOLEONS WITH KIWIFRUIT AND MANGO SAUCE

SERVES 6

An adaptation of a classic napoleon, this dessert has the contrasting textures of crisp filo and hazelnut layers, cool and creamy pastry cream, and fresh kiwi and mango. Feel free to alter the flavors and fruits. Replace the lemon extract with almond extract and use peaches instead of kiwi, for example.

LEMON-CARAMEL CREAM

1 cup Sucanat

3/4 cup soy milk

12.3 ounces low-fat silken tofu

1 1/2 tablespoons lemon extract

1 1/2 teaspoons vanilla extract

1/8 teaspoon sea salt

3 1/2 tablespoons agar agar flakes

1 1/2 cups water

FILO LAYERS

1 cup hazelnuts, toasted and peeled (see page 234)

1/2 cup Sucanat

8 sheets filo, thawed

1/8 cup canola oil for brushing

1 recipe Mango Sauce (page 224)

6 kiwifruits, peeled and cut into 1/8-inch-thick slices

To make the lemon caramel cream: In a large saucepan, combine the Sucanat and the soy milk. Heat over medium heat and stir until the Sucanat has completely dissolved in the soy milk.

In a blender, combine the tofu, lemon extract, vanilla extract, and salt. Carefully pour the Sucanat mixture into the blender. Blend on medium speed for 2 minutes

In a large saucepan, combine the agar agar and water and boil, then reduce heat and simmer over low heat, stirring occasionally, for 10 minutes, or until the agar agar is fully dissolved. Pour the mixture into the blender with the previously blended ingredients. Blend on high speed for 2 minutes until the mixture is completely smooth.

Refrigerate the cream for 5 hours, or until firm. Blend it again until smooth. Cover and refrigerate until used, up to 10 days.

To make the filo layers: Preheat the oven to 350°. Line an 11 x 17-inch sheet pan with parchment paper.

In a blender or food processor, combine the hazelnuts and Sucanat and grind to a meal. Lay 2 sheets of filo on top of the parchment paper and brush the top sheet with oil. Sprinkle some of the hazelnut mixture on top. Repeat with the remaining filo, ending up with a layer of hazelnut mixture.

Cut the filo stack into 20 rectangles. Bake for 10 to 15 minutes, or until golden brown. Let cool. Store in an airtight container for up to 4 days.

To assemble: For each serving, make a large pool of mango sauce on a plate. Place 1 filo rectangle in the center of the sauce. Spoon 2 tablespoons of the lemon cream on top of the filo and then some sliced kiwi. Repeat to make 2 more layers. Repeat to make 5 more napoleons and serve at once.

NUTRITIONAL INFORMATION PER SERVING:

517 Calories (30% from fat), 9 g Protein, 82 g Carbohydrate, 17 g Fat, 0 mg Cholesterol, 229 mg Sodium, 6 g Fiber

Mocha Mud Slide

Makes one 8-inch cake, serves 10

An espresso-flavored cake with a very dark chocolate sauce, the mud slide has a number of accompaniments, so be sure to read all the steps carefully in advance. The idea and name for this cake came from former assistant pastry chef Tauna Riggins. She envisioned the espresso sorbet sliding down the side of a slice of cake.

Espresso Sponge Cake

2 cups unbleached all-purpose flour

1 teaspoon baking powder

1/2 teaspoon baking soda

1 tablespoon finely ground espresso

1 1/2 teaspoons ground cinnamon

Pinch sea salt

1/3 cup canola oil

3/4 cup maple syrup

1 cup soy milk

1 1/2 teaspoon vanilla extract

1/8 teaspoon lemon juice

Chocolate Sauce (page 223)

Espresso Sorbet (page 217)

Lemon Tuiles (page 209)

Fresh berries or sliced fruit for garnish

To make the espresso sponge cake: Preheat the oven to 350°. Lightly oil an 8-inch round, 2 1/2-inch deep pan with a false bottom. In a large bowl, sift the flour, baking powder, baking soda, espresso, cinnamon, and salt together. In a medium bowl, blend the oil, maple syrup, soy milk, vanilla, and lemon juice together. Pour the wet ingredients into the dry ingredients and whisk until combined. Pour the batter into the prepared pan and bake for 45 to 55 minutes, or until a toothpick inserted into the center comes out clean and the cake pulls away from the edges of the pan. Turn out onto a wire rack and let cool completely.

Cut the cake into 10 slices. For each serving, lay a slice of cake, cut-side down, on a plate. Spoon 1 tablespoon of the chocolate sauce on top of the cake and pour 1 1/2 tablespoons of the sauce on the plate. Place a scoop of the espresso sorbet next to the cake, place a lemon tuile on top of the sorbet, and add any fruit or berries that you desire.

Nutritional information per serving:

392 Calories (28% from fat), 4 g Protein, 67 g Carbohydrate, 12 g Fat, 0 mg Cholesterol, 171 mg Sodium, 3 g Fiber

MILLENNIUM FRUIT CRISP

MAKES 8 SERVINGS

We serve this dessert throughout the year with a gamut of different fruit combinations. During the winter, we serve some combinations of apples, pears, persimmons, cranberries, and blueberries, and in the spring, apples, strawberries, blueberries, and ginger. In the summer, we use peaches, plums, and fresh berries, and in the fall, we are back to apples, pears, ginger, and perhaps some figs. The oat topping given in the main recipe is oil-free; for a different version, try the streusel topping given at the end of the recipe.

OAT TOPPING

2 cups rolled oats

2 teaspoons ground cinnamon (optional)

1/8 teaspoon sea salt

1/3 cup maple syrup

FILLING

8 cups berries and/or cubed seasonal fruit

2 teaspoons ground cinnamon

1/2 teaspoon ground nutmeg

3/4 cup maple syrup

One 2-inch-piece fresh ginger, peeled and minced

1/4 cup fresh lemon juice

2 tablespoons arrowroot

To make the oat topping: Preheat the oven to 350°. Line a sided baking sheet with parchment paper. In a small bowl, combine the oats, cinnamon, and sea salt. Stir until combined, then stir in the maple syrup. Spread the oats on the prepared pan and toast for 10 minutes, or until the oats appear dry. Let cool. Leave the oven at 350°.

To make the fruit filling: In a large bowl, combine the berries and fruit. Add the cinnamon, nutmeg, maple syrup, ginger, and lemon juice. Mix until combined. In a blender, combine one third of the fruit mixture with the arrowroot and purée until smooth. Pour the puréed mixture back into the bowl and mix.

Pour the fruit mixture into an ungreased 9 x 9-inch baking dish and bake for about 35 minutes, or until the mixture begins to bubble and has thickened. Remove from the oven, top with the oat topping, and bake again for 5 minutes.

Remove the crisp from the oven and allow to cool for 5 to 10 minutes. If you like, serve with Vanilla Sauce (page 223), frozen vanilla Rice Dream, or any sorbet in this book.

VARIATION:

To substitute a streusel topping for the oat topping, combine 1 cup whole-wheat pastry flour, 1/2 cup Sucanat, 2 teaspoons ground cinnamon, and 1/8 teaspoon sea salt in a bowl. Whisk together, then stir in 1/4 cup canola oil. Sprinkle this mixture on top of the fruit crisp for the last 5 minutes of cooking.

NUTRITIONAL INFORMATION PER SERVING:

(oat topping) 310 Calories (6% from fat), 4 g Protein, 69 g Carbohydrate, 2 g Fat, 0 mg Cholesterol, 75 mg Sodium, 7 g Fiber

(streusel topping) 356 Calories (20% from fat), 3 g Protein, 68 g Carbohydrate, 8 g Fat, 0 mg Cholesterol, 80 mg Sodium, 6 g Fiber

Baklava with Pomegranate Sorbet

Makes 13 servings

Our version of baklava is sweetened with a mixture of maple and brown rice syrups. Canola oil replaces the butter. The pomegranate sorbet is divine and is definitely worth the effort to make. Serve this with a good strong cup of coffee.

3/4 cup maple syrup

3/4 cup brown rice syrup

Minced zest of 1 orange

1/2 cup fresh orange juice

3 cups hazelnuts, toasted and skinned (page 234)

3 cups walnuts

12 sheets filo dough, thawed

1/4 cup canola oil, plus more as needed

Pomegranate Sorbet (page 219)

Ground cinnamon for dusting

Pomegranate seeds or other fresh fruit, for garnish

In a medium saucepan, combine the maple syrup, rice syrup, orange zest and juice. Simmer for 10 minutes. Set aside and let cool.

Preheat the oven to 350°. In a blender or food processor, chop the nuts until coarsely ground. Then pour 3/4 of the simmered syrup into the food processor, and pulse until nuts and syrup are combined. Unwrap the filo and lay it flat on a flat work surface. Cut the stacked sheets in half crosswise. Cover the sheets with a kitchen towel. Place 1 sheet of filo in an 8 x 11-inch baking dish and lightly brush it with oil.

Repeat with 5 sheets of filo, brushing each sheet with oil. Sprinkle 2 cups chopped nut mixture evenly over the top sheet of filo. Repeat this procedure 2 more times until there are 3 layers of nuts and 4 layers of 6 sheets of filo dough each. With a sharp knife, cut the baklava into 40 pieces by cutting it into 4 lengthwise sections and 5 crosswise sections, and then cut each piece in half on the diagonal. Bake for 25 to 30 minutes, or until lightly browned. Remove from the oven, leaving the oven on. Pour the remaining syrup mixture over the baklava. Return to the oven and bake for 15 minutes.

Remove from the oven and let cool. Baklava is best eaten the day it was made, but may be stored in an airtight container in the refrigerator for up to 1 week.

Serve each piece with a scoop of pomegranate sorbet and garnish with ground cinnamon and pomegranate seeds or other fruit. (Don't forget the coffee!)

Nutritional information per serving:

595 Calories (59% from fat), 8 g Protein, 53 g Carbohydrate, 39 g Fat, 0 mg Cholesterol, 94 mg Sodium, 4 g Fiber

MAD GOOD
CHOCOLATE CAKE

MAKES 7 INDIVIDUAL CAKES

This cake actually rivals our Chocolate Almond Midnight in the eyes of chocolate junkies. It is served warm over rum caramel sauce with coconut sorbet. The hidden bonus is the creamy chocolate ganache filling that oozes out when the warm cake is cut. Note that this is an individual cake: you will need seven 2-inch ring molds that need to be oiled and placed on a parchment-lined baking pan, or seven 1-cup muffin slots, oiled and filled with cake.

1½ cups unbleached all-purpose flour

½ cup unsweetened cocoa powder

1 teaspoon baking powder

½ teaspoon baking soda

⅛ teaspoon sea salt

4 ounces extra-firm low-fat silken tofu

¾ cup soy milk

¾ cup maple syrup

½ cup canola oil

2 teaspoons vanilla extract

¼ teaspoon fresh lemon juice

7 tablespoons Chocolate Ganache (page 223)

Caramel-Rum Sauce (page 272)

Fresh berries of choice

Coconut Sorbet (page 216)

Unsweetened cocoa powder for dusting

Preheat the oven to 350°. Into a large bowl, sift the flour, cocoa powder, baking powder, and soda together. Add the salt and stir well until combined.

In a blender, combine the tofu, soy milk, maple syrup, oil, vanilla, and lemon juice. Purée until smooth. Pour the wet mixture into the dry mixture and whisk until smooth, scraping the sides of the bowl with a rubber spatula as needed.

Fill each of 7 greased muffin cups half-full. Place 1 tablespoon Chocolate Ganache in a ball on top of the batter. Top with more batter to fill each cup just over three-quarters full.

Bake the cakes for 35 to 45 minutes, or until they are firm and begin to pull away from the side. Let cool to the touch. Remove from the muffin cups, using a paring knife if necessary. If making ahead, rewarm in a 300° oven for 5 minutes.

For each serving, make a spiral of Caramel-Rum Sauce on a plate. Place a warm cake in the middle of the plate, place some berries around the cake, top the cake with a scoop of Coconut Sorbet, dust with cocoa powder, and enjoy.

NUTRITIONAL INFORMATION PER SERVING:

511 Calories (41% from fat), 6 g Protein, 70 g Carbohydrate, 23 g Fat, 0 mg Cholesterol, 223 mg Sodium, 3 g Fiber

PUMPKIN CAKE WITH CHOCOLATE-HAZELNUT GANACHE AND CINNAMON-COFFEE SAUCE

MAKES ONE 8-INCH CAKE; SERVES 10

A great cake for those times when pumpkin pie comes to mind but you want something a little different.

CHOCOLATE-HAZELNUT GANACHE
1 cup hazelnuts, toasted and skinned (see page 234)
2 cups soy milk
1 pound semisweet nondairy chocolate, melted

CINNAMON-COFFEE SAUCE
3/4 cup freshly brewed coffee
1/2 teaspoon ground cinnamon
3 tablespoons Sucanat or fructose

PUMPKIN CAKE
2 cups unbleached all-purpose flour
1 tablespoon ground cinnamon
3/4 teaspoon baking powder
1/2 teaspoon baking soda
1/2 teaspoon sea salt
1/2 cup pumpkin purée (see page 230)
1/3 cup canola oil
3/4 cup maple syrup
1/2 cup soy milk
3 tablespoons minced fresh ginger
1 1/2 teaspoons vanilla extract
1/4 teaspoon lemon juice

Chopped fresh fruit or berries for garnish
Ground cinnamon for garnish

Chop the hazelnuts in a blender or food processor. Add the soy mild and combine with the nuts. Turn the blender on and slowly pour in the melted chocolate. When fully blended, pour into a bowl, cover, and refrigerate until firm, about 4–6 hours.

To make the cinnamon-coffee sauce: In a bowl, combine the coffee, cinnamon, and Sucanat. Whisk together and cook over medium heat. Let cool and refrigerate until needed—up to 2 days if you make it ahead.

To make the pumpkin cake: Preheat the oven to 350°. Oil an 8-inch round springform or false bottom cake pan. Into a large bowl, sift the flour, cinnamon, baking powder, and baking soda. Stir in the salt until well combined. In a blender, combine the pumpkin purée, oil, maple syrup, soy milk, ginger, vanilla, and lemon juice. Blend until well combined.

Pour the wet mixture into the dry mixture and whisk until combined. Pour the batter into the prepared pan and bake for 55 to 65 minutes, or until golden brown and a toothpick inserted in the center comes out clean. Let cake cool completely in the pan, then remove it from the pan.

Slice the cake horizontally into 3 even layers. Place the bottom layer of the cake on a cake pan. Drizzle 1/4 cup coffee-cinnamon sauce onto the bottom cake layer. Spread one half of the hazelnut ganache on the cake layer (if the ganache is too hard to spread, place the container in a warm water bath). Place the second layer of cake on top of the ganache layer. Drizzle 1/4 cup coffee-cinnamon sauce onto the middle cake layer and spread it with the remaining half of the hazelnut ganache. Place the third layer of cake on top. Wrap the cake with plastic wrap and refrigerate at least 1 hour.

To serve, cut the cake into 10 pieces. For each serving, place slices of cake on serving plates and garnish with chopped fruit or fresh berries and a sprinkle of cinnamon.

NUTRITIONAL INFORMATION PER SERVING:

582 Calories (46% from fat), 7 g Protein, 71 g Carbohydrate, 30 g Fat, 0 mg Cholesterol, 135 mg Sodium, 5 g Fiber

PINE NUT AND ANISE CAKE WITH BLOOD ORANGE COMPOTE

MAKES ONE 8-INCH CAKE; SERVES 10

This cake was inspired by the combination of two of my favorite flavors, anise and pine nuts. They lend a rustic quality to this cake, which was originally created for Valentine's Day. The blood orange compote paired with this cake is sure to win many hearts. Blood oranges are available from early to late winter; they have a blood-red color and a berry-like flavor. Try this cake with a glass of Cassis liqueur.

PINE NUT AND ANISE CAKE

2 cups unbleached all-purpose flour

1 teaspoons baking powder

3/4 teaspoon baking soda

1/8 teaspoon sea salt

3/4 cup maple syrup

1 cup soy milk

1/2 cup canola oil

2 1/2 ounces silken tofu

1 tablespoon anise extract

1 teaspoon vanilla extract

1/2 teaspoon fresh lemon juice

1/2 cup pine nuts, toasted (see page 234)

BLOOD ORANGE COMPOTE

8 blood oranges or Valencia oranges

1/2 cup Sucanat or unrefined sugar

1 tablespoon arrowroot dissolved in 3/4 cup cold water

To make the cake: Preheat the oven to 350°. Lightly oil an 8-inch round springform or false bottom cake pan. Into a large bowl, sift the flour, baking powder, and baking soda. Add the salt and stir until well combined. In a blender, combine the maple syrup, soy milk, oil, tofu, anise and vanilla extracts, and lemon juice. Purée until smooth. Pour the wet mixture into the dry mixture, and mix well. Fold in the pine nuts. Pour into the prepared pan. Bake for 55 to 65 minutes, or until the cake is golden brown and a toothpick inserted in the center comes out clean.

Let the cake cool completely in the pan on a rack, then remove it from the pan.

To make the compote: Juice 4 of the oranges. Peel the remaining 4 oranges and cut them into segments. In a small saucepan, combine the orange juice and Sucanat. Bring the mixture to a simmer and stir in the arrowroot mixture. Stir until the sauce becomes translucent. Remove from heat and let cool. Stir in the orange segments.

To serve, cut the cake into 10 slices. Heat the orange compote until warm. For each serving, pool orange compote in the center of a plate, place a slice of cake on top of the compote.

NUTRITIONAL INFORMATION PER SERVING:

411 Calories (33% from fat), 6 g Protein, 63 g Carbohydrate, 15 g Fat, 0 mg Cholesterol, 139 mg Sodium, 4 g Fiber

BROWNIES À LA MODE

MAKES 12 BROWNIES

We feature these truly amazing fudgy brownies in our upstairs lunchtime cafe and often on our evening dessert menu. The prunes in this dessert mean there doesn't have to be oil in the recipe; they also combine with the cocoa powder to add a depth to the chocolate flavor. You can bake these brownies with all prunes to replace all of the canola oil (for a lower-fat version) or 1 cup of oil and no prunes. The flaxseeds are another interesting ingredient. In this recipe they serve as an emulsifier.

PRUNE PURÉE

1/2 cup prunes, pitted and roughly chopped
1/2 cup water, plus more if needed

BROWNIES

2 cups unbleached all-purpose flour
1 cup unsweetened cocoa powder
1 1/2 tablespoons baking powder
1 1/2 cups Sucanat
1/8 teaspoon sea salt
1 1/2 tablespoons flaxseeds
1/2 cup canola oil
1 1/4 cups soy milk
1 cup maple syrup
1 tablespoon vanilla extract
1/2 cup nondairy chocolate chips (optional)

Chocolate Sauce (page 223)
Raspberry Sauce (page 224)
1 pint frozen vanilla Rice Dream
Fresh berries or chopped fruit, and cocoa powder, for garnish

To make the prune purée: In a small saucepan, combine the prunes and 1/2 cup water and simmer for 5 minutes, or until the prunes are plump and soft. Add more water as needed. In a blender, purée the prunes with their simmering liquid until smooth.

To make the brownies: Preheat the oven to 350°. Oil an 8 x 11-inch baking pan and line it with parchment paper.

Into a large bowl, sift the flour, cocoa powder, and baking powder. Add Sucanat and salt and stir until combined. In a blender, grind the flaxseeds until they resemble coarse meal, about 1 minute. Add the prune purée, oil, soy milk, maple syrup, and vanilla. Purée until smooth. Pour the wet mixture into the dry mixture. Mix until combined, then fold in the chocolate chips and pour into the prepared pan.

Bake for 40 to 55 minutes, or until brownies are firm to the touch and have pulled away from the sides of the pan. Cut the brownies into 12 even pieces. For each serving, place 2 in a bowl, embellish with Chocolate Sauce and Raspberry Sauce and top with Rice Dream. Garnish with fresh berries, and a dusting of cocoa powder.

VARIATION:

For a lower-fat version, double the recipe for prune purée and use the second 1/2 cup to replace the canola oil.

NUTRITIONAL INFORMATION PER SERVING (BROWNIE ONLY):

(with oil) 437 Calories (27% from fat), 6 g Protein, 74 g Carbohydrate, 13 g Fat, 0 mg Cholesterol, 223 mg Sodium, 5 g Fiber

(lower-fat) 381 Calories (12% from fat), 6 g Protein, 78 g Carbohydrate, 5 g Fat, 0 mg Cholesterol, 223 mg Sodium, 5 g Fiber

Alpine Torte

Let 1 pint of frozen Rice Dream sit out at room temperature for 25 minutes, or until it becomes slightly soft. Spoon it into a bowl. Mince 1 bunch stemmed mint, mix the mint into the Rice Dream, and refreeze. For each serving, scoop 2/3 cup of this mixture into the center of a brownie that has been sliced in half, top with the second half of the brownie, and serve with Chocolate Sauce or Chocolate Ganache.

NUTRITIONAL INFORMATION PER SERVING:

612 Calories (29% from fat), 6 g Protein, 102 g Carbohydrate, 20 g Fat, 0 mg Cholesterol, 353 mg Sodium, 5 g Fiber

(with lower-fat brownie) 556 Calories (19% from fat), 6 g Protein, 106 g Carbohydrate, 12 g Fat, 0 mg Cholesterol, 353 mg Sodium, 5 g Fiber

HAWAIIAN MUD TORTE

MAKES 6 SERVINGS

This dessert was inspired by one of the many great desserts created by Catherine Burke, Millennium's former pastry chef. Though simple, it's outright decadent: coconut macaroons sandwiched with vanilla Rice Dream and topped with chocolate ganache. Try using any of the fruit sorbets in this book in place of the Rice Dream.

MACAROONS

2 1/2 cups unsweetened coconut flakes

1 1/4 cups Sucanat

6 tablespoons unbleached all-purpose flour

1/8 teaspoon sea salt

6 tablespoons water

3 tablespoons egg replacer powder

1 teaspoon vanilla extract

Chocolate Ganache (page 223) 1/2 recipe

1 pint vanilla frozen Rice Dream, or your favorite nondairy ice cream

Fresh berries of choice and mint sprigs for garnish

To make the macaroons: Preheat the oven to 350°. Line a baking sheet with parchment paper. In a large bowl, combine the coconut, Sucanat, flour, and salt. In a blender, combine the water, egg replacer, and vanilla. Blend on a high speed for about 2 minutes. Fold into the dry ingredients and blend well with a rubber spatula (use your hands if necessary).

Scoop 2 tablespoons of batter for each of 6 macaroons, placing them 4 inches apart on the prepared sheet. Using a piece of plastic wrap, press each round to the thickness of 1/4 inch. Bake for 17 to 22 minutes, or until golden brown but still slightly soft. Immediately remove the cookies and the parchment paper from the baking sheet and place on a rack to cool to the touch. Repeat to bake the remaining batter. Store in an airtight container for up to 2 weeks.

For each serving: Place a macaroon in the center of a plate, spoon or scoop about 1/3 cup frozen Rice Dream on top of the macaroon and top with 2 tablespoons Chocolate Ganache; then another cookie and 2 tablespoons more ganache. Garnish with some seasonal berries and mint and enjoy.

VARIATION:

For wheat-free macaroons: substitute rice flour for the all-purpose flour in the macaroon recipe.

NUTRITIONAL INFORMATION PER SERVING:

587 Calories (35% from fat), 4 g Protein, 91 g Carbohydrate, 23 g Fat, 0 mg Cholesterol, 208 mg Sodium, 4 g Fiber

CHOCOLATE-ALMOND MIDNIGHT

MAKES ONE 8-INCH CAKE; SERVES 12

Chocolate-Almond Midnight is served with raspberry sauce and maple almond praline. Creamy, rich, and chocolatey, this chocolate mousse cake really has no match. It's been on the menu every single day and night since Millennium opened.

CASHEW CRUST

1/3 cup unsalted cashew nuts

3 tablespoons Sucanat

3 tablespoons canola oil

1/2 teaspoon vanilla extract

1 cup unbleached all-purpose flour

1/8 teaspoon sea salt

CHOCOLATE MOUSSE

2 cups (16 ounces) malt-sweetened, nondairy
  chocolate chips

24.6 ounces (2 boxes) extra-firm low-fat silken tofu

3/4 cup Sucanat

1 teaspoon vanilla extract

1/8 teaspoon sea salt

MAPLE ALMOND PRALINE

1/4 cup maple syrup

1 cup slivered almonds

Raspberry Sauce (page 224)

Fresh fruit, cocoa powder, and finely shredded
  fresh mint for garnish

To make the cashew crust: Preheat the oven to 350°. Lightly oil an 8-inch round springform or false bottom pan. In a food processor, grind the cashews until they resemble fine meal. Add the Sucanat, oil, and vanilla. Process again until well combined. In a small bowl, stir the flour and salt together. Add the cashew mixture and mix into the flour, beginning with a spatula and ending with your hands. Press the crust into the prepared pan. Bake for 20 to 25 minutes, or until light brown and dry.

To make the chocolate mousse: In a double boiler over barely simmering water, melt the chocolate chips. In a blender or food processor, combine the silken tofu, Sucanat, vanilla, and salt. Process, then add the melted chocolate and blend for 2 minutes, or until very smooth and completely combined.

Preheat the oven to 350°. Lightly oil the sides of the cake pan above the prebaked crust. Pour the mousse mixture into the pan and bake for 35 minutes. Let cool for 10 minutes, then run a paring knife around the inside of the pan. Let the cake cool to the touch, refrigerate for at least 2 hours before serving. Unmold just before serving.

To make the praline: In a heavy-bottomed saucepan, bring the maple syrup to a boil. Boil for 1 minute. Add the almonds and stir constantly until the maple syrup has completely crystallized onto the almonds and the almonds appear dry.

Pour the almonds onto a baking sheet and let cool. Store in an airtight container for up to 5 weeks.

To serve, cut the cake into 12 pieces. For each serving, pool Raspberry Sauce on a plate and top with a slice of cake. Top with 1 tablespoon maple-almond praline and garnish with fresh fruit, cocoa powder, and mint.

NUTRITIONAL INFORMATION PER SERVING:

431 Calories (40% from fat), 9 g Protein, 56 g Carbohydrate, 19 g Fat, 0 mg Cholesterol, 121 mg Sodium, 4 g Fiber

VARIATION:

For a wheat-free version of Chocolate Almond Midnight, replace the all-purpose flour in the cashew crust with rice, barley, or spelt flour.

Warm Shortcake with Winter Fruit Compote

MAKES ONE 8-INCH CAKE; SERVES 8

The idea of using corn in place of oil in this cake was developed by Catherine Burke, the former pastry chef at Millennium. We serve this with a compote of winter fruits: cranberries, pears, and persimmons. This recipe will make a lot of fruit compote, but that's the idea.

SHORTCAKE

1²/₃ cup unbleached all-purpose flour

¹/₂ teaspoon baking soda

¹/₈ teaspoon sea salt

²/₃ cup maple syrup

³/₄ cup water

¹/₃ cup fresh or frozen corn kernels

¹/₂ teaspoon vanilla extract

¹/₄ teaspoon lemon juice

WINTER FRUIT COMPOTE

³/₄ cup port wine

3 cups (12 ounces) fresh cranberries

2 Fuyu persimmons or apples, finely diced

2 pears, peeled, cored, and finely diced

¹/₂ cup Sucanat

¹/₂ cup apple juice

¹/₂ teaspoon ground allspice

2 teaspoons ground cinnamon

¹/₂ teaspoon ground nutmeg

Pulp from ¹/₂ split vanilla bean or 2 teaspoons vanilla extract

One-inch piece fresh ginger, minced

1 recipe Vanilla Sauce (page 224)

8 fresh mint sprigs

To make the shortcake: Preheat the oven to 350°. Lightly oil an 8-inch square or round cake pan. Into a large bowl, sift the flour and baking powder. Stir in the salt. In a blender, combine the maple syrup, water, corn, vanilla, and lemon juice. Pour the wet ingredients into the dry ingredients and mix well. Pour into the prepared pan.

Bake for 40 to 45 minutes, or until the cake is golden brown and a cake tester inserted in the center comes out clean. Let cool. Run a paring knife around the edge of the cake and unmold. Cut into 8 pieces.

To make the compote: In a large saucepan, combine the port and cranberries and simmer for 7 minutes, or until the cranberries are all popped open. In a blender, purée half of this mixture and set aside. Add the persimmons, pears, Sucanat, apple juice, allspice, cinnamon, nutmeg, vanilla, and ginger to the cranberries in the pan. Mix well and simmer for 15 to 20 minutes, until the fruit is al dente. Add the puréed cranberries. Set aside and keep warm.

Warm the cake just before serving. For each serving, center a square of shortcake on a plate. Spoon an eighth of the compote on top of the shortcake. Garnish with Vanilla Sauce and a mint sprig.

NUTRITIONAL INFORMATION PER SERVING:

297 Calories (3% from fat), 3 g Protein, 69 g Carbohydrate, 1 g Fat, 0 mg Cholesterol, 127 mg Sodium, 4 g Fiber

BAKED HAZELNUT-CRUSTED PEARS WITH DRIED FRUIT COMPOTE

MAKES 6 SERVINGS

This dessert was created on the spur of the moment one incredibly busy Saturday night in December. It later became one of our New Year's Eve desserts. Omit the compote for a simple warm fruit dessert.

BAKED HAZELNUT-CRUSTED PEARS

6 Bosc, d'Anjou, or other pears

1 cup dry red wine or grape juice

2 cups apple juice

1 cup Sucanat

One 2-inch piece fresh ginger, minced

1 teaspoon ground pepper (optional)

2 cinnamon sticks, or 2 teaspoons ground cinnamon

1 teaspoon ground allspice

DRIED FRUIT COMPOTE

2 tablespoons orange liqueur or orange juice

1 cup apple juice

$1/2$ cup Sucanat

1 teaspoon ground cinnamon

$1/2$ teaspoon ground allspice

Pinch sea salt

$1 1/2$ cups dried pears

1 cup golden raisins

1 cup fresh cranberries, or 1 cup dried cranberries and $1/4$ cup apple juice

$1/2$ cup hazelnuts, toasted, skinned, and coarsely chopped (see page 234)

Persimmon Sorbet (page 218) or frozen vanilla Rice Dream

Finely shredded fresh mint and pomegranate seeds for garnish

To bake the pears: Preheat the oven to 350°. Core the pears with a corer or melon baller, then peel the lower half of the pears. Cut a thin slice from the bottom of each pear so it will stand straight up. In a medium bowl, whisk the wine, apple juice, Sucanat, ginger, pepper, cinnamon, and allspice together. Place the pears in a baking dish that is large enough to hold them. Pour the liquid into the dish and cover with aluminum foil.

Bake the pears for 20 minutes, or until tender when pierced with a fork. Remove the foil, remove the pears from the dish, and let them cool to the touch. Pour the baking liquid into a small, heavy saucepan and simmer until reduced to a syrup, about 10 minutes.

To make the compote: In a medium saucepan, combine the orange liqueur, apple juice, Sucanat, cinnamon, allspice, and salt. Stir well and add the dried fruit. Simmer until the fruit is plump, about 10 minutes. Pour onto a sided baking sheet to cool.

Stuff the dried fruit compote into the hollow of each pear. Dip the lower part of the pear in the chopped hazelnuts and roll it around until it is completely coated.

To serve, warm 6 bowls and divide the reduced liquid among them. Stand a hazelnut-crusted pear up in each bowl and place a scoop of Persimmon Sorbet at the base of the pear. Garnish with some mint and pomegranate seeds and serve.

NUTRITIONAL INFORMATION PER SERVING:

544 Calories (13% from fat), 3 g Protein, 115 g Carbohydrate, 8 g Fat, 0 mg Cholesterol, 133 mg Sodium, 12 g Fiber

MEYER LEMON BUNDT CAKES WITH BLACKBERRY SORBET AND MEYER LEMON SAUCE

MAKES 6 INDIVIDUAL BUNDT CAKES

Meyer lemons have thinner skins and a sweeter taste than regular lemons. When these cakes are made with Meyer lemons, the flavor is great; though regular lemons can also be used. Using a high-quality lemon extract will enhance the flavor dramatically. Blackberry sorbet is a natural accompaniment. If you can't make your own, use a high-quality commercial sorbet. The cake is incredibly light, thanks to the egg replacer powder. If you have any of this cake left over after a day or two, it tastes great toasted and spread with blackberry jam.

MEYER LEMON BUNDT CAKE

2 cups unbleached all-purpose flour

1 teaspoon baking powder

$1/2$ teaspoon baking soda

$1/8$ teaspoon salt

Minced zest of 2 Meyer lemons

2 tablespoons egg replacer powder

$1/4$ cup water

$1/3$ cup fresh Meyer lemon juice

$3/4$ cup maple syrup

$1/2$ cup canola oil

$1/2$ cup soy milk

1 tablespoon lemon extract

$1^1/2$ teaspoons vanilla extract

Meyer Lemon Sauce (page 222)

Blackberry Sorbet (page 216)

Finely shredded fresh mint and fresh blackberries for garnish

To make the cakes: Preheat the oven to 350°. Lightly oil 6 mini bundt cake pans. Into a large bowl, sift the flour, baking powder, and soda. Stir in the salt and lemon zest until well combined. In a blender, combine the egg replacement powder and water and blend well for about 2 minutes. Add the lemon juice, maple syrup, oil, soy milk, lemon and vanilla extracts, and blend again. Pour the wet ingredients into the dry ingredients and whisk until combined.

Pour the batter into the prepared pans and bake for 35 to 45 minutes, or until the cakes are golden brown and pull away from the edges of the pans. Let cool completely.

For each serving: Pool 1 tablespoon of the Meyer lemon sauce in the center of a large dinner plate. Place an individual bundt cake on top of the sauce. Top with a scoop of blackberry sorbet and garnish with some mint and blackberries.

NUTRITIONAL INFORMATION PER SERVING:

471 Calories (36% from fat), 5 g Protein, 70 g Carbohydrate, 19 g Fat, 0 mg Cholesterol, 347 mg Sodium, 2 g Fiber

MELON FRUIT SOUP WITH LEMONGRASS

MAKES 6 SERVINGS

We serve chilled fruit soup as a fruit-driven dessert when the fruit crisp is not offered. This one has a South Pacific flavor and is a good ending to any of our Asian-inspired meals.

1 cup water
1/2 cup fructose
4 lemongrass stalks, coarsely chopped
One 3-pound Sharlyn, cantaloupe, honeydew, or other ripe melon, quartered, seeded, and peeled

Fresh berries and diced fruit, finely shredded fresh mint, and ground cinnamon for garnish
6 Sesame Lace Tuiles (page 210)

In a small saucepan, combine the water and fructose and simmer until the fructose is completely dissolved. Add the lemongrass and simmer for 10 minutes. Strain through a fine-meshed sieve. Reserve the liquid and discard the lemongrass. Let cool. Cover and refrigerate at least 2 hours, or until chilled.

In a blender, combine the melon flesh and half the lemongrass syrup. Blend until smooth. Add more of the syrup to taste. Any remaining syrup will last indefinitely refrigerated in an airtight container. Cover and refrigerate at least 1 hour.

To serve, pour the soup into 6 chilled soup bowls. Garnish with some berries and sprinkle with some mint and cinnamon. Place a cookie on the rim of the bowl and enjoy.

NUTRITIONAL INFORMATION PER SERVING:

156 Calories (0% from fat), 1 g Protein, 38 g Carbohydrate, 0 g Fat, 0 mg Cholesterol, 26 mg Sodium, 2 g Fiber

PEACH AND GINGER SOUP

MAKES 6 SERVINGS

This fruit soup is an elegant conclusion to a summer meal.

6 large peaches, peeled, pitted, and coarsely chopped (about 3 cups)
One 2-inch piece ginger, peeled and coarsely chopped
2 cups water
2 tablespoons fresh lemon juice
1/3 cup fructose

Fresh berries, diced fruit, finely shredded fresh mint, and ground cinnamon for garnish
6 Pine Nut and Anise Cookies (page 210)

In a large saucepan, combine the peaches, ginger, water, lemon juice, and fructose. Simmer for 10 minutes. Let cool to the touch. Remove the pieces of ginger. In a blender, purée the mixture until smooth. Cover and refrigerate for at least 2 hours.

To serve, pour the soup into 6 chilled soup bowls. Garnish with some berries and diced fruit, and sprinkle with some mint and cinnamon. Place a cookie or two on the rim of each bowl and enjoy.

NUTRITIONAL INFORMATION PER SERVING:

95 Calories (0% from fat), 0.8 g Protein, 23 g Carbohydrate, 0 g Fat, 0 mg Cholesterol, 3 mg Sodium, 2 g Fiber

PECAN PIE

MAKES ONE 9-INCH PIE;
SERVES 10

This is the pecan pie that we serve at our Thanksgiving Day meal. It is as traditional as it gets: rich, thick, and moist, with a great toasted pecan taste. Try serving it with some Persimmon Sorbet (page 218) or Vanilla Sauce (page 223).

$2^1/_2$ cups pecans, toasted and coarsely chopped
    (see page 234)
$3/_4$ cup maple syrup
$1/_3$ cup brown rice syrup
1 tablespoon vanilla extract
1 tablespoon minced fresh ginger
$1/_4$ teaspoons sea salt
3 tablespoons flaxseeds
$1^1/_2$ teaspoons arrowroot
$1/_3$ cup soy milk
Prebaked Pie Crust (page 233)

To make the filling: Place the pecans in a large bowl. In a medium saucepan, combine the maple syrup, rice syrup, vanilla extract, ginger, and salt. Simmer the mixture for 5 minutes, then remove from heat and allow to come to room temperature. In a spice grinder, grind the flaxseeds to a powder. Combine the arrowroot, soy milk, and flaxseed meal with the maple syrup mixture, pour into a blender, and blend until smooth. Pour the liquid from the blender over the pecans. Mix well and pour into the prebaked pie shell. Bake at 350° for 30 minutes, or until the filling has firmed up. Let cool.

NUTRITIONAL INFORMATION PER SERVING:
    503 Calories (55% from fat), 5 g Protein, 51 g Carbohydrate, 31 g Fat, 0 mg Cholesterol, 144 mg Sodium, 3 g Fiber

PUMPKIN PIE

MAKES 8 SERVINGS

This is our Thanksgiving pumpkin pie. It is simple to prepare and should not be reserved for Thanksgiving, but enjoyed at any time.

$1^1/_2$ cups pumpkin purée (see page 230)
$2/_3$ cup maple syrup
3 tablespoons molasses
$1/_2$ teaspoon vanilla extract
1 teaspoon ground cinnamon
1 tablespoon minced fresh ginger
$1/_4$ teaspoon ground nutmeg
1 teaspoon ground allspice
2 teaspoons arrowroot
$1/_2$ cup soy milk
Prebaked Pie Crust (page 233)

1 recipe Vanilla Sauce (page 223)
Vanilla Frozen Rice Dream (optional)

In a food processor, combine the pumpkin purée, maple syrup, molasses, vanilla, cinnamon, ginger, nutmeg, allspice, arrowroot, and soy milk, in batches if necessary. Process until the mixture is well combined and smooth. Pour into the prebaked pie crust and bake for 30 minutes, or until the filling has firmed up. Let cool.

Serve with Vanilla Sauce and frozen Rice Dream.

NUTRITIONAL INFORMATION PER SERVING PIE:
    334 Calories (38% from fat), 3 g Protein, 49 g Carbohydrate, 14 g Fat, 0 mg Cholesterol, 140 mg Sodium, 2 g Fiber

STRAWBERRY-RHUBARB GALETTES

MAKES 7 GALETTES

A galette is a freeform tart in which the dough is folded over the filling instead of being baked in a pan. Galettes look rather rustic; no two will ever be the same. They are a nice way to provide everyone with an individual dessert. If you have any left over, serve them for breakfast.

STRAWBERRY-RHUBARB FILLING

1 1/2 pounds rhubarb, finely diced (about 4 cups)

1/2 cup maple syrup

2 tablespoons minced ginger

1 teaspoon balsamic vinegar

4 cups fresh strawberries, hulled and chopped

2 teaspoon arrowroot dissolved in 2 tablespoons cold water

WALNUT PASTRY DOUGH

3 cups unbleached all-purpose flour

1/2 cup walnuts, toasted and finely chopped (see page 234)

1/4 cup Sucanat

1/4 teaspoon sea salt

1/4 teaspoon ground pepper

3/4 cup canola oil

1/2 cup soy milk

Vanilla Rice Dream or Vanilla Sauce (page 223)

To make the filling: In a large saucepan, combine the rhubarb, maple syrup, ginger, and vinegar. Simmer over medium heat for about 5 to 7 minutes, or until the rhubarb begins to break down. Add the strawberries and mix them into the filling thoroughly. Add the arrowroot and cook for 3 more minutes, stirring continuously. Pour the filling onto a sided baking sheet and let cool.

To make the dough: Preheat the oven to 350°. Sift the flour into a medium bowl. Add the walnuts, Sucanat, salt, and pepper. Drizzle the oil into the dry ingredients, covering as much surface area as possible. Mix lightly with a spatula until the flour and oil form into little dough balls about the size of marbles. Drizzle 1/2 cup of the soy milk into the bowl, and stir until the mixture forms a ball. Add more soy milk in 1-tablespoon increments if more liquid is needed. Wrap the ball in plastic wrap. Knead lightly in the plastic until the ingredients adhere and refrigerate for 15 to 30 minutes.

To make the galettes: Preheat the oven to 350°. Line a baking sheet with parchment paper. Divide the dough into 7 pieces. Roll 1 piece between 2 sheets of parchment or waxed paper to a rough circle 6 inches in diameter. Keep the remaining dough covered with a towel. Remove the top sheet of parchment to break the seal of the dough. Replace the paper on top of the dough lightly, flip the dough over, and remove the parchment paper now on top. With a paring knife, cut the dough into a 5-inch-diameter circle, using a small plate as a guide. Remove the excess dough.

Place 1/4 cup filling in the center of the circle. Fold the sides of the circle over the filling, leaving the center open and creating a square galette. Using a large metal spatula, transfer the galette to the prepared sheet. Repeat with the remaining dough and filling.

Bake for 35 minutes, or until the crust is golden brown and the filling bubbles. Let cool slightly on a rack. Serve warm with Rice Dream or Vanilla Sauce.

NUTRITIONAL INFORMATION PER GALETTE:

536 Calories (40% from fat), 7 g Protein, 73 g Carbohydrate, 24 g Fat, 0 mg Cholesterol, 265 mg Sodium, 5 g Fiber

CRANBERRY-WALNUT GALETTES

MAKES 7 GALETTES

Cranberries and walnuts are an extraordinary combination for a fall dessert. The richness of the walnuts complements the tartness of the cranberries nicely.

WALNUT PASTRY DOUGH

1/2 cup walnuts, toasted (page 234)

3 cups unbleached all-purpose flour

1/4 cup Sucanat

1/4 teaspoon sea salt

3/4 cup canola oil

1/2 to 3/4 cup soy milk

CRANBERRY-WALNUT FILLING

1/4 cup orange liqueur (optional)

1/2 water

1/4 cup fresh lemon juice

1 1/2 cups Sucanat

1 teaspoon ground cinnamon

2 tablespoons minced fresh ginger

1 1/2 pounds fresh or frozen cranberries

7 tablespoons walnuts, toasted and chopped (page 234)

Vanilla Sauce (page 223), or frozen vanilla Rice Dream

To make the pastry dough: Finely chop toasted walnuts by hand or grind them in a blender or food processor. Sift the flour into a bowl. Add the walnuts, Sucanat, and salt. Stir the dry ingredients together. Drizzle the oil into the dry ingredients, covering as much surface area and possible, and mix lightly with a spatula until the flour and oil form dough balls about the size of marbles. Drizzle 1/2 cup soy milk into the bowl and stir until the mixture forms a ball. If the dough does not come together, add more soy milk 1 tablespoon at a time. Wrap the ball in plastic wrap. Knead lightly in the plastic and refrigerate for at least 30 minutes.

To make the filling: In a medium saucepan, simmer the liqueur for 1 minute to remove some of the alcohol. Add the remaining ingredients and simmer until the cranberries have broken down, 15 to 20 minutes. Pour the hot filling onto a sided baking sheet and let cool.

To make the galettes: Preheat the oven to 350°. Line a baking sheet with parchment paper. Divide the dough into 7 pieces. Roll 1 piece between 2 sheets of parchment or waxed paper to a rough circle 6 inches in diameter. Keep the remaining dough wrapped in plastic.

Remove the top sheet of paper to break the seal of the dough. Replace it on top of the dough lightly, flip the dough over, and remove paper that is now on top. With a paring knife, cut the dough into a 5-inch-diameter circle, using a small plate as a guide. Remove the excess dough.

Place 1/4 cup filling in the center of the circle and top with 1 tablespoon chopped walnuts. Fold the sides of the circle over the filling, leaving the center open and creating a square galette.

Using a large metal spatula, transfer the galette to the prepared sheet. Repeat with the remaining dough and filling. Bake for 35 minutes, or until the crusts are golden brown. Let cool slightly on a rack. Serve warm with Vanilla Sauce or Rice Dream.

NUTRITIONAL INFORMATION PER GALETTE:

781 Calories (38% from fat), 10 g Protein, 111 g Carbohydrate, 33 g Fat, 0 mg Cholesterol, 110 mg Sodium, 7 g Fiber

WARM CARAMELIZED APPLE GALETTES WITH SPICED RICE DREAM

MAKES 7 GALETTES

This dessert was created for a fall equinox celebration dinner. It has a great rustic appeal. It's just like apple pie, only individual portions.

APPLE BUTTER

5 tart apples, preferably Gala, Fuji, or Granny Smith, peeled, cored, and coarsely chopped

$1/2$ cup maple syrup

1 teaspoon ground cinnamon

SPICED RICE DREAM

1 pint vanilla Rice Dream, or your choice of nondairy frozen dessert

2 teaspoons ground cinnamon

$1/4$ teaspoon ground allspice

$1/8$ teaspoon ground nutmeg

PASTRY DOUGH

3 cups unbleached all-purpose flour

$1/2$ cup Sucanat

$1/4$ teaspoon sea salt

$3/4$ cup canola oil

$1/2$ to $3/4$ cup soy milk

CARAMELIZED APPLES

4 apples, preferably Gala or Granny Smith, peeled, cored, and cut into $1/8$-inch sliced

$1/4$ cup maple syrup

To make the apple butter: In a medium saucepan, combine the apples, maple syrup, and cinnamon. Bring to a simmer, reduce heat to low, cover, and simmer for about 40 minutes, or until the apples have softened and the mixture has no excess moisture. Set aside and let cool.

To make the spiced Rice Dream: Spoon the Rice Dream into a bowl and let sit for 15 minutes.

Add the spices and mix thoroughly with a spatula. Spoon back into the container and freeze again for at least 3 hours.

To make the pastry: Sift the flour into a medium bowl and stir in the Sucanat and salt. Drizzle the oil into the dry ingredients, covering as much surface area as possible, and mix lightly with a spatula until the flour and oil form dough balls about the size of marbles. Drizzle in $1/2$ cup soy milk, stirring until the mixture forms a ball. Stir in more soy milk in 1-tablespoon increments if needed. Wrap the ball in plastic wrap. Knead lightly and refrigerate for 30 minutes or longer.

To make the caramelized apples: In a heavy, medium saucepan, combine the apples and syrup. Bring to a simmer and cook for 5 minutes. Set aside and let cool.

To make the galettes: Preheat the oven to 350°. Line a baking sheet with parchment paper. Divide the dough into 7 pieces. Roll 1 piece out between 2 sheets of parchment or waxed paper to a rough circle 6 inches in diameter. Cover the remaining dough with a towel. Remove the top sheet of paper to break the seal of the dough. Put it on top of the dough lightly, flip the dough over, and remove the piece of paper that is now on top. With a paring knife, cut the dough into a 5-inch-diameter circle, using a small plate as a guide. Remove the excess dough.

Place $1/4$ cup apple butter in the center of the circle and top with a fan of caramelized apple slices. Fold the sides of the circle over the filling, leaving the center open and creating a square galette. Place the galette on the prepared pan. Repeat with the remaining dough and filling.

Bake for 35 minutes, or until the crusts are golden brown. Let cool slightly on a rack. Serve warm with the spiced Rice Dream.

NUTRITIONAL INFORMATION PER GALETTE:

731 Calories (33% from fat), 7 g Protein, 115 g Carbohydrate, 27 g Fat, 0 mg Cholesterol, 286 mg Sodium, 6 g Fiber

ALMOND BISCOTTI

MAKES ABOUT 20 BISCOTTI

A perfect companion for your afternoon cup of double espresso. These biscotti do not get as hard as traditional biscotti, but I think that is an improvement. Try serving these with Espresso Sorbet (page 217) after dinner.

2 cups unbleached all-purpose flour
2 cups slivered almonds, toasted (see page 234)
1/4 cup Sucanat
1 1/2 teaspoons baking powder
1/8 teaspoon sea salt
1/2 cup plus 2 tablespoons soy milk
1 1/2 teaspoons egg replacement powder
1/4 cup maple syrup
1/4 cup canola oil
1 teaspoon vanilla extract
1 teaspoon fresh lemon juice

Preheat the oven to 350°. Line a baking sheet with parchment paper. In a large bowl, stir together the flour, almonds, Sucanat, baking powder, and salt. In another bowl, whisk together the soy milk, egg replacement powder, maple syrup, oil, vanilla extract, and lemon juice. Pour the wet mixture into the dry mixture and mix gently to form a dough.

On a lightly floured board, roll the dough with your hands into a log that is 10 inches long and about 1 inch high. Knead extra flour into the dough if it is too sticky to handle. Place on the prepared baking sheet and bake for 35 minutes, or until the biscotti are just beginning to firm. Let cool to the touch (leave the oven on). Slice the log into 1/2-inch-thick slices. Place the slices flat on the baking sheet. Bake again for 15 minutes. Turn on the second side for 10 to 15 minutes, or until they seem to have dried. Let cool on racks. Store in an airtight container.

NUTRITIONAL INFORMATION PER SERVING:

153 Calories (53% from fat), 3 g Protein, 15 g Carbohydrate, 9 g Fat, 0 mg Cholesterol, 63 mg Sodium, 2 g Fiber

VARIATION:

Melt 1/2 pound nondairy dark chocolate and dip half of each biscotti into it. Place on a baking sheet or cooling rack until set.

LEMON TUILES

MAKES ABOUT 25 COOKIES

These cookies go well with chocolate desserts.

1/4 cup rice syrup
1/4 cup maple syrup
Minced zest of 1 lemon
Juice of 1 lemon
1/4 cup canola oil
1/2 cup unbleached all-purpose flour
2 tablespoons arrowroot
1/8 teaspoon sea salt

Preheat the oven to 350°. Line a baking sheet with parchment paper. In a small bowl, combine the rice syrup, maple syrup, lemon zest and juice, and canola oil. Whisk together. In another small bowl, stir the flour, arrowroot, and salt together. Pour the wet ingredients into the dry ingredients and whisk until well combined. Spoon 1/2-tablespoonfuls of batter 4 inches apart on the prepared sheet. Bake for 6 minutes. Rotate the sheet and bake for 7 more minutes, or until the tuiles are golden brown around the edges. Allow the cookies to cool on the sheet. Remove and serve, or store in an airtight container for up to 7 days.

NUTRITIONAL INFORMATION PER TUILE:

46 Calories (39% from fat), 0 g Protein, 7 g Carbohydrate, 2 g Fat, 0 mg Cholesterol, 25 mg Sodium, 0.1 g Fiber

SESAME LACE TUILES

MAKES ABOUT 25 COOKIES

We always keep these cookies around for garnish. They are also served with Melon Fruit Soup with Lemongrass (page 203).

¹/₂ cup canola oil
¹/₃ cup brown rice syrup
²/₃ cup maple syrup
¹/₂ cup unbleached all-purpose flour
¹/₂ cup mixed black and white sesame seeds
1 teaspoon arrowroot
¹/₄ teaspoon sea salt

Preheat the oven to 350°. Line a baking sheet with parchment paper. In a medium bowl, combine the canola oil, rice syrup, and maple syrup. Whisk until blended. In a small bowl, stir together the flour, sesame seeds, arrowroot, and sea salt. Pour the wet mixture into the dry mixture and stir until well combined. Drop half-teaspoonfuls 3 inches apart on the prepared sheet. Bake for 6 minutes. Rotate the sheet and bake for 7 more minutes, or until golden brown. Allow to cool on the sheet. The cookies will firm as they cool. If they seem soft after cooling, bake again for 3 minutes. Store in a sealed container for up to two weeks.

NUTRITIONAL INFORMATION PER TUILE:

93 Calories (48% from fat), 0 g Protein, 12 g Carbohydrate, 5 g Fat, 0 mg Cholesterol, 30 mg Sodium, 0.1 g Fiber

PINE NUT AND ANISE COOKIES

MAKES ABOUT 20 COOKIES

Incredibly flaky and rich, these cookies go well with dessert wines, port, coffee, or tea. Serve them also with sorbet or as an accompaniment to one of our fruit soups. This recipe is based on the Anise Cookies with Pignoli in Lorna Sass's Cooking Recipes from an Ecological Kitchen *(Morrow). If I could only eat one kind of cookie for the rest of my life, these would definitely be the one.*

3 cups unbleached all-purpose flour
¹/₄ teaspoon sea salt
1¹/₂ teaspoons baking powder
1 tablespoon aniseed
1 cup pine nuts, toasted (see page 234)
³/₄ cup plus 2 tablespoons maple syrup
¹/₂ cup canola oil
¹/₄ cup water
1 tablespoon plus 1 teaspoon anise extract
1 teaspoon vanilla extract

Preheat the oven to 350°. Line a baking sheet with parchment paper. In a large bowl, sift together the flour, salt, and baking powder. Mix in the aniseed and pine nuts. In a small bowl, whisk together the remaining ingredients. Pour the wet mixture into the dry mixture and stir until combined. Form a ball of dough with about 2 tablespoons batter and place on the prepared sheet. Press with your hand to a thickness of ¹/₃ inch. Repeat, placing the cookies 3 inches apart. Bake for 20 to 30 minutes, or until lightly brown. Let cool on a wire rack. Store in an airtight container for up to 2 weeks.

When making these cookies for the peach and ginger fruit soup, cut the recipe in half. When forming the cookies, place the dough between two sheets of parchment paper. Roll the dough until it is about 1/3 inch thick. Remove the top layer of parchment payer and cut the dough into pieces that are about 1 inch by 1 inch. Place the parchment paper with the cookie squares onto a cookie sheet and bake for 15 to 20 minutes, or until the cookies are lightly brown. Cool on a wire rack.

NUTRITIONAL INFORMATION PER COOKIE:

193 Calories (42% from fat), 3 g Protein, 25 g Carbohydrate, 9 g Fat, 0 mg Cholesterol, 128 mg Sodium, 1 g Fiber

DOUBLE CHOCOLATE CHIP COOKIES

MAKES ABOUT 25 COOKIES

These double chocolate chip cookies are great when you want that familiar chocolate cookies taste that haunts us all from childhood, but could use a lighter version.

3 1/2 cups unbleached all-purpose flour
3/4 cup rolled oats
3/4 teaspoon baking soda
1/2 cup unsweetened cocoa powder
1 cup Sucanat
1/8 teaspoon sea salt
1 cup nondairy chocolate chips
1/2 cup low-fat soy milk
3/4 cup apple sauce
1/2 cup brown rice syrup
1 tablespoon vanilla extract

Preheat the oven to 350°. Line a baking sheet with parchment paper. In a large bowl, stir together the flour, rolled oats, baking soda, cocoa powder, Sucanat, and salt until well combined. Add the chocolate chips and stir until well combined. In a medium bowl, whisk together the soy milk, apple sauce, rice syrup, and vanilla extract.

Pour the wet mixture into the dry mixture and mix well until combined (start with a rubber spatula and end with your hands). Drop balls of dough, about 3 tablespoons each, 3 inches apart on the prepared sheet. Press the dough flat with a piece of plastic wrap until the cookies are 1/3 inch thick.

Bake for 20 to 25 minutes, or until the bottoms are golden brown. Let cool on a rack. The cookies will firm as they cool.

The best method for baking these is on a parchment paper-lined sheet pan. These cookies adhere to whatever they are baked on. When parchment paper is used, it can be peeled away from the bottoms of the cookies easily.

NUTRITIONAL INFORMATION PER COOKIE:

167 Calories (16% from fat), 3 g Protein, 32 g Carbohydrate, 3 g Fat, 0 mg Cholesterol, 70 mg Sodium, 2 g Fiber

FIG AND ALMOND TART WITH RED WINE AND PEAR CREAM

SERVES 10

This interesting tart uses a layer of red wine pear cream under fresh figs and over an almond crust. Serve it with Blackberry Coulis (page 222)—use the optional black pepper. This tart could be made with dried black figs plumped in red wine and a bit of Sucanat if you desire.

RED WINE AND PEAR CREAM

5 pears, such as Bosc or d'Anjou, peeled, cored, and coarsely chopped (about 5 cups)

$1/4$ cup dry red wine

$1/2$ cup maple syrup

$1/2$ teaspoon ground allspice

$1/4$ teaspoon ground pepper

ALMOND TART SHELL

1 cup whole almonds

$1^{1}/2$ cups all-purpose flour

$1/4$ teaspoon sea salt

$1/2$ cup maple syrup

$1/4$ cup canola oil

2 tablespoons water

1 teaspoon vanilla extract

2 cups fresh mission figs

Blackberry Coulis with black pepper (page 222)

To make the pear and red wine cream: In a medium, heavy saucepan, combine all the ingredients. Bring to a simmer, cover, and cook for about 25 minutes, or until the pears are soft. Remove the cover and cook for about 10 minutes, or until any excess liquid has evaporated. Pour the mixture onto a sided baking sheet and let cool. Purée in a blender or food processor until smooth. Set aside.

To make the tart shell: Preheat the oven to 350°. In a food processor, grind the almonds to a fine meal. In a small bowl, stir the flour, ground almonds, and salt together. In a second bowl, whisk the maple syrup, oil, water, and vanilla extract together.

Pour the wet mixture into the dry mixture. Mix well with a spatula. Press the dough into a 9-inch false-bottom tart pan, or five 3-inch tart pans. With a fork, make 6 or 7 sets of holes in the dough. Bake 25 to 35 minutes, or until the crust is golden brown. Let cool on a rack.

Cut the figs into $1/8$-inch round slices. Spread the red wine and pear cream in the prebaked shell. Arrange the fig slices on top of the cream. Remove the tart from the ring of the pan but keep it on the metal bottom. Cut the tart into 10 pieces or serve each person an individual 3-inch tart.

Spoon some Blackberry Coulis onto each serving plate, place a piece of tart on the plate, and enjoy.

NUTRITIONAL INFORMATION PER SERVING:

373 Calories (31% from fat), 5 g Protein, 59 g Carbohydrate, 13 g Fat, 0 mg Cholesterol, 64 mg Sodium, 6 g Fiber

SORBETS

The sorbets in this section can be made either in an ice cream maker or in the freezer. Making sorbets is fun and easy, so make your own combination of fruits and flavorings. When making a sorbet mixture, it should be a little sweeter than you want the sorbet to be. A little liqueur will highlight flavors. and make the mixture softer when frozen. Try adding 1 or 2 teaspoons orange liqueur to lemon, peach, plum, or persimmon. Try a bit of rum with coconut or espresso, and some framboise with blackberry or pomegranate.

If you don't have an ice cream maker, sorbet can be made granita style, as follows:

Pour the sorbet mixture into a large, shallow dish, cover with plastic wrap, and freeze overnight. When ready to serve, scrape the frozen mixture with a fork, and serve. You can also pour the sorbet mixture into a shallow dish, place the dish in the freezer, and stir the mixture every hour until it is frozen.

Because the sorbet that you make will not have the starches or stabilizers that commercial sorbets have, their shelf life is shorter. They will become overly icy in about 4 days, so either eat them before then, or melt and refreeze them.

BLACKBERRY SORBET

MAKES ABOUT 4 CUPS

Blackberry sorbet is a real treat on its own or garnished with some fresh berries—raspberries and strawberries create a wonderful contrast of taste and color. You can serve this sorbet in a wine glass with some Cabernet Sauvignon drizzled over the sorbet. This recipe can be easily halved.

6 cups fresh blackberries
1 cup water
1/4 cup fresh lemon juice
1/2 cup Sucanat
Pinch sea salt

In a blender, purée the blackberries. Strain them through a fine-meshed sieve into a bowl. Rinse the blender and pour the blackberry purée back into it. Add the water, lemon juice, Sucanat, and salt. Blend until well combined.

Freeze in an ice cream maker according to the manufacturer's instructions.

To make granita-style, pour the mixture into a large shallow baking dish and place it in the freezer. Stir the mixture every hour for 4 to 6 hours, or until frozen. Store in an airtight container in the freezer for up to 4 days. After 4 days, the sorbet may become icy; when this happens, the sorbet can be melted and refrozen.

NUTRITIONAL INFORMATION PER 1/2 CUP:

104 Calories (0% from fat), 0.4 g Protein, 26 g Carbohydrate, 0 g Fat, 0 mg Cholesterol, 5 mg Sodium, 1 g Fiber

COCONUT SORBET

MAKES 2 CUPS

This wonderful sorbet likes chocolate, but it pairs well with almost anything else that you might think to serve it with. It complements any fruit-based dessert wonderfully. We serve it with our Mad Good Chocolate Cake.

1 14-ounce can light coconut milk
6 tablespoons fructose
Pinch sea salt
1/4 scraped vanilla bean or 1/4 teaspoon vanilla extract

In a medium bowl, combine all the ingredients and whisk until well combined. Freeze in an ice cream maker according to the manufacturer's instructions.

To make granita-style, pour the mixture into a large shallow baking dish and place it in the freezer. Stir this mixture every hour for 4 to 6 hours, or until frozen. Store in an airtight container in the freezer for up to 4 days. After 4 days, the sorbet may become icy; when this happens, the sorbet can be melted and refrozen.

NUTRITIONAL INFORMATION PER 1/2 CUP:

136 Calories (53% from fat), 0 g Protein, 16 g Carbohydrate, 8 g Fat, 0 mg Cholesterol, 8 mg Sodium, 0 g Fiber

LOWER-FAT COCONUT SORBET

MAKES 2 CUPS

The flavor of this sorbet is intense and rich even though the coconut milk is replaced with rice milk.

1$1/2$ cups rice milk
$1/4$ cup fructose
1 teaspoon coconut extract
$1/2$ teaspoon vanilla extract or $1/4$ scraped vanilla bean
Pinch sea salt

In a small bowl, combine all of the ingredients and whisk until well combined. Freeze in an ice cream maker according to the manufacturer's instructions.

To make granita-style, pour into a large shallow baking dish and place it in the freezer. Stir every hour for 4 to 6 hours, or until frozen. Store in an airtight container in the freezer for up to 4 days. After 4 days, the sorbet may become icy; when this happens, the sorbet can be melted and refrozen.

NUTRITIONAL INFORMATION PER $1/2$ CUP:

84 Calories (7% from fat), 0.4 g Protein, 19 g Carbohydrate, 0.7 g Fat, 0 mg Cholesterol, 34 mg Sodium, 0 g Fiber

ESPRESSO SORBET

MAKES 4 CUPS

This is the sorbet that we serve with our Mocha Mud Slide (page 189). It is equally at home on its own or with some biscotti or other cookies.

1$1/2$ cups cold brewed espresso
$3/4$ cup Sucanat
1 14-ounce can light coconut milk
2 teaspoons vanilla extract
$1/4$ teaspoon finely ground espresso

In a medium bowl, combine all the ingredients and whisk until well blended. Freeze in an ice cream maker according to the manufacturer's instructions.

To make granita-style, pour into a large shallow baking dish and place it in the freezer. Stir this mixture every hour for 4 to 6 hours, or until it is frozen. Store in an airtight container in the freezer for up to 4 days. After 4 days, the sorbet may become icy; when this happens, the sorbet can be melted and refrozen.

NUTRITIONAL INFORMATION PER $1/2$ CUP:

110 Calories (33% from fat), 0.5 g Protein, 18 g Carbohydrate, 4 g Fat, 0 mg Cholesterol, 3 mg Sodium, 0 g Fiber

PEACH SORBET

MAKES 4 CUPS

Peach sorbet goes well with either of our fruit soups (page 203). For an interesting twist, try adding some minced fresh herbs to the sorbet mixture before freezing it. This works equally well with nectarines—white nectarines especially create a beautiful color when made into sorbet.

4 large ripe peaches (about 2 pounds),
    pitted, and coarsely chopped
3/4 cup water
2 tablespoons fresh lemon juice
1/2 cup fructose
1 tablespoon minced fresh rosemary, basil,
    or tarragon (optional)
Pinch sea salt

In a blender, combine all the ingredients and purée until smooth, pulsing if necessary. Freeze in an ice cream maker according to the manufacturer's instructions.

To make granita-style, pour the mixture into a large shallow baking dish and place it in the freezer. Stir this mixture every hour for 4 to 6 hours, or until it is frozen. Store in an airtight container in the refrigerator for up to 4 days. After 4 days, the sorbet may become icy; when this happens, the sorbet can be melted and refrozen.

NUTRITIONAL INFORMATION PER 1/2 CUP:

120 Calories (0% from fat), 0 g Protein, 30 g Carbohydrate, 0 g Fat, 0 mg Cholesterol, 5 mg Sodium, 1 g Fiber

PERSIMMON SORBET

MAKES 4 CUPS

Persimmons make a great-tasting sorbet with an interesting texture. Their flavor comes through well in this sorbet, though it does require a bit more added sweetener than other sorbets. Fuyu persimmons work best in this recipe.

7 Fuyu persimmons (about 3 pounds), chopped
1 cup water
2 tablespoons fresh lemon juice
1/2 cup fructose
Pinch sea salt

In a blender, combine all the ingredients and purée until completely smooth, about 3 minutes.

Freeze in an ice cream maker according to the manufacturer's instructions.

To make granita-style, pour the mixture into a large shallow baking dish and place it in the freezer. Stir this mixture every hour for 4 to 6 hours, or until frozen. Store in an airtight container in the freezer for up to 4 days. After 4 days, the sorbet may become icy; when this happens, the sorbet can be melted and refrozen.

NUTRITIONAL INFORMATION PER 1/2 CUP:

140 Calories (0% from fat), 0 g Protein, 35 g Carbohydrate, 0 g Fat, 0 mg Cholesterol, 5 mg Sodium, 4 g Fiber

218

POMEGRANATE SORBET

MAKES 4 CUPS

Fresh pomegranate juice can be made by placing ripe pomegranates in a plastic bag and rolling them around until they feel soft, then piercing the pomegranate with the prongs of a fork and squeezing all of the juice out. Strain the juice through a fine-meshed sieve. You'll need about 6–8 pomegranates for 3 cups juice.

3 cups fresh or bottled pomegranate juice
¹⁄₄ cup maple syrup

In a medium bowl, whisk the ingredients together. Freeze in an ice cream maker according to the manufacturer's instructions.

To make granita-style, pour the mixture into a large shallow baking dish and place it in the freezer. Stir this mixture every hour for 4 to 6 hours or until frozen. Store in an airtight container in the freezer for up to 4 days. After about 4 days, the sorbet may become overly icy; when this happens, the sorbet can be melted and refrozen.

NUTRITIONAL INFORMATION PER ¹⁄₂ CUP:

72 Calories (0% from fat), 0 g Protein, 18 g Carbohydrate, 0 g Fat, 0 mg Cholesterol, 3 mg Sodium, 0 g Fiber

HEART PLUM SORBET

MAKES 4 CUPS

Elephant heart plums are a bit larger than the average plum, and they really are heart-shaped. Their most striking quality is their intense red color, which makes a beautiful sorbet. If you can't get elephant heart plums, you can use Santa Rosas or any other local variety. Enjoy this sorbet with a ginger cookie.

¹⁄₄ cup port
¹⁄₂ cup Sucanat
2 pounds elephant heart plums (about 6), or your favorite variety, pitted and chopped

In a small saucepan, simmer the port and Sucanat until the Sucanat dissolves, about 3 minutes.

In a blender, combine the port mixture and the plums. Purée until smooth. Freeze in an ice cream maker according to the manufacturer's instructions.

To make granita-style, pour into a large shallow baking dish and place it in the freezer. Stir every hour for 4 to 6 hours, or until frozen. Store in an airtight container in the freezer for up to 4 days. After 4 days, the sorbet may become icy; when this happens, the sorbet can be melted and refrozen.

NUTRITIONAL INFORMATION PER ¹⁄₂ CUP:

124 Calories (0% from fat), 1 g Protein, 30 g Carbohydrate, 0 g Fat, 0 mg Cholesterol, 4 mg Sodium, 2 g Fiber

RED WINE AND BLACK PEPPER SORBET

MAKES 3 CUPS

You might not associate red wine and black pepper with dessert, but they make a great sorbet with an incredibly refined taste. Try serving it with a Warm Caramelized Apple Galette (page 208) or with some fresh or poached figs.

1 bottle (750 ml) dry red table wine
1/2 teaspoon ground pepper
1/3 cup fructose
Pinch sea salt

In a heavy, medium saucepan, simmer the red wine for 20 minutes or until reduced by about one-third. Add remaining ingredients and whisk together.

Refrigerate for at least 2 hours, or until well chilled. Freeze in an ice cream maker according to the manufacturer's instructions.

To make granita-style, pour the mixture into a large shallow baking dish and place it in the freezer. Stir every hour for 4 to 6 hours, or until it is frozen. Store in an airtight container in the freezer for up to 4 days. After 4 days, the sorbet may become icy; when this happens, the sorbet can be melted and refrozen.

NUTRITIONAL INFORMATION PER 1/2 CUP:

128 Calories (0% from fat), 0 g Protein, 13 g Carbohydrate, 0 g Fat, 0 mg Cholesterol, 5 mg Sodium, 0 g Fiber

SPICED GREEN APPLE SORBET

MAKES 4 CUPS

Apple sorbet is refreshing, refined, and loaded with texture. This recipe has a lot of spice, so you might want to reduce it if the sorbet is to accompany something delicate. This goes well with our Pumpkin Cake with Chocolate Hazelnut Ganache (page 194).

3 apples, such as Granny Smith or substitute your favorite apple, peeled, cored, and chopped
1 1/2 cups apple juice
1/2 cup fructose
1/2 teaspoon ground allspice
Pinch ground pepper
Pinch sea salt

In a blender, combine all the ingredients and purée until smooth. Freeze in an ice cream maker according to the manufacturer's instructions.

To make granita-style, pour the mixture into a large shallow baking dish and place it in the freezer. Stir every hour for 4 to 6 hours, or until frozen. Store in an airtight container in the freezer for up to 4 days. After about 4 days, the sorbet may become overly icy; when this happens, the sorbet can be melted and refrozen.

NUTRITIONAL INFORMATION PER 1/2 CUP:

108 Calories (0% from fat), 0 g Protein, 27 g Carbohydrate, 0 g Fat, 0 mg Cholesterol, 3 mg Sodium, 1 g Fiber

CHANTERELLE MUSHROOM SORBET

MAKES 2 CUPS

We serve this sorbet at our annual mushroom dinner. This sorbet works best with fresh, clean golden chanterelles. Their unique woodsy-apricot flavor is highlighted in this slightly sweet, orange-perfumed sorbet.

8 ounces golden chanterelles, brushed well to clean

2 tablespoons orange liqueur, such as Grand Marnier or Grand Torres

$1/3$ cup fructose

$1/2$ cup water

$1/4$ teaspoon sea salt

2 tablespoons fresh lemon juice

Coarsely chop the chanterelles and place in a bowl. Toss with the orange liqueur.

In another bowl, whisk the sugar, water, and salt together. Add to the mushrooms. In a blender, purée until smooth.

Freeze in an ice cream maker according to the manufacturer's instructions.

To make granita-style, pour the mixture into a large shallow baking dish and place it in the freezer. Stir every hour for 4 to 6 hours, or until frozen. Store in an airtight container in the freezer for up to 4 days. After 4 days, the sorbet may become icy; when this happens, the sorbet can be melted and refrozen.

NUTRITIONAL INFORMATION PER $1/2$ CUP:

112 Calories (0% from fat), 1 g Protein, 27 g Carbohydrate, 0 g Fat, 0 mg Cholesterol, 160 mg Sodium, 0.6 g Fiber

SAUCES

BLACKBERRY COULIS

MAKES 1 CUP

The black pepper gives this sauce a subtle spiciness, but you can omit it if you like.

2 cups fresh blackberries, or 10 ounces frozen
    unsweetened blackberries, thawed
1/4 to 1/2 cup Sucanat
1/4 teaspoon ground pepper (optional)

In a blender, combine the blackberries with the Sucanat and pepper. Blend to a smooth sauce. Pass the sauce through a fine-meshed sieve. Store in an airtight container in the refrigerator for up to 7 days.

NUTRITIONAL INFORMATION PER
1/4 CUP SERVING:

139 Calories (0% from fat), 0.8 g Protein, 34 g Carbohydrate, 0 g Fat, 0 mg Cholesterol, 3 mg Sodium, 3 g Fiber

CARAMEL SAUCE

MAKES 1 CUP

A sauce that we use as a complement for many different flavors in the desserts served at Millennium, depending on the liquid used.

1 cup fructose
1/3 cup water or other liquid such as
    Meyer lemon juice or rum

In a small, heavy saucepan combine the fructose and the water or other liquid. Place the saucepan over a medium high heat. Cook until the mixture comes to simmer, allow to turn a light brown, then remove from heat. Pour into an airtight container and refrigerate. The caramel sauce will thicken when chilled, about 3 hours. Store in the refrigerator for up to 2 months.

NUTRITIONAL INFORMATION PER 1/4 CUP:

192 Calories (0% from fat), 0 g Protein, 48 g Carbohydrate, 0 g Fat, 0 mg Cholesterol, 1 mg Sodium, 0 g Fiber

CARAMEL RUM SAUCE: In place of water, add a mixture of 2 tablespoons water and 2 tablespoons rum to the caramelized fructose.

MEYER LEMON SAUCE: In place of the water, use the juice of 1 Meyer lemon.

222

CHOCOLATE GANACHE

MAKES 4 CUPS

Our version of the classic ganache is simple to make and goes with everything. It can be used as a cake filling or icing, or you can dip bread in it or eat it with a spoon.

1 pound semisweet nondairy dark chocolate, chopped
2 cups soy milk

Melt the chocolate in a double boiler over barely simmering water. Pour the soy milk into a blender, then pour in the melted chocolate and purée until smooth. Or whisk half the soy milk into the chocolate, then whisk in the second half and continue whisking until the mixture is smooth. Pour the ganache into an airtight container and refrigerate for 6 hours, or until firm. Will keep for 1 week refrigerated.

NUTRITIONAL INFORMATION PER 1/4 CUP:

161 Calories (50% from fat), 2 g Protein, 18 g Carbohydrate, 9 g Fat, 0 mg Cholesterol, 4 mg Sodium, 2 g Fiber

CHOCOLATE SAUCE

MAKES 1 1/2 CUPS

This sauce has a rich cocoa flavor. Serve it with our brownie (page 196) or use it any time you want to highlight or add chocolate flavor.

1 cup water
3/4 cup Sucanat
6 tablespoons unsweetened cocoa powder
1 teaspoon vanilla extract
Pinch sea salt

In a small saucepan, combine the water and Sucanat. Heat the mixture until the Sucanat dissolves. Pour into a medium bowl and add the cocoa powder, vanilla, and salt. Whisk until well combined. Refrigerate until well chilled. Store in an airtight container in the refrigerator for up to 1 week.

NUTRITIONAL INFORMATION PER 1/4 CUP SERVING:

125 Calories (7% from fat), 1 g Protein, 28 g Carbohydrate, 1 g Fat, 0 mg Cholesterol, 58 mg Sodium, 2 g Fiber

VANILLA SAUCE

MAKES 1 1/2 CUPS

Our version of crème anglaise is an all-purpose sauce that goes with everything from fresh fruit to Chocolate Almond Midnight (page 198).

One 12.3-ounce box low-fat extra-firm silken tofu
3/4 cup soy milk
1/3 cup fructose
1 tablespoon vanilla extract
Seeds scraped from 1/4 split vanilla bean
Pinch sea salt

In a blender combine all the ingredients and blend until smooth. Store in an airtight container in the refrigerator for up to 1 week.

NUTRITIONAL INFORMATION PER 1/4 CUP:

69 Calories (13% from fat), 4 g Protein, 11 g Carbohydrate, 1 g Fat, 0 mg Cholesterol, 65 mg Sodium, 0.4 g Fiber

MANGO SAUCE

MAKES ABOUT 1 1/2 CUPS

Mango sauce adds color and a bit of tropical flavor to almost any dessert. We serve it as an integral part of our Lemon Caramel Napoleon. It would be equally delicious with a slice of Chocolate Almond Midnight.

1 ripe mango
1/2 to 1 cup fresh Lemonade (see page 237)

Peel the mango and remove its flesh. Either cut off the peel with a knife and slice the flesh from around the pit, or cut off flesh and skin together in large slices, then score the flesh in cubes with a knife, invert the skin, and slice the mango cubes away from the skin.

In a blender, combine the flesh of the mango with 1/2 cup of lemonade. Purée until smooth, adding more lemonade if needed. Store in an airtight container in the refrigerator for up to 8 days.

NUTRITIONAL INFORMATION PER 1/4 CUP:

40 Calories (0% from fat), 0 g Protein, 10 g Carbohydrate, 0 g Fat, 0 mg Cholesterol, 2 mg Sodium, 1 g Fiber

RASPBERRY SAUCE

MAKES 1 CUP

Raspberry sauce is served with our Chocolate Almond Midnight. It would also work well tossed with some diced fruit to garnish just about any other dessert.

2 cups fresh or 10 ounces unsweetened frozen raspberries, thawed
1/4 cup Sucanat or fructose

In a blender, combine the raspberries and Sucanat, then blend to a smooth sauce. Strain the sauce through a fine-meshed sieve. Store in an airtight container in the refrigerator for up to 1 week.

NUTRITIONAL INFORMATION PER 1/4 CUP:

88 Calories (0% from fat), 1 g Protein, 21 g Carbohydrate, 0 g Fat, 0 mg Cholesterol, 1 mg Sodium, 2 g Fiber

BASICS

This chapter features the building blocks of many of our dishes. From vegetable stocks and braised garlic to making seitan from scratch to smoking tofu, these are essential to completing some of the recipes in this book. Some basics, such as marinated tempeh and seitan or vegetable stocks, are commercially available and make acceptable time-saving substitutes. But many of these recipes are worth preparing just to add to your food skills and knowledge.

BASIC VEGETABLE STOCK

MAKES 3 QUARTS

Vegetable stocks are the foundation for many of our soups, sauces, and entrées. We make them every day with the vegetable trimmings and scraps saved from the previous day. Our stocks vary with the seasons, though onions, garlic, tomatoes, carrots, and celery are a constant. Here is our basic stock, and three variations. The basic vegetable stock is a good starting point for any number of variations. A few words of caution though: Stay away from strong-tasting vegetables like broccoli, kale, and other members of the cabbage. They tend to lend an unpleasant ("skunky") quality to a stock. Also, don't use too many onion peels in a stock, as this can make a stock bitter. Stocks freeze quite well. Prepare a large batch, portion it into pints, and remove from the freezer when you need it.

6 quarts cold water
4 yellow onions, halved
4 cloves garlic
4 carrots, peeled and coarsely chopped
2 stalks celery
2 tomatoes, chopped
8 ounces button mushrooms and/or mushroom stems
2 bay leaves
6 allspice berries
1/2 bunch thyme stems or 1/2 teaspoon dried thyme
3 rosemary stems or 1/2 teaspoon dried rosemary
Optional ingredients: Root vegetables, fennel bulbs, corn, wild mushrooms, basil stems, tarragon stems, fresh ginger, lemon zest, peppercorns

In a large pot, combine all the ingredients. Bring to a boil, reduce heat to simmer, and cook for 1 hour. Strain through a fine-meshed sieve. Store in the refrigerator for up to 3 days, or freeze for up to 3 months.

NUTRITIONAL INFORMATION PER CUP:

20 Calories (0% from fat), 0 g Protein, 5 g Carbohydrate, 0 g Fat, 0 mg Cholesterol, 25 mg Sodium, 0 g Fiber

Asian Vegetable Stock

Prepare the Basic Vegetable Stock, replacing the thyme and rosemary with 4 stalks lemongrass, crushed; 1/2 cup coarsely chopped fresh ginger, 1 cup shiitake mushroom stems; 1 teaspoon Schezuan peppercorns, 1 bunch cilantro stems; and 1 bunch basil stems.

Tomato-Corn Stock

Prepare the Basic Vegetable Stock, replacing the mushrooms with 8 chopped tomatoes, 6 to 8 corn cobs, and 1 bunch basil stems.

Mushroom Stock

Prepare the Basic Vegetable Stock, adding 1 ounce dried porcini; 8 ounces fresh button or cremini mushrooms, chopped; and 1 cup shiitake mushroom stems.

DARK VEGETABLE STOCK

MAKES 3 QUARTS

4 red onions, halved
2 leeks, washed and sliced
4 cloves garlic
4 carrots, peeled and coarsely chopped
1 cup shiitake mushroom stems
8 ounces button mushrooms
2 cups dry red wine or nonalcoholic red wine
1 tablespoon olive oil (optional)
6 quarts cold water
2 bay leaves
6 allspice berries
$1/2$ bunch thyme stems, or 1 teaspoon dried thyme
3 rosemary stems, or $1/2$ teaspoon dried rosemary

Preheat the oven to 400°. In a baking pan, combine the onions, leeks, garlic, carrots, and mushrooms with 1 cup of the red wine and the olive oil. Toss to coat. Bake for 45 minutes to 1 hour, stirring the vegetables after 30 minutes.

In a large pot, combine the vegetables, the remaining 1 cup red wine, the bay leaves, allspice berries, thyme, and rosemary. Boil for 1 hour, skimming the oil and foam from time to time. Strain through a fine-meshed sieve. Store in the refrigerator for up to 3 days, or freeze for up to 3 months.

NUTRITIONAL INFORMATION PER CUP:

17 Calories (26% from fat), 0 g Protein, 3 g Carbohydrate, 0.5 g Fat, 0 mg Cholesterol, 25 mg Sodium, 0 g Fiber

CARAMELIZED ONIONS

MAKES 2 CUPS

Like our braised garlic, caramelized onions add body and richness to oil-free recipes. Purée them to use in everything from salad dressings to stews.

3 yellow onions, cut lengthwise into thin crescents
$1/2$ cup dry white wine, nonalcoholic white wine, or vegetable stock
$1/2$ teaspoon sea salt
Vegetable stock as needed

In a medium nonstick skillet, combine all the ingredients. Bring to a boil, reduce heat and simmer until all the liquid is evaporated, about 15 minutes, stirring often. Continue cooking over low heat, stirring frequently to prevent scorching, until the onions are very soft and a light caramel brown, about 15 to 20 minutes. Let cool and store in an airtight container in the refrigerator for up to 4 days, or freeze.

NUTRITIONAL INFORMATION PER SERVING:

46 Calories (0% from fat), 1 g Protein, 7 g Carbohydrate, 0 g Fat, 0 mg Cholesterol, 635 mg Sodium, 1 g Fiber

MILLENNIUM BRAISED GARLIC

MAKES 1 CUP

This staple is indispensable for our oil-free cookery. The soft and slightly caramelized cloves of garlic add both depth of flavor and, when puréed, creamy texture to many dishes. Keep this on hand to blend into soups, pasta sauces, and condiments.

4 large heads garlic
1 cup vegetable stock, or dry white wine, or nonalcoholic white wine
1 teaspoon minced fresh rosemary
1 teaspoon minced fresh thyme

Preheat the oven to 350°. With a large knife, cut off the top 1/2 inch from each garlic bulb. Place the garlic heads in a small baking dish. Add the stock, thyme, and rosemary. Cover tightly with aluminum foil. Bake for 1 1/2 hours, or until the heads are soft and slightly browned. Let cool to the touch. Squeeze the soft garlic out of the sliced-open top. Store in airtight container in the refrigerator for up to 1 week.

NUTRITIONAL INFORMATION PER TABLESPOON:

16 Calories (0% from fat), 0 g Protein, 4 g Carbohydrate, 0 g Fat, 0 mg Cholesterol, 10 mg Sodium, 0.2 g Fiber

PUMPKIN PURÉE

MAKES 1 1/2 CUPS

2 cups pumpkin flesh, cut into 1/2 inch cubes
1 cup water

Places the pumpkin cubes and the water in a saucepan with a tight-fitting lid. Bring to a boil, then reduce the heat to low and simmer, covered, for 20 minutes, or until the cubes are very soft. Drain well and purée in a food processor until smooth.

NUTRITIONAL INFORMATION PER 2 CUP SERVING:

178 Calories (10% from fat), 4 g Protein, 36 g Carbohydrate, 2 g Fat, 0 mg Cholesterol, 20 mg Sodium, 15 g Fiber

GINGER JUICE

MAKES ABOUT 1 TABLESPOON

4 tablespoon grated fresh ginger

Place the ginger in a very fine strainer and press to extract the juice, or wrap in cheesecloth or a very fine linen napkin, and squeeze over a bowl.

MARINATED SEITAN MEDALLIONS

SERVES 8

Seitan is a wheat gluten preparation that has been used as a protein source and meat substitute in Asia for hundreds of years. The traditional procedure for making seitan involves making a flour and water dough and then rinsing it under running water to remove the starch components of the flour, leaving behind the high-protein gluten. The dough is then wrapped in cheese cloth and poached until it is firm; then it is sliced and marinated. Our procedure removes the rinsing step, and saves about 40 minutes. Give it a try!

SEITAN

4 cups pure gluten flour
2/3 cups unbleached white flour
2 tablespoons bran flakes
3 1/2 cups cool water
Cheesecloth for wrapping the seitan

MARINADE

1 cup red wine or nonalcoholic red wine
2 quarts vegetable stock or water
1/2 cup tamari or Bragg Liquid Aminos
2 cloves garlic, minced
1 sprig fresh rosemary
8 allspice berries (optional)
1 teaspoon dried sage
1 teaspoon dried thyme
1/4 teaspoon red chile flakes
2 teaspoons maple syrup, honey, or Sucanat

Combine the flours and bran flakes in a large mixing bowl. Knead the dough with your hands, slowly adding the 3 1/2 cups of water until it is absorbed. Continue kneading the dough for 2 minutes, until it is firm and springy.

Bring 4 to 6 cups of water to a rolling boil. Meanwhile, divide the dough into 3 equal portions. Knead each portion into a cylindrical loaf shape, about 5 to 6 inches long. Cut the cheesecloth into three 10-inch lengths and open it up. Place a seitan loaf at the bottom center of each piece of cheesecloth. Roll the cheesecloth up over the seitan, so that it is wrapped snugly but not tightly (the seitan needs a little room to expand). Cut off the excess cheesecloth at the ends of the roll and tie each end with kitchen twine, sealing the seitan in.

Carefully immerse the seitan rolls in the boiling water. Lower the heat slightly, cover the pot leaving the cover slightly ajar, and cook the seitan for 1 1/2 hours, or until seitan is very firm.

Drain the seitan rolls and allow them to come to room temperature, or immerse them in an ice water bath until cool. You can either store the wrapped seitan in an airtight container for up to 2 days in the refrigerator, or use it as soon as it has cooled to room temperature.

To marinate the seitan, unwrap the cooled seitan rolls. If the cheesecloth sticks, immerse the roll under warm running water to loosen it. Slice the seitan into 1/4-inch thick medallions.

Combine all the marinade ingredients in a deep pot and bring to a boil. Add the seitan medallions and simmer, covered, for 40 minutes. Either use the seitan medallions or store them in an airtight container in the refrigerator with enough marinade to cover for up to 4 days.

NUTRITIONAL INFORMATION PER SERVING:

164 Calories (0% from fat), 31 g Protein, 10 g Carbohydrate, 0 g Fat, 0 mg Cholesterol, 590 mg Sodium, 1 g Fiber

BAKED TOFU

MAKES 6 SERVINGS

This recipe yields tofu with a firm texture and a lacquered skin. It's great for sautéing, smoking, or adding to salads, stews, and soups because it will not disintegrate like raw tofu.

1 pound firm tofu
1/4 cup tamari soy sauce
2 teaspoons maple syrup or honey

Preheat the oven to 400°. Drain the tofu. Cut the tofu in half and then in thirds along the width to make 6 slices about 1/2 inch thick. Line a baking pan with parchment paper.

In a shallow bowl, combine the tamari and maple syrup. Dip the tofu in the marinade and place on the baking pan. Bake for 20 to 30 minutes. Turn the tofu over, brush with any remaining marinade, and bake for 20 minutes, or until caramel brown. Let cool. Store in an airtight container in the refrigerator for up to 4 days.

NUTRITIONAL INFORMATION PER SERVING:

135 Calories (47% from fat), 13 g Protein, 5 g Carbohydrate, 7 g Fat, 0 mg Cholesterol, 550 mg Sodium, 0.1 g Fiber

BAKED MARINATED TEMPEH

MAKES 6 SERVINGS

We bake or braise tempeh in this all-purpose marinade for over an hour to remove most of the bitter flavor associated with tempeh. Bake a double recipe of tempeh and freeze what you will not use in a week. When you are ready to use it, just thaw.

MARINADE
1 cup red of nonalcoholic red wine
4 cups vegetable stock or water
1/2 cup tamari
4 cloves garlic, minced
1 tablespoon Dijon mustard
1 teaspoon dried sage
2 teaspoons dried thyme
1/2 teaspoon nutmeg
1/4 teaspoon dried red chile flakes
2 teaspoons maple syrup, honey, or Sucanat
6 four-ounce portions tempeh

Preheat the oven to 350°. Mix all the marinade ingredients together. Place the tempeh in a baking dish and pour the marinade over the tempeh. Bake for 1 1/2 hours. Either remove the tempeh from the remaining marinade to serve or freeze, or store the tempeh in the marinade for up to a week in the refrigerator.

NUTRITIONAL INFORMATION PER 4-OUNCE SERVING:

285 Calories (28% from fat), 24 g Protein, 27 g Carbohydrate, 9 g Fat, 0 mg Cholesterol, 385 mg Sodium, 6 g Fiber

SMOKING FOODS

This method works for vegetables, tofu, and a number of other things in this book. Smoked foods add warmth and depth of flavor to many dishes. We've smoked almost every product we have in the Millennium larder with varying degrees of success. We regularly smoke onions, tomatoes, eggplant, portobello mushrooms, and reconstituted dried chiles. We regularly smoke tofu as a staple for our spinach salad and have smoked seitan and tempeh for entrées.

Hot smoking is not rocket science. All you need is a heat source, a heatproof container to hold the wood chips, a rack to suspend the food above the chips, a cover to contain the smoke, and either a good exhaust fan or the wide-open spaces of the outdoors.

Home cooking units are available in many sporting goods and outdoors specialty shops. These units are simply boxes or cylinders with electric heating elements on the bottom and three to five racks to hold the food. You can also use your charcoal or gas grill.

For a charcoal grill, soak wood chips in water to cover for 30 minutes, then drain and sprinkle over a low fire. Push the coals and wood chips to one side of the grill. Add the food to the cooking rack on the side opposite the coals and wood chips, cover the grill, and smoke for 30 to 40 minutes after the chips start smoking. Some gas grills have built-in containers for soaked wood chips. Otherwise, place the drained wood chips in an aluminum foil package. Poke holes in the bottom and set the package directly on the lava rocks. A third method is to use an electric wok outdoors. Place the soaked chips in a disposable aluminum pan in the bottom of the wok. Set the food on a rack that suspends the food at least 6 inches above the chips. Heat the wok just hot enough to smolder the chips and place the cover slightly ajar over the wok.

PREBAKED PIE CRUST

MAKES 1 CRUST

1^1/$_2$ cups unbleached all-purpose flour
^{1}/$_4$ cup Sucanat
^{1}/$_4$ teaspoon sea salt
6 tablespoons canola oil
4 to 5 tablespoons soy milk

Sift the flour into a bowl and add the Sucanat and salt. Stir the dry ingredients together. Drizzle the oil into the dry ingredients, covering as much surface area as possible, and mix lightly with a spatula until the flour and oil form dough balls about the size of marbles. Drizzle the soy milk into the bowl. Mix until a ball is formed. Wrap the ball in plastic wrap and knead lightly. Refrigerate for 30 minutes or longer.

Preheat the oven to 350°. Unwrap the dough and place it between 2 sheets of parchment or waxed paper. Roll the dough out to make a circle roughly 12 inches in diameter. Gently remove the top sheet of paper, replace it lightly, flip the dough over, and gently remove the bottom sheet of paper.

Flip the dough over on top of a pie pan and remove the top sheet of paper once again. Press the dough into a 9-inch pie pan and trim and flute the edges. Pierce the dough with the tines of a fork. Place a sheet of parchment paper over the crust and fill with ^{1}/$_2$ cup dried beans or pie weights. This is called blind baking and will keep the tart shell flat in the pie pan. Bake for 15 minutes. Remove the parchment paper and beans or weights. Bake for 5 to 10 minutes, or until the crust is a light golden brown.

TOASTING NUTS

Small quantities (under 1/2 cup) of nuts can be toasted in a dry saute pan over medium heat. Shake the pan constantly to prevent scorching. Larger quantitiies are best toasted in an oven, as described below.

Walnuts

Soaking walnuts before you toast them removes some of the bitter tannins from the nuts, and makes them crisper.

1 cup walnuts
2 cups warm water

Soak the walnuts in the water for thirty minutes. Drain. Place nuts on a baking sheet and bake ina 350° oven for 30 minutes, or until dry and light brown. Rotate every 10 minutes. Allow to cool to room temperature before serving.

Hazelnuts

To toast and skin hazelnuts, pour the shelled nuts onto a sided baking sheet and bake in a preheated 350° oven until toasted and fragrant, about 15 minutes. Place the hazelnuts in a bowl, cover the bowl with plastic wrap, and allow them to steam for a few minutes. Pour the nuts out onto a clean kitchen towel, and rub them together until the skins come off. Repeat the process with any nuts that have stubborn skins. (Remember it's okay to leave some of the skin on the nuts.) Try blanching unskinned hazelnuts (before roasting) in boiling water with one tablespoon baking soda, for three minutes. This helps loosen the skin.

Other Nuts

Almonds and pine nuts should take about 10 minutes to toast. Pecans and pistachios should take about 12 to 15 minutes.

TOASTING BREAD CRUMBS

MAKES 1 CUP
12 1/4-inch-thick slices of French bread

Preheat the oven to 250°. Place the bread slices in one layer on a baking sheet and bake until crisp and lightly browned, about 15 minutes (dry bread will be done more quickly). Remove from the oven and let cool to room temperature. Pulse the bread in a food processor until reduced to relatively uniform crumbs. Store in an airtight container at room temperature; will keep for two weeks.

TOASTING SPICES

Toast the spices in a dry sauté pan over high heat, shaking the pan constantly, until the spices darken slightly and give off fragrant wisps of smoke. This usually takes no more than a minute and a half. Remove spices from pan immediately.

TOASTING SEEDS

Seeds can be toasted in a dry sauté pan over medium heat, following same procedure as with spices, although the time will be 3 to 6 minutes. They can also be toasted in a 350° oven until the color darkens slightly. Time varies by seed, so check frequently.

ROASTING PEPPERS AND CHILES

Preheat broiler. Place the peppers on a baking sheet, or directly on the broiler rack, and broil until the skin blisters and chars. Turn the peppers and repeat until uniformly charred. You can also do this over a grill or open flame. Place the peppers in a paper bag or a bowl cover with plastic wrap, and let stand for 15 minutes. Peel off the charred skin and remove the stems and seeds. Use immediately, or store refrigerated, drizzled with a little olive oil if you wish, in an air-tight container for up to 1 week.

PEELING AND SEEDING TOMATOES

Cut an "X" in the bottom of each tomato and blanch them in boiling water for 30 seconds, then immerse them in an icewater bath until cool. Use a paring knife to peel back the skin, starting at the X. Seed tomatoes by cutting them in half and squeezing or scooping out the seeds.

SALTING EGGPLANT

Salting eggplant removes its bitter acids.

Cut the eggplant as required for the recipe (sliced, cubed, in half, etc.), and sprinkle with salt, allowing one teaspoon for each medium eggplant. Allow to stand for 20 minutes in a colander. Rinse the salt off the eggplant and pat dry.

SMOKING EGGPLANT

Prepare a smoker according to the manufacturer's directions, or as discussed on page 233. Place salted and rinsed eggplant slices in the smoker, and smoke for 30 to 40 minutes after the chips start to smoke.

SMOKING TOFU, TEMPEH, OR SEITAN

Prepare a smoker according to the manufacturer's directions, or as discussed on page 233. Place baked tofu, marinated tempeh, or marinated seitan in the smoker, and smoke for 40 to 60 minutes after the chips start to smoke.

SOAKING AND COOKING BEANS

Most beans benefit from presoaking before they are cooked; this speeds up cooking time and improves their digestibility. Small to medium beans should generally be soaked for a minimum of 4 hours, while larger ones should be soaked at least 6 hours. With beans of any size, it's often easiest to soak them overnight. Soak beans in three parts water to one part beans; after soaking, drain them and discard the water.

Quick-Soaking Beans

Bring the beans and water (three times as much water as beans) to a boil, and boil for 5 minutes. Remove from heat and cover; allow to soak for 2 hours. Drain the beans, discarding the soaking water.

On Cooking Beans

To cook, use 3 cups of water for every cup of soaked beans, or 4 cups for unsoaked beans. One cup of dried beans will yield $1\frac{1}{2}$ to 2 cups when cooked. Cooking time varies according to length of soaking time, and how old the beans are. Properly cooked beans should hold their shape, yet smash between your fingers with little resistance. Following is a table of approximate cooking times for presoaked beans:

BEAN	COOKING TIME
Aduki	45 min to 1 hour
Anasazi	1 to $1\frac{1}{2}$ hours
Black	$1\frac{1}{2}$ to 2 hours
Chestnut lima	1 to $1\frac{1}{2}$ hours
Calypso	1 to $1\frac{1}{2}$ hours
Flageolet	1 to $1\frac{1}{2}$ hours
Garbanzo	$1\frac{1}{2}$ to 2 hours
Pinto	1 to $1\frac{1}{2}$ hours
White (navy)	$1\frac{1}{2}$ to 2 hours
White (cannellini)	1 to $1\frac{1}{2}$ hours

COOKING GRAINS

Brown Basmati and Other Long-Grain Brown Rice

MAKES 2 CUPS

**1 cup brown basmati or
    other long-grain brown rice**
2 cups water

Toast the rice over medium-high heat in a saucepan for 2 minutes. Add the water and bring to a boil, then reduce to a simmer and cook, covered, for 30 to 35 minutes. Remove from heat and let stand for 10 minutes before serving.

Barley

MAKES 2^1/2 CUPS

1 cup hulled barley
3 cups water

Bring water to a boil, add barley, and reduce to a simmer. Cook covered for 1 hour. Remove from heat and let stand 5 to 10 minutes before serving.

Note: For pearled barley, use 2 1/2 cups of water and cook for 35 to 40 minutes.

Wild Rice

MAKES 2^1/2 CUPS

1 cup wild rice
2^1/2 cups water

Bring water to a boil, add wild rice, and reduce to a simmer. Cook covered for 40 to 45 minutes, or until the rice's outer kernels open up.

Quinoa

MAKES 3 CUPS

1 cup quinoa
2^1/2 cups water

Bring water to a boil and add quinoa. Reduce to a simmer and cook covered for 10 minutes. Let stand 10 minutes before serving.

Israeli Cous Cous

MAKES 2^1/2 CUPS

1 cup Israeli cous cous
2 quarts water
Salt

Add a pinch of salt to the water and bring to a boil. Add the cous cous and stir. Cook for 7 minutes. Drain, then cool under cold running water.

LEMONADE

MAKES 1 CUP

^{1}/4 cup fresh lemon juice
2 tablespoons unrefined sugar
^{3}/4 cup water

Mix all ingredients together.

GLOSSARY AND BASIC PROCEDURES

You'll find a list of ingredients below. Some may be unfamiliar, but all should be available in specialty (Asian, Mexican, gourmet, etc.) or natural-food stores. Ingredient quality is very important to us at Millennium, so here are a few notes about general issues before getting into the specific ingredient-by-ingredient glossary.

Beans: We always have a large variety of dried beans at our disposal. We have access to purveyors that specialize in heirloom varieties. Most natural foods and specialty grocers carry an ever-increasing supply of heirloom varieties, too. Many beans are interchangeable in recipes, dependent on the size and texture you desire. See below, under "Beans and Legumes," for information on specific varieties.

Chiles, dried: We use a number of dried chiles at Millennium, usually more for their depth of flavor than for the addition of heat alone. Many of the mild- to medium-heat dried chiles like anchos, guajillos, New Mexicos, and poblanos add warm earthy qualities and subtle dried-fruit flavors to their respective recipes. One indispensable ingredient is the chipotle. Chipotle refers to any number of variety of chiles that are dried by smoking, adding warm pronounced smoky qualities to any dish. The traditional and most commonly available chipotles are made from smoked jalapeños, though we use milder varieties, such as New Mexican and Hungarian wax, grown and smoked by our friends at Tierra Vegetables in Healdsburg, California (see "Resources").

Chiles, fresh: The serrano and the jalapeño, while different in size are similar in heat. Hot without being searing (the heat varies, depending on how old the peppers are and when and where they are grown), serranos have a slight herbal flavor to them and are probably my all-around favorite chile.

I also like the Thai bird's-eye, a small chile that packs a wallop. It has a clean searing heat, key in Southeast Asian cuisine.

Habanero and Scotch bonnet chiles are the kings of Caribbean cuisine. While absolutely explosive in heat, these squat yellow and orange chiles have the most distinct fruity flavor of any chile, making them worth the potential pain.

Mushrooms: We're very mushroom-friendly here at Millennium. I love mushrooms of all varieties, and as a mycologist wannabe living and cooking in an area noted for its abundance of wild mushrooms during the rainy season, it shows in our menus. Come winter in these parts you can find me on my time off turning my running and biking excursions into mushroom forays. At the restaurant we buy many of our wild mushrooms from reputable foragers, straight out of the woods. Also we have a camaraderie with the San Francisco Mycological Society, a group of amateur and professional fungophiles, with whom we've had special dinners and cooking classes showcasing wild and specialty mushrooms.

These days you should be able to find specialty domestic mushrooms like shiitakes, oyster mushrooms, and portobellos, as well as some of the more popular wild varieties such as porcini, cepes, chanterelles, and morels in specialty food stores throughout the country.

For resources on mushrooms I recommend, Jack Czarnecki's *A Cook's Book of Mushrooms* for how to cook with specific varieties and David Arora's *Mushrooms Demystified* as thc biblc on wild mushroom identification.

GLOSSARY

Agar (agar-agar): A tasteless dried seaweed that can be used in place of gelatin and acts as a setting agent. It is widely used in Asia and sold in the form of blocks, flakes, or strands. Agar can be purchased in Asian markets and natural-food stores.

Almond milk: A milk substitute made from almonds; it can be purchased in natural-food stores.

Arrowroot: A starch obtained from the rhizomes or roots of various tropical plants. The finely powdered starch is an excellent natural thickening agent for soups, sauces, and other cooked foods in lieu of flour or cornstarch. Unlike cornstarch, arrowroot does not alter the taste of foods prepared with it. It is tasteless and becomes clear when cooked. Arrowroot can be purchased in supermarkets and natural-food stores.

Barley malt: A very mild sweetner with a dark, "malty" flavor, it can be found in natural-food stores in either powder or syrup form.

Beans and Legumes:

Adzuki beans: A small brownish bean with a sweet flavor used frequently in Japanese and macrobiotic cooking. Adzuki beans can be purchased in Asian markets and natural-food stores.

Anasazi beans: Native to the Americas, this bean is a speckled cranberry-and-white color and can used anywhere you would use pinto beans. With its sweetish taste and meaty texture, it goes well with Southwestern and Latin American flavors. You'll find Anasazis in specialty and gourmet food stores.

Chickpeas: Also commonly called "garbanzo beans," these legumes now come in many sizes, from baby split chickpeas, which take fifteen minutes to cook, to large beans that can take upwards of two hours to cook, even after soaking. For hummus or other purées, try substituting white beans.

Lentils: The quickest cooking beans, they require no soaking. They come in several varieties.

Brown and green: The most common lentils, they have a pronounced earthy flavor.

French and black: Smaller than brown or green lentils, these remain al dente, with a chewy texture and nutty flavor, and are great in salads. The black or "black beluga" lentil makes a great garnish because of its jet-black color and small size.

Red: These cook in as little as fifteen minutes and quickly go from al dente to mush. Bright orange and "lighter" (less earthy) in flavor than other lentil varieties.

Mung beans: A close relative of the split pea, mung beans have a slightly "grassy" flavor.

Split peas: Dried peas that have been hulled and are split in half. They are available in green or yellow varieties and are often used in soups.

Blood orange: A number of varieties of oranges with flesh ranging from pink to a dark burgundy. Some varieties are slightly sweeter than common oranges, with a subtle raspberry flavor.

Boca Burgers: A fat-free vegetarian burger that has a meatlike taste and texture. Boca Burgers can be purchased in natural-food stores and in some supermarkets.

Bragg Liquid Aminos: A commercial unfermented soy sauce–like all-purpose seasoning that has a salty and unique flavor. It is used like soy sauce in cooking and as a condiment. Bragg Liquid Aminos are sold in natural-food stores and in some supermarkets.

Canola oil: The commercial name for rapeseed oil–which is a vegetable oil expressed from rape seeds. Canola oil is bland-tasting, lower in saturated fat than any other vegetable oil on the market, and very high in monounsaturated fat.

Celery root: Celery root, also known as celeriac, comes from a variety of celery having a large edible root. The root has a taste that is a cross between strong celery and parsley. The root can be eaten raw or cooked, and it is a wonderful ingredient in salads, soups, and purées.

Chickpea flour: A flour made from chickpeas or garbanzo beans.

Coconut extract: A concentrated natural flavoring (in liquid form) derived from coconut. It is used to deliver a natural coconut flavor to foods.

Corn flour: A finely ground cornmeal milled from the whole yellow or white corn kernel, or from kernels from which the germ has been removed. Corn flour is available in either yellow, white, or blue varieties.

Couscous: A popular staple of the North African countries of Algeria, Morocco, and Tunisia. Couscous is quick cooking granular semolina. It is available in refined and whole-wheat varieties.

Egg replacer: A powdered, egg-free commercial product made with starches and used as a substitute for eggs in many recipes. Egg replacer can be purchased in natural-food stores and in many supermarkets.

Fermented black beans: Whole black soybeans that are fermented then salted, along with orange peel and ginger. Makes for a pungent addition to Asian cookery. Try substituting dark red miso.

Flaxseed: A small shiny brown seed originating from the Mediterranean region. The tiny seeds are a rich source of omega-3 fatty acids. Flaxseeds can be purchased at natural-food stores.

Fructose: A natural sugar also called "fruit sugar" because it occurs naturally in many fruits. It is sweeter than sucrose (common table sugar) and is commercially derived from corn.

Galangal: a spicier and more pungent relative of ginger.

Ginger: a rhizome indispensable to Asian cookery. Look for younger roots that are moist and unbruised.

Gluten flour: A high-protein, starch-free flour made by removing the starch from hard wheat flour. Gluten flour can be used as an additive to dough or used to make vegetarian protein foods such as seitan.

Grains and Rice:

Arborio rice: The Italian variety most often used with risotto, noted for its creamy yet starchy quality.

Barley: An ancient grain that is highly nutritious and mild in taste. Barley has a chewy quality and a somewhat nutty flavor and is frequently used in dishes such as cereals, breads, stews, and soups. Look for pearled—all hull removed, hulled—with the bran or unhulled, which takes the longest to cook.

Basmati rice: An aromatic long-grain rice with a light, dry texture and a delicate nutlike flavor. It is the standard variety of rice used in Indian cooking. Basmati rice can be purchased in Indian and Middle Eastern markets, natural-food stores, and some supermarkets.

Grains and Rice (continued),

Black japonica or black rice: This rice comes in a few different varieties, usually fairly starchy. A native of Asia, it makes for striking presentations.

Brown basmati rice: An unhulled version of Indian basmati rice, a long grain rice that is usually domestically grown. It has a warm nutty flavor.

Jasmine rice: An aromatic rice from Thailand that has a unique pleasant flavor.

Millet: A quick-cooking, nutty-flavored grain from African. These small couscous-shaped "pellets" are great used like couscous or in pilafs.

Quinoa: This tiny, round, sand-colored grain has a light texture and cooks in under ten minutes; it has a delicate nutlike flavor and an earthy, herbaceous quality. Also look for the smaller, black-hulled black quinoa.

Short-grain brown rice: Starchy and sweeter than long-grain varieties, this works well as an alternative to white sushi rice.

Triticale: A nutritious whole grain that is a hybrid of wheat and rye and has a nutlike, sweet flavor.

Wehani or red rice: Firm textured and nutty flavored, wehani is a great complement to brown basmati in pilafs.

Wheat berries: Like their relatives spelt, kamut, rye, and triticale berries, wheat berries need long cooking times and have chewy textures. Flavors vary with the variety, but all make great additions to rice pilafs and hearty salads.

Wheat bran: The outer covering of a wheat kernel, which is separated from wheat flour during milling, wheat bran is a rich source of dietary fiber.

Wild rice: Wild rice really is not a rice at all, but comes from a grass that grows in marshes along the banks of freshwater lakes. Wild rice grains are blackish in color and have a nutlike flavor and crisp chewy texture.

Kaffir lime leaf: Usually found fresh or frozen in Asian markets, though sometimes found dried, a poor substitute for fresh. Adds a distinctive floral, citrus accent to Asian cookery.

Leeks: A mild and subtle-flavored onion that looks like giant scallion. Leeks can be used as flavorful ingredient in soups, salads, and many other dishes, or cooked whole as a vegetable.

Lemongrass: Stalks of a woody grass that lend a lemon-citrus flavor to Thai and Vietnamese cuisines.

Maple Syrup: The boiled-down sap of the sugar maple which is used as a natural flavoring and sweetener. 100% pure maple syrup which is certified organic is used in Millennium cooking. It should not be confused with "maple-flavored" syrup, which is made with less expensive sugar or corn syrup containing only a small amount of pure maple syrup.

Miso: A fermented soybean paste that is often used in Japanese cooking to make miso soup or to flavor various dishes. Barley and rice are also sometimes used in miso. Miso comes in several varieties. Lighter-colored varieties are used in delicate soups and sauces, and darker-colored varieties are stronger in flavor and used in heavier dishes.

Mushrooms:

Black trumpet: A fragile, trumpet-shaped mushroom that has a waxy, charcoal gray outer surface and is blackish brown and velvety on the inside. Black trumpet mushrooms are considered a great delicacy. They can be purchased in some produce markets on the West Coast

Blewit: A lavender/brown wild mushroom with a slightly fruity, hazelnut-like flavor. They are grown commercially in France.

Crimini: Also called "brown mushrooms." A brown-capped, slightly more flavorful cousin of the white button mushroom.

Chanterelle: A wild mushroom harvested throughout the country, depending on the season, found on the West Coast during the winter. It is a small- to medium-sized, usually gold or yellow (white and red species do exist), mushroom with a very firm flesh and a slightly fruity (apricot) flavor and aroma.

Cepe: Also known as porcini, this mushroom is most commonly found dried, though found fresh in the fall and spring. Perhaps the most prized of all wild mushrooms. The flavor is rich, earthy, smoky, slightly nutty, and luxurious. When fresh the flesh should be dense and white, with a soft yellow/olive sponge (under the cap).

Enoki: A delicate-tasting mushroom that has long, spaghetti-like stems topped with a tiny white cap. The mushroom grows in clusters, has a crunchy texture, and is prominently used in many Asian dishes. Enoki mushrooms can be purchased in Asian markets and in some supermarkets.

Hedgehog: A wild mushroom found under pine trees in the Pacific Northwest, the hedgehog is gold in color and has an earthy, slightly piny flavor. It derives its name from the fact that there are small spines under its cap instead of gills.

Lobster: A very firm and crunchy white-fleshed mushroom with the outer color of cooked lobster. The flavor to my taste is somewhat like shellfish. Actually this mushroom is a variety of russalie invaded by another parasitic fungus, thus giving it its bright red color. Found nationwide and picked and sold primarily on the West Coast.

Matsutake: A highly prized (especially in Japan) wild mushroom, foraged in the Pacific Northwest, with firm, off-white caps with a unique pine-floral scent and flavor.

Morel: A unique wild variety with a hollow, conical, honeycombed cap. These mushrooms have a chewy texture and an earthy, dusky, and slightly eggy flavor.

Oyster: A fan-shaped or oyster shell–shaped mushroom that is gray-brown in color and tastes peppery when raw but has a subtle taste when cooked. They are popular in Asian cooking. Oyster mushrooms can be purchased in Asian markets and some supermarkets.

Portobello: A very large, dark brown mushroom that has an open flat cap. The caps can be grilled and cut into thick slices or served whole. They have a meaty texture and flavor and can be served as an appetizer, in salads, or as an entrée. The woody stem should be removed but can be used in soup stocks. Portobello mushrooms can be purchased in many supermarkets and produce markets.

Shiitake: A popular mushroom used in Asian cuisine. Shiitake mushrooms have a brownish convex or almost flat cap and a meaty flesh. They can be purchased fresh or dried in Asian markets and some supermarkets.

Pasta and Noodles:

Capellini: Thin pasta noodles that are slightly thicker than "angel hair" (capelli d'angelo) pasta.

Fettuccini: A pasta cut into long, thin, flat strips. While most fettuccini noodles are made with egg, Millennium uses fettuccini noodles made without eggs.

Linguine: A long, narrow, flat, eggless pasta. Linguine has the appearance of a flat spaghetti.

Penne: Large straight pasta tubes cut at a diagonal.

Soba noodles: Japanese noodles made from buckwheat.

Pine nuts: An edible seed found inside the pine cone. Pine nuts grow in southern Europe, China, Mexico, and in the southwestern United States.

The pine nut has a soft texture and sweet flavor. Some varieties are stronger in flavor.

Plantain: A cousin of the banana. Unless very ripe (the skin will be black), plantains are usually cooked before eating. Used as a savory starch throughout Latin America.

Polenta: A popular specialty from northern Italy that is made from cornmeal. Polenta can be sliced and grilled or baked and served as an appetizer or side dish.

Rice Dream: A dairy-free commercial ice cream substitute made from rice milk. It is served like ice cream as a dessert.

Rice milk: A dairy-free milk substitute made from rice.

Rice syrup: A sweet syrup made from brown rice. Rice syrup can be used as a natural sweetener in desserts.

Sea Vegetables:

Arame: A mildly flavored sea vegetable that is frequently served as a vegetable side dish in Japanese meals. It is yellowish brown when fresh and becomes blackish when cooked. Its wide leaves are finely shredded, precooked, and sun-dried. Arame can be purchased in Asian markets and some natural-food stores.

Dulse: A coarse, dark-red edible seaweed native to the northern waters of the Atlantic and Pacific Oceans. Mildly salty tasting, it is used in its dried state or lightly toasted to intensify its crunchy texture and slightly smoky flavor. It dissolves almost completely when added to soups as a thickener.

Hiziki: A dried sea vegetable available from Asian markets or natural-food stores; can be used interchangeably with arame, though hiziki has a more pronounced briny flavor. Pour boiling or very hot tap water over it and allow it to soak for 10 to 20 minutes before using.

Sea palm: A wild seaweed harvested on the Mendocino coast. It has a crunchy texture that is a great addition to salads, and a lightly briny flavor. Pour boiling water over it and allow it to soak 10 to 20 minutes.

Seitan: Also called "wheat meat," seitan is a protein-rich food made from gluten (wheat protein). Seitan has a chewy texture and is used as a meat substitute in many vegetarian dishes. It can be prepared in the kitchen or is commercially prepared and sold in natural-food stores and Asian markets.

Soy milk: A nondairy milk made from soybeans. It is used as a substitute for cow milk and can be made in the kitchen or sold commercially in natural-food stores, Asian markets, and in some supermarkets. Commercially it is available in several varieties, including low-fat and non-fat versions, with or without added natural flavors. Some soy milk products can also be fortified with nutrients such as vitamins A and D, vitamin B12 and calcium.

Sucanat: A commercial product used as a natural sweetener and made from evaporated sugarcane juice.

Sundried tomatoes: Tomatoes that have been sun-dried or dried by other methods, producing a chewy texture. They are rich in flavor and can be used in many dishes.

Tahini: A popular ingredient used in Middle Eastern cooking, made from sesame seeds ground into a thick paste.

Tamari: A dark, thick, fermented sauce made from soybeans. Tamari soy sauce is made without the wheat used in the more commercially common shoyu soy sauce.

Tamarind paste: Paste of the very pungent tamarind fruit. Used in Asian sauces.

Tempeh: A fermented soybean cake traditionally used in Indonesia. Tempeh is high in quality protein and has a yeasty and nutlike flavor that is popular in vegetarian cooking. Tempeh can be purchased in natural-food stores.

Tiger lily buds: A dried flower bud used in Asian soups and sauces—it lends a slightly sour and floral flavor.

Tofu: A soybean curd made from soy milk. Tofu is prominent in Asian food. It is very versatile and can be used as an ingredient in many ways in vegetarian cooking. Tofu has a custardlike texture and a somewhat bland taste on its own; however, its flavor can be modified, as it easily absorbs the flavors of other foods and ingredients. Tofu comes in many textures, such as soft, firm, and extra-firm. It is also now available in low-fat versions. A commercial product called Mori-Nu Silken Tofu Lite is now available and is often used at Millenium. Silken tofu has a creamy, smooth texture that can be easily prepared as dips, puddings, soups, and many other dishes that require a more creamy and smooth texture. Tofu is usually sold, packaged in containers, in the form of a rectangular block. In vegetarian cooking tofu is recognized as an excellent source of vegetable protein, containing all eight essential amino acids.

Tomatillos: A Mexican fruit resembling a small green tomato with a husk, often used in salsa. Tomatillos are popular in Mexican and Southwestern cooking.

Unrefined sugar: A general term used to describe a type of granulated cane sugar that has not been refined, or has been only minimally refined, retaining some of the nutrients naturally occurring in cane sugar juice. Commercial products such a Sucanat and Florida Crystals are examples of this type of sugar. It is used as a natural sweetener in many Millennium recipes.

Vinegars:

Balsamic vinegar: A very fine Italian vinegar made from white Trebbiano grape juice. Balsamic vinegar is dark brown in color and mellow and subtle in flavor.

Champagne vinegar: A light, high acid vinegar with a clean slightly grape taste, an excellent all-around vinegar.

Red wine vinegar: Seek out quality brands made from specific varietals of red wine for their distinct flavor.

Rice vinegar: Low to moderate in acid, yet has a mellow warm flavor.

Sherry vinegar: Varies greatly in flavor sweetness and acidity, depending on the brand. The better brands have a very complex flavor.

COOKING TERMS AND PROCEDURES

Brunoise : To slice into small cubes approximately $1/6$ to $1/8$ of an inch.

Blanch: To quickly immerse in boiling water for no more than thirty seconds, usually followed by shocking or immersing in an ice-water bath to arrest the cooking process.

Braise: To cook in the oven or covered on the stove-top in small quantities of liquid, usually for longer cooking times.

Chiffonade : To slice into very fine strips. Usually used with leafy herbs like basil and mint.

Dice: To slice into small uniform cubes.

Julienne: To cut into uniform long and thin slices; usually $1/8$ to $1/4$ inch in width.

Sauté: To quickly cook foods in a minimum of fat or another liquid over high heat on the stovetop.

Roast: To dry cook in an oven.

A Note on Cooking with Wine and Other Alcohol-Containing Products

We do utilize a good deal of wine, sherry, marsala, and other liquors in our cookery, although we virtually always cook these products down to burn off the alcohol and reduce them to their very flavorful essence.

When reduced, the sugars in the wines caramelize, adding extra depth and warmth to sauces and soups. The tannins and fruit components add a subtle pungent and fruity note to whatever they are added to. With wines and sherry in savory cookery, I prefer drier varietals; they provide more than enough residual sugars without being too cloying or sweet. Dessert wines and flavored liquors usually provide sweeter flavors.

When choosing wines and liquors, the better the quality you start with, the better your finished product will be. This is especially true with flavored liquors. The inexpensive versions usually taste like cheap flavorings and extracts. With wine, if you wouldn't drink it, don't cook with it. Stay away from anything labeled cooking wine.

For those that want or need to stay away from alcohol, there are some nice alternatives to choose from, dry grape juices made from specific wine grape varietals, such as those from Navarro Vineyards or dealcoholized wine from Sutter Home and Ariel, as well as a few other vintners. With flavored liquors you might want to try extremely small quantities of glycerine-based flavor extracts or substitute, where appropriate, their fresh counterpart.

MAIL ORDER SOURCES

MUSHROOMS

Fungi Perfecti

P. O. Box 7634

Olympia, WA 98507

(800) 780-9126

Philipps Mushroom Place

909 East Baltimore Pike

Kennet Square, PA 19348

(800) 243-8644

BEANS AND GRAINS

Indian Harvest Specialty Foods

P. O. Box 428

Bemidji, MN 56601

(800) 346-7032

BEANS, GRAINS, CHILI AND
SOUTHWESTERN FOOD PRODUCTS

Manitou Trading

2013 Swanson Court

Gurnee, IL 60031

(847) 244-9595

SPECIALTY CHILES AND CHIPOLTES

Tierra Vegetables

13684 Chalk Hill Road

Healdsburg, CA 95548

(707) 837-8366

SPECIALTY FOODS

Dean and Delucca

560 Broadway

New York, NY 10012

(800) 221-7714

Afterword: On the Vegetarian Lifestyle

Since the beginning of time, people from cultures all over the world have eaten vegetarian diets. There are several types of vegetarian diets, but the purest form is the *vegan* way of eating. When people who don't know much about this diet hear the word vegan, they tend to think you're some sort of science fiction character from another planet, or, if they have a little more knowledge, a health or animal-rights enthusiast. This latter is the real truth, but people have all sorts of reasons for embracing this way of eating—concern about their own health, the health of the planet, helping world hunger, and caring about animals.

Indeed, I don't know a vegan (pronounced *vee-gan*) who isn't motivated by either a strong desire to live a healthy life or an equally strong desire to avoid causing pain and harm to other creatures. (In many cases, of course, both wishes are present.) And I don't know a meat-eater who doesn't pause, at least for a moment, when considering vegan principles and say to him- or herself, "Well, it's too hard for me to do, but it certainly does make sense."

What we have shown in the *Millennium Cookbook,* of course, is that not only does it indeed make perfect sense, but it isn't too hard for *anyone* to do! Though many of the recipes in this book may stray from the purest low-fat guidelines by incorporating some oils and fats, they possess all the other virtues that conscientious pure vegetarian eating embraces: they include no meat, poultry, fish, eggs, or dairy products, and are built instead on a foundation of grains, legumes, fruits, vegetables, nuts, and seeds. And even the fats included in some recipes are used very sparingly indeed—and all are cholesterol-free. We have also included low-fat, oil-free variations for many of our recipes, for those of us trying to keep our fat intake to the bare minimum.

At Millennium, we have created a vegetarian cuisine that is closely aligned with important vegan principles, and, not coincidentally, delicious and creative in its use of ingredients and combinations of flavors. Chef Eric Tucker deserves enormous credit for blending rigorous restaurant technique with a forward-looking, conscious approach to recipe development. As staff nutritionist at Millennium, I try to complement his innovation behind the scenes with the several roles I play. First, I analyze the menu items for their nutritional value (the results of this can be seen in the nutritional analyses of every recipe in this book). Second, I make time to visit the dining room floor, to discuss our approach to vegetarian cooking with customers, and to answer any nutritional questions they may have. Third, I collaborate with Eric on the vegetarian cooking classes we give on occasional weekend mornings: he cooks and teaches culinary techniques, while I add comments or answer questions about the nutritional strategy behind each dish.

And finally, Eric and I have created what we

call the Millennium Lifestyle Program, a comprehensive month-long class designed to help people achieve optimal health through delicious gourmet vegetarian cuisine and a healthy lifestyle.
The program includes a cooking class and four weekly evening class sessions: participants attend nutrition and health lectures, watch video presentations, and take part in group discussions. Each participant also receives a personal nutritional consultation with me, a complete course syllabus, a copy of the course textbook, Dr. John A. McDougall's landmark guide *The McDougall Program: 12 Days to Dynamic Health,* and a year's subscription to *Veggie Life* magazine, for which I am the nutrition editor.

There are class lectures and homework assignments, based on materials from Dr. McDougall's book, as well as daily dietary and lifestyle records to be kept. Students are also encouraged to exercise, and to cook dishes at home on non-class days that follow the principles of Millennium's low-fat vegetarian cuisine. (Each student receives a complete set of all the recipes served in the program—did I forget to mention that Eric prepares a special delicious low-fat meal at each of the four classroom sessions?)

Some participants elect to have medical tests and fitness evaluations performed at the beginning and the conclusion of the program, to monitor their progress. It's always a pleasure to see the improvement made by individuals who follow the program's guidelines strictly for the month. We frequently see significant improvements in their blood cholesterol and blood pressure, weight level and proportion of body fat, and overall appearance and feeling of well-being. (A 25 percent or better drop in cholesterol is not atypical for participants who start the program with total cholesterol readings of 200 mg/dl or more—the equivalent, if maintained over time, to a 50 to 75-percent decrease in the risk of death from coronary heart disease. And overweight participants

easily and safely lose 4 to 8 pounds or more by the end of the class.)

The recipes that Eric prepares for program participants are low-fat, oil-free variations of the same ones he's currently preparing for the restaurant. They are prepared under stricter guidelines than are the dishes that appear on Millennium's menu, although our customers always can—and often do—ask for oil-free meals to be prepared for them. In addition to proscribing all animal foods and products—including red meat, poultry, fish and shellfish, eggs, milk, cheese, yogurt, and the like—the dishes in the program exclude all added fats (including vegetable oils) as well. High-fat plant foods such as nuts, seeds, olives, avocados, and soybean products are either avoided entirely during the month, or used very sparingly indeed—the goal of the Millennium Lifestyle Program being to create a diet in which no more than 10 percent of the total daily calories consumed come from fat. These are similar to the dietary guidelines that Dr. John McDougall and Dr. Dean Ornish recommend for reversing serious health problems.

Those participants who stick closely to our recommended guidelines make the best progress during the month toward reaching their personal goals, whether those relate to weight, fitness, or mood. They also lay the best foundation toward maximizing the health benefits of this diet over time. Healthy vegetarian diets like Millennium's have a protective role in preventing—and can even be said to help in treating—diseases and conditions such as heart disease, cancer, stroke, and diabetes. Because the program's dietary plan is so healthy and so low in fat, participants can eat and enjoy as much as they want, without feeling deprived, without the fear of gaining weight, and without guilt.

For those outside the San Francisco Bay Area who can't attend our Millennium Lifestyle Program or even dine occasionally at Millennium restaurant, the recipes in this book provide a healthy start on a new way of cooking…and of living. If you're already committed to a vegetarian approach to eating and health, then I'm sure you've found a great many superb recipes to add to your repertoire. And if you're feeling like you want to improvise a bit now, to head out on your own in the kitchen while still observing vegan principles as closely as possible, just visualize what we call the Millennium Lifestyle Pyramid.

Those who follow nutritional developments will recognize the Millennium pyramid as a variant of the Vegetarian Food Guide Pyramid first unveiled at the Third International Congress on Vegetarian Nutrition in 1997. That pyramid was designed to provide a conceptual framework to aid consumers in selecting the types and quantities of various foods that, taken together, will provide a healthful diet and promote optimal health. It followed the form established by

the familiar Food Guide Pyramid developed by the USDA, with foods nearer the broad base of the pyramid being recommended for frequent and substantial consumption, and those near the narrow apex being recommended only occasionally, and in small quantities. The Vegetarian Food Guide Pyramid's upper portion was marked off from its lower area with a dotted line; included above the line were optional foods such as eggs, dairy products, and refined products such as vegetable oils and sweets. We've done much the same with our own pyramid, but have eliminated dairy products and eggs entirely.

So, the health benefits of a vegan vegetarian diet are clear. But what about other benefits of this way of eating? They do exist, and are quite important to many vegan vegetarians. For instance, food safety is a growing concern in this country, and safety concerns usually center on meat, eggs, or dairy. Overall, plant-based

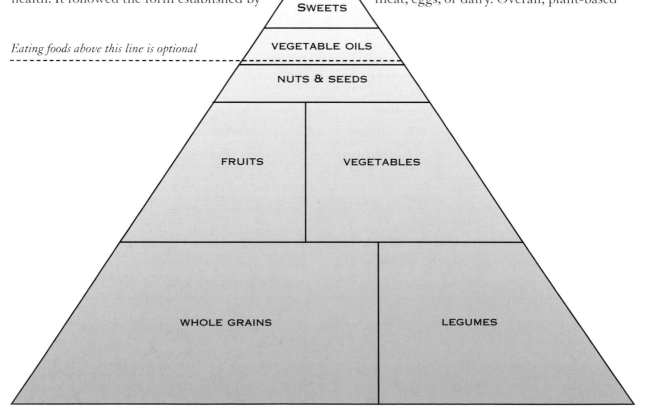

Eating foods above this line is optional

SWEETS

VEGETABLE OILS

NUTS & SEEDS

FRUITS

VEGETABLES

WHOLE GRAINS

LEGUMES

Note: A reliable source of vitamin B12 (available to vegetarians from supplements or fortified foods) should be included.

foods are much safer, cleaner, and healthier. Widening our focus, we see that eating low on the food chain is also beneficial to the environment. A plant-based diet decreases pollution, reduces soil erosion and fuel usage, and helps promote better stewardship of agricultural land.

The stewardship ties directly in to another benefit, that of helping to feed the world. We can grow much more food per acre when that land is used for growing plants rather than raising animals. So, as the number of vegetarians grows, so does the amount of food available for the world's population. Finally, there is the issue of kindness to animals. Mahatma Gandhi once said, "The greatness of a nation and its moral progress can be judged by the way its animals are treated. A vegan diet is a more humane diet.

Still, the question is often raised, even by people who embrace all of these benefits, Can a diet based on all plant foods provide a person with all the essential nutrients? Don't vegetarians run the risk of shortchanging their bodies—and their health? Not according to the American Dietetic Association, which in 1997 took the formal position that "…appropriately planned vegetarian diets are healthful, are nutritionally adequate, and provide health benefits in the prevention and treatment of certain diseases." The ADA's report was careful to specify that such diets are appropriate not just for some idealized "healthy adult," but for pregnant and lactating women, as well as infants, children, and adolescents.

The ADA's rigorous review of the medical and scientific literature led it to the following conclusions:

- Protein from plant sources can provide adequate amounts of essential amino acids if a variety of plant foods are consumed and energy needs are met.

- Protein intake by both vegans and lacto-ovo vegetarians (those who consume dairy products and eggs) appears to be adequate.

- Vegan diets can provide adequate calcium if the diet regularly includes foods rich in calcium (such as beans and legumes, soyfoods like tofu, tempeh, and soybeans, certain nuts and seeds, dried fruits, and a number of vegetables).

- Vitamin D intake—long believed to be the "Achilles heel" of vegan diets because its most common source is fortified cow's milk—in fact is controlled more specifically by exposure to sunlight. Only those who do or must limit such exposure will need to take vitamin D supplements or consume vegan foods specially supplemented with vitamin D.

- By consuming sufficient amounts of certain readily available breads, grains, cereals, legumes, vegetables, and soyfoods, vegetarians can counteract the low bioavailabililty of zinc from plant foods in general.

Likewise, the low availability of Vitamin B-12 to vegetarians who avoid or limit their intake of animal foods can be offset by supplements or the use of fortified foods.

All of this leaves the vegan-inspired diner and the creative cook with a wealth of ingredients to combine, more than enough to guarantee both variety and satisfaction. With chefs like Eric Tucker at work in more and more vegetarian kitchens, doing their best to track down the finest produce and the most tantalizing flavor combinations from cuisines around the globe, no one need fear for the future of vegetarian dining—either in the home kitchen, or in pacesetting restaurants like Millennium.

—John Westerdahl, M.P.H., R.D., C.N.S.

INDEX